Praise for *What Every Pare*
College Admissions

"This is the go-to guide for students to find the right path, at the right time, for the right tuition, to lead to their best career outcome. Implementing Individualized Career and Academic Planning in middle and high school helps identify interesting, high-paying careers in growth fields. Barnes's book is the first available for parents and students to plan for a successful future."

—Anna Costaras and Gail Liss, authors of *The College Bound Organizer* and the forthcoming *The College Bound Planner*

"In *What Every Parent Needs to Know About College Admissions*, Barnes examines how our education systems are adapting to today's workforce demands by combining practical experience with traditional approaches to create more opportunities for any student to access high-paying, in-demand jobs in modern fields. She walks students and parents past the limiting notion of 'college or bust' and explores how work-based learning in combination with related instruction can be an options multiplier for students. It's that kind of endless possibility we're building with CareerWise—students can start with a youth apprenticeship and end with a PhD or a corner office—and Barnes's book helps students find the career and education paths that are right for them. Apprenticeship can be a powerful enhancement to education or a fast-track to a top career, or both."

—Noel Ginsburg, founder, CEO, and chairman of the board at CareerWise Colorado, the nonprofit tasked with running the statewide youth apprenticeship system in Colorado

"When it comes to college planning, some parents are like passengers sitting on deck chairs on the *Titanic* as it sinks, convinced the ship is unsinkable. We need a book like this to explain new realities, new changes, and new opportunities for higher education and college success."

—Laura Miller, counseling coordinator and CTE Campus Administrator at Cherry Creek Innovation Campus, Centennial, Colorado

"As a higher education professional with six years of experience working in admissions, assessment, advising, and presently as a financial aid specialist, I have witnessed the considerable strain navigating the college process causes for students and their parents. The internet is full of advice, but so much of it is outdated or incorrect. It is evident that Christie Barnes spent many years gathering information that will vastly improve the preparation and transition process from high school to college."

—Natalie Eck, financial aid specialist at Valencia College in Orlando, Florida

"The path from high school to higher education to a successful career is no longer a straight line. This planner is a map that will help you navigate these treacherous waters."

—Scott Horn, PhD in Geospatial Information Sciences from the University of Texas at Dallas, Geographic Information Systems (GIS) Lecturer

"A valuable book that examines how elitism affects college and career choices."

—Bonnie Timmermann, producer/casting director

"I'd be honored to say my kid goes to Harvard. But with my kids, I have learned you wind up where you are supposed to be. And this book explains 'where you are supposed to be.' We have to stop labeling, 'reach' schools, 'safety' schools—labeling is setting yourself up for disappointment. This book is great when the kid doesn't get in somewhere, doesn't want to go to their only options, or when they get in—is the college really the right place? This book is about understanding and running with the options that present themselves. As Barnes says, there isn't a one-size-fits-all magic college that will bestow the perfect future on anyone who enters. Every college or higher ed experience can get you there if you are not always fixated on what you might be missing somewhere else. As Barnes says,

'Hide the name of the college and consider the program; would it inspire my student to learn?' The student's learning, not the school name, is what matters in today's world."

—Nina Kleinert, graduate of Beverly Hills Public Schools, mom of four Beverly Hills Public Schools children

"As a mental health professional who works with teens and families, it has been disheartening and concerning to see how much the pressure to succeed in the classroom and achieve high grades and GPA scores to get into the top-name colleges has been damaging the self-esteem of many students and contributing to high levels of anxiety and depression, and even self-harming behaviors. Barnes's book is such a helpful and impactful read for parents, students, teachers, and school administrators as it gives insight not only into the problem with the culture of academic success and its negative impact, but more importantly the solutions and multiple options to help teens thrive in the right way with the right mindset that keeps their mental health and self-esteem intact."

—Talisa Stowers, licensed marriage and family therapist and owner of 3 In One Health Counseling and Wellness Practice

What Every Parent
Needs to Know About
College
Admissions

What Every Parent Needs to Know About

College

Admissions

How to Prepare Your Child to Succeed in College
and Life—With a Step-by-Step Planner

By Christie Barnes

CORAL GABLES

Cover Design: Roberto Nuñez
Cover illustration: Sky Motion/Shutterstock
Layout & Design: Katia Mena

For permission requests, please contact the publisher at:
Mango Publishing Group
2850 S Douglas Road, 2nd Floor
Coral Gables, FL 33134 USA
info@mango.bz

For special orders, quantity sales, course adoptions and corporate sales, please email the publisher at sales@mango.bz. For trade and wholesale sales, please contact Ingram Publisher Services at customer.service@ingramcontent.com or +1.800.509.4887.

What Every Parent Needs to Know About College Admissions: How to Prepare Your Child to Succeed in College and Life—With a Step-by-Step Planner

Library of Congress Cataloging-in-Publication number: 2021936122
ISBN: (print) 978-1-64250-315-9, (ebook) 978-1-64250-316-6
BISAC category code FAM034000, FAMILY & RELATIONSHIPS / Parenting / General

Printed in the United States of America

Table of Contents

Preface

I write books about perceptions versus reality. My books have been acclaimed by the *New York Times*, ABC, and NPR. Recently I have appeared in *Forbes* and the *Reader's Digest*. Primarily, I focus on parents' beliefs about the "best" and "worst" for their children and whether those clung-to beliefs match facts. One example is "Do parents' perceptions of the greatest dangers to their children match with the most prevalent dangers that actually befall children?" Sensational news stories, flashy marketing, social media, and rumors lead us parents to beliefs that are far from reality.

As a parent of college-bound high school-aged triplets plus one, I felt it was time to turn my scrutiny to college admissions, college outcomes, and career success to best help my children and those heading to college soon.

Okay, I have been really, really busy raising triplets and troubleshooting parent problems, mine and others'. I knew I was operating on assumptions about college choice and admissions that I accepted from my personal college experience, and more relevant, high school meetings, college admissions books, and college websites. For example, I took for granted that the goal was for my triplets to get accepted at the "best college," as college has been the Golden Ticket to a high-paying career for life with an "elite" college (also known as the "best," the "most prestigious," the "highest-ranking," the "most selective") being added insurance of a glowing future. But when my cousins' brilliant, selective-college graduate children did not get anticipated job offers, my curiosity was piqued. Were they just unlucky? They were excellent students graduating from the nation's top colleges. But now they were filling out job applications three hours a day, taking part-time jobs, and eventually attending graduate school after of a year of rethinking. Then friends, and grown children of friends, showed me two loans—their mortgage figure and their student debt figure—and I could not tell which was which, the amounts were both so colossal and eerily similar. Was it time for a new book?

It was certainly time to engage in some "fact-checking." Based on statistics showing what works, how do students gain the advantage to make the dream college a reality that will then guarantee making that dream career a reality?

What I found in researching this book was totally unexpected. All my meticulous research on college admissions and outcomes showed dramatically different—dramatically negative—results contradicting my preconceptions of what were the most valuable aspects of college. Researched facts and statistics contrasted significantly with the information in college admissions guides, on rankings websites, in college mailings, and in information I got from my triplets' high school's Thursday ten o'clock College Coffee with our high school's post grad expert that I attended for three years.

I ran and reran numbers—graduation statistics, job outcomes, salaries, profiles of college success, who got top-earning jobs in growth industries and how. Little of it matched generally accepted assumptions about college, admissions, and careers. Was I the only writer in the country who had discovered this shocking information about college admissions and outcomes? Was there a national cover-up? So many of us with kid-centered lives are trying so hard to get this right—but were we just wrong?

Braving a Colorado blizzard, I drove fifty miles in a white-out snowstorm to barge into a college and career think tank session at the annual Colorado counselor convention. When it came time to introduce myself, I just stood up and blurted out, "Tell me—am I nuts?—but my statistics say…" The group leader and everyone in the room listened, and then they started laughing at me. Then the lead educator put up a slide on the huge lecture-hall screen. There were "my" bad college outcome statistics. They knew. Counselors in every single state, principals, the Superintendents Association of America, educators, and education policy makers nationwide all know.

"Why didn't I know this? Why don't parents know this?" I asked. The leader answered, "This think tank is brainstorming that problem: How do we communicate current information about college admissions, outcomes, and career planning to parents and students?" This was a think tank program leading to certification as a college and career specialist, requiring each of us to write marketing/advocacy plan creation templates, a sample email, and brochure evidence to get the improved higher education information to parents and students.

> Why do we think that planning for one lifetime career with four-year college will work in a new age of seven to eleven completely new careers in a work lifetime? Those multiple careers have two requirements: higher education and continuous lifelong learning.
>
> Why do we think our teen should learn traditional five- and ten-year business planning methods when the Technology Age's exponential change means six-month planning cycles? Why do we prepare to work in segregated, autonomous departments working separately when all forms of work now are turning to interdisciplinary, agility-oriented teams to innovate quickly?
>
> Instead, we double down on having our students be even more competitive: leaders striving to be at the top when the new age is of equal team members—we know the world is changing but cling to tradition. Traditional education is excellent, but it is not surprising that it is slightly out of line with careers, STEM or non-STEM, today. Excelling at old tests and old-style courses, slightly off the "future of work" targets, is not leading to stellar outcomes. We have made our students strive to reach higher and higher standards—the problem is that they are now somewhat irrelevant standards.

Under the direction of the think tank mentors, I ended up getting post-master's certificates and education hours in college admission planning. I became certified in college and career counseling through one of the new career counseling initiatives being launched in most states. I interviewed educators from local school districts across the country and policy makers in Washington, DC. During the first six months of the COVID-19 quarantine, I had three or more Zoom meetings (or private webinar meetings) with college deans and presidents and their CFOs and college admissions officers, planning their college's or university's survival and planning their next five years. I ended up advocating and testifying about paths to better education outcomes to senators and congressmen funding programs to get Americans in high-paying careers in growth fields.

Every school district in the US, and education systems across the world, are moving in new directions driven by poor college outcomes and a need to fill great, high-paying jobs in newly invented growth fields. Asian and European countries now make career pathways a policy to get every single person entering the workforce into an upper-middle-class salaried job in a high-growth business or industry. The information, the tools, and the opportunities are available in America too. No one will say college-for-all isn't a success because *everyone* needs higher education/college! College is excellent, but it has to be the right path to college with the right courses—not an elite college as a one-size-fits-all guarantee to a top career. So, uninformed as to the complicated nuances of "the best college," many parents approach college as if it were 1999, or even 1969.

This book has become more than just another "how to get into an elite college" book. My book is a news story, a history of change, a discussion of the future of work. But primarily it is a guide, full of solutions to problems that some do not realize exist. About 80 percent of parents are missing crucial information their students need. This is the Technology Age, and old rules don't apply. Parents and their teens at each economic level are using the wrong information.

College (higher education) is necessary, but with today's worker having seven to eleven entirely different careers, college is no longer "one four-year degree" to prepare for one job for life, because technology destroys and creates jobs at exponentially increasing speed. And we can't exactly do seven to eleven bachelor's degrees for the seven to eleven careers. We need to plan college differently.

College admissions guides, usually sponsored by the selective college industry, are still saying that there are two choices: one four-year college education, meaning higher salaries, and a high school education, meaning lower salaries. And usually those guides focus on ages twenty-five to sixty-five, or thirty-five to sixty-five, and not twenty to thirty-five—Technology Age workers. A sixty-five-year-old probably did have one degree and one job, the forty-five-year-old, one or two careers. Now we are in the Technology Age—a gig economy, accelerated technological change, six-month agile planning as careers can change that fast. College is vital but requires different planning.

In fairness to our high school's post grad expert—who is one of the nation's top college admissions experts—he spoke the truth, but we parents heard what we wanted to hear. He oversaw sessions at the high school about new real opportunities, new curriculum, "best" colleges. These got an audience of fifteen or twenty in a school of nearly four thousand. He held "highly selective college" information sessions, and these got audiences of over five hundred parents of juniors. And, though both he and the principal told these hundreds of parents that entrance to "elite" colleges carried worse odds than winning the lottery—"Apply, but don't plan on admission"—their teens applied. On decision day, many turned up in the principal's office crying—virtually all of these highly-qualified kids were rejected. This high school turns out academically "perfect" students. But they hadn't listened when told that, for example, 40,000 academically perfect students apply for 1,000 places (at an elite college), or 135,000 apply for 5,900 places (at a selective state university).

This has gotten crazy. Kids with perfect ACT scores and 4.78 GPAs have been turned down by colleges from state schools to Ivies for bizarre reasons we will look at in the book. The parents, devastated by rejections, act as though their teen is now a failure, forever unemployable, destined to live in a tent down by some river flowing with toxic waste. We've seen parents pay six million dollars for a place at the "best school" and others go to jail for trying. How do you plan for "unfair"? A fact-check book is long overdue.

And, with the COVID-19 disruption, planning the best pathway to a high-paying career in a growth field is even more important, for those starting college and also for any adult working, rethinking career advancement or contemplating a new career entirely.

This is vital information for anyone wanting to succeed in the labor market—it is a rare bipartisan issue, as was presented at the National Policy Symposium I attended in Washington, DC (virtually in 2021).

This is still a book about your teen getting into the "best" college, and getting set up for the "best" future. But higher education in the Technology Age requires education for a lifetime that includes seven to eleven completely different careers. Not seven promotions, but seven careers. Getting a new bachelor's for each new career is a ludicrous idea.

So, what are the "best colleges"? How do we find them? What are the outcomes we want from college? How do we plan a "secure" future for our teens that is of more value than an admissions letter to a top college? Will things get back to normal after the COVID-19 disruption, and do we want them back to "normal"?

The first half of the book explains what is happening, why, and how parents and teens are inadvertently getting it wrong by being swept into toxic aspects of old norms. The second half of the book is the "Ninth Grade through Career" planner to help readers get on a pathway that has a chance for better outcomes.

Successfully Navigating the First Change to College in Fifty Years

College as the Golden Ticket to a high-paying secure career and sure entry to the upper classes has been perceived as true for more than fifty years, with the selective college being the Platinum Ticket. It has been predominantly true for decades. No wonder that parents and teens were desperate for that "best college" acceptance letter, even before the current pandemic disruption. Now, uncertainty and confusion push that desperation to new heights.

Emergency online learning followed by remote, hybrid, or an emotionally taxing in-person educational experience have ranged from a hugely disappointing compromise to a profound hardship and even trauma—all challenges we have been forced to accept. Alongside medical and college experts, including Dr. Anthony Fauci and college presidents, in wide-ranging publications from the *Reader's Digest* to *Forbes*, I have written about unanticipated fundamental changes that will endure.

After years of hard work by dedicated students and years of saving by devoted parents, the guarantee of a successful future is put in question by the pandemic disruption and its aftermath.

On so many levels, college norms are on pause, in question, or gone for good:

- What happens to entry chances and scholarships? Even some sports scholarships are gone, since competitive teams turn recreational or are simply canceled. Many colleges are short of funds for National Merit Scholars.

- Do you drive across several states to find a coveted ACT or SAT test spot? These are scores required for scholarship consideration—tests optional for admission but required for scholarship eligibility. ("Test-blind" colleges may even penalize students who submit even "truly exceptional" scores.)

- Will COVID-19 pass/fail grades disqualify the excellent candidate when the selective college wants only a high GPA acceptance average, as it's vital to their rankings and therefore the college's future?

- Many colleges are now described as "the walking dead" or "on the death row march." What happens if your college goes bankrupt?

- What happens when your college abolishes your major, as it is a financial drain?

- Will the parents' job uncertainty impact college savings and therefore choices?

- Whether the student is rich or poor, overall economic uncertainty prompts questions of whether college is "value for money."

- Is a self-imposed "gap year" to wait for normality to be restored a life-impacting, disastrous choice?

- Will the student have to break up college to work? Will the college place be lost, or the scholarship lost?

- What will be the emerging high-earning growth careers? And can the student afford enough education to enter those careers?

These few issues don't even begin to capture the wide-ranging impact that is transforming higher education.

However much we would love everything to return to normal, the college experience will never fully go back to that decades-old "normal." This is affirmed unanimously by the college deans, presidents, and administrators that I "meet" in daily college information sessions for professionals, meetings held nearly every day since March 2020.[1]

Students will find still colleges that they love and that will love them back, but parents and students will have to cope with profound changes to a system that has not changed in fifty years or more.

The "New Normal"

Likely long-term changes to college:

- As many as a thousand colleges, one-fifth of colleges, may close, merge, or be bought by larger colleges.

- A 25 percent minimum of most degree programs may be permanently online (which allows for higher student enrollment and/or earlier graduation).

- Higher or even double enrollment numbers may be needed to bring in more revenue—even for Ivies and elite colleges.

- Colleges may cut places by 20 percent or more to create higher enrollment rates, knowing the economic hit is driving down enrollment on all levels.

- Summer terms/semesters may be offered to accommodate more students or lead to quicker graduations.

- An increased importance of community colleges, which have more professional programs with local industry and business/school partnerships, will provide quicker entry to growth careers and a transferable foundation for future higher degrees.

- More colleges may partner with businesses and industries.

- Degrees may be more in line with careers.

- There may be more emphasis on learning and credentials more aligned with growth careers for success and less on the "brand prestige" that used to propel success.

- Planning should aim for stackable credits in case the planned education path is broken, for whatever reason, so credits lead to credentials (if needed) that lead to higher degrees.

- Lifelong upskilling and retooling through higher education will be available for everyone.

We are already seeing all of these being initiated or adopted, not as temporary measures, but as permanent changes to college as we know it.

Under enormous stress and faced with uncertainty, the first reaction of most people is to cling to past truths and rules, or even double down on "old methods and tradition." But following "old ways" isn't always the best guiding principle for coping with pervasive change.

It is crushing. Metaphorically, parents and teens are watching the planks fall out one by one from the rope bridge that was the traditional route to college admissions and a sure future. They can double down with old traditional methods and try leaping to the remaining shaky planks on the swinging bridge to get across, all while the ropes of the bridge are fraying and starting to snap. But the normal route is gone. Parents and teens, literally and figuratively, need to make course corrections immediately—"course" corrections as in curriculum course corrections, perhaps by adding more dual enrollment and CTE courses than APs (and reducing college test prep courses) and course correction as in life planning: who you will be after college, not the person you are when you are accepted. Acceptance isn't the ultimate defining achievement we think it is. It is barely the first step. But what direction leads to success?

Whether you're new or experienced with the college process, this book is about how to take control. It lays out college admissions changes, high school curriculum changes, emerging careers, and the new emerging Technology Age normal, which is very different from the pre-Recession normal or Industrial Age normal. Parents and teens can make informed decisions in planning for high school, "the best" college, and beyond. This book will also point to the education on-ramps to new growth careers, both for the college-bound and for anyone looking for a promotion or even a complete career change. So, the book also works for the 60 percent of adult American workers, of all education levels, who are reevaluating their current jobs, wanting to upskill to higher-paying positions in their fields or transition to more in-demand careers. The pandemic and the Technology Age mean "new rules" for employment and advancement that affect most of us. Any person entering or in the work force can target the path that suits him or her.[2]

This book is about how to cope with "the new." "I don't want you to underestimate just how hard this is going to be," said a college president. "You're asking people to do something different."[3]

> In this Technology Age, even non-STEM careers require a custom-fit education, not the one-size-fits-all college experience of the past. It isn't complicated—it is finding a college program that matches the individual student's interests, learning style, funds, and internship opportunities. The alternative is turning your student into some perceived "ideal college applicant" to pursue an ill-fitting degree, usually ending in a less-than-successful outcome.

In addition to changes already mentioned, the immediate "different" includes:

- The new criteria for college admissions selection.

- The "degree" concept is giving way to proof of the ability to apply academic study, like credentialing and experience. Like the popular meme: You have a college degree…so tell me again, why should I hire someone with no experience?

- Colleges recognize the need to make sure an education leads to a job and the need to prove that success with real data metrics, not their current, advertising-company-manipulated, misleading "data."

- Parents need to evaluate college financials to predict bankruptcy. Will the student's major get cut? Which majors at the college are loss leaders which will be cut?

- Which schools will reform to allow stackable courses leading to degrees that are transferable to other college systems?

- Acceptance of professional degrees as equal to academic degrees.

- A new definition of prestige; new elements defining "the best."

- The rewriting of job requirements by departments of education working with growth industries from kindergarten to career—grade school, middle school, high school, college. The Human Resources departments of business and industry are all on the same page, use the same terminology, and agree on the education needed to enter top-paying growth careers for every education level.

If your student needs to earn a living—hopefully, a great living, at some point—then planning needs to be done with care to account for pandemic-driven change and the fundamental changes brought by the shift from the Industrial Age to the Technology Age. Surprisingly, genuinely wanting a student to be self-supporting is not to be assumed when the majority of parents say they are willing to help support "their baby" until age thirty or beyond.

Certifications, career planning, student services, making majors interdisciplinary, applied and in-the-field learning, and more transferable credits are recent high school innovations. Some states are embedding community college, trade schools, professional credentialing, three-year degrees, and four-year and graduate programs all into the university system because "we are all learners" and will have to continue to upskill for the Technology Age working life. Great careers have on-ramps at every education level, from credentialing and college courses with certifications available in high school to the selective college degree.

Academic overpreparation and striving for ever-higher scores for college admissions are no guarantee of a successful outcome for admission, nor college performance, nor career and life outcomes. In this time of complex change, students and parents have to do more than just prepare for college admission when planning for the future. Making an "individualized" plan for your student will bring better results than the simplistic "just do everything you can to get into the best college" college and career planning many currently adhere to. That used to work—it doesn't now.

This Book

This book is about how students can get the best life and career outcomes through the best planning for the twenty-first century: K through 12, through college and beyond—or, really, "K through *careers*."

- What are colleges looking for, now that some admissions goals (like scores, sports, and activities that would make your teen *someone no college could turn down*) are "optional" or gone?
- What are the "best" high school courses?
- What are the best colleges?
- What are new growth careers and what education is needed, now that "any" college degree will no longer work for most jobs, as it did in the past?

As I wrote in a recent article in *Forbes*, success will not come from hoping life will go back to the way it was twenty or fifty years ago—or even a year ago.

Doing "everything you are supposed to do" to get into college wasn't working before the COVID-19 disruptions, and it isn't working now. Learn what you need to learn to do the job, then learn it.

An example of individualized planning that breaks common college admissions perceptions of high scores and beating other students

A sixth-grader wanted to be a marine biologist. Every school year, she sat down with her teachers to make sure she could learn what she needed to be a marine biologist. She didn't concentrate on years of exam prep, or taking courses colleges prefer, like AP courses.

She spent homework time learning material beyond the test. Even if she had not been so focused, learning beyond the test is a better foundation for a college and career than devoting study time to a college admissions test simply to impress a big-name college with a high score. The exemplary learning was more impressive and valuable than high scores.

She prepared specifically to be a marine biologist. She was awarded a full scholarship to a Florida private college with a top marine biology program. Her master's and PhD were paid for because she was an expert with a deep knowledge of the material. She now has her dream job—half-time researching and tagging pythons and alligators in the Everglades, the other half doing deep-sea shark research.

What if, in her senior year of high school, she had decided she didn't want marine biology? That can look like a mature decision based on experience. It showed she could plan and achieve. Much of her in-depth knowledge was transferable. She had seriously applied herself. So, instead of a looking like an "average" student with high scores and vague direction, she demonstrated intention and application. Demonstrating vision and persistence has as much value as twisting and turning oneself into someone else's concept of ideal. Being truly special isn't a process of homogenization. It is going beyond "average."

Taking a dozen AP courses, spending homework time on college admission test prep, and going to a highly selective college would not have gotten her this career. It can for a few, but it will require additional specialized study at a specialized university—highly selective schools are not one-size-fits-all for success. She could get there via the selective school route, but reaching her level of expertise would have been more "costly" in time and tuition. If you have the time and the money, take any route you wish. **But planning can get you farther, faster, cheaper.**

Specialization is a key. Middle East oil moguls' children wanting to go into the family business go to the top programs in petroleum engineering in Texas and New Mexico, and not to Ivies. *Value is not how much it costs.* There are great engineering courses at elite colleges, selective colleges, tech colleges, state universities—at the bachelor's level. Find the best route for the individual and his or her needs and constraints.

My Statistics Methodology

So many of our decisions are based on information. But the college industry employs high-end advertising going for the "hard sell." The rosy picture painted from selective college industry information drowns out statistics. While their statistics may be "true," industry statistics may paint a skewed picture.

Make sure the statistics are complete and applicable to your student.

- Check the rubric. It is no good if a statistic only factors in students from private schools, only athletes, no athletes, students with "above 3.9 GPAs," Pell grant students, etc.

- Make sure the statistics mean what you think they do. For example, "selective completion" used to mean "in four years," Now it usually means within six years, but sometimes even eight. Most colleges now use six years as the normal time it takes to graduate a "four-year" program, but that will be in a footnote. The entry will give the "successful graduation percentage."

- The definition of "best value" college changed a few years ago. Different rankings define it radically differently than most parents assume. Most parents think it means that the "excellence" of the student's degree will lead to a career that will cover the cost in a reasonable time frame. Best value did mean that; now in some rankings it signifies which college gives the most extra money to "poor" students. This is essential information for Pell grant students, but it could be seen as deliberately misleading to middle-class parents, "tricked" into believing a $400,000 education is worth selling the family home—because the college is "best value for the money." Giving the most extra money to a seriously economically disadvantaged student is excellent, but that "best value" ranking has no relevance to the majority of students—though it did with the old definition.

- Find out the criteria used for any rankings you plan to use for your decisions. Ranking guides can contain great descriptions of the school, like the number and kind of clubs, student demographics, information on political and religious persuasions, kinds of sports, activities, concerts, attitude to partying, etc. But don't let the rankings numbers dictate the "best" college—best for whom?

Much more on rankings later.

It's the Flaw of Averages and Not the Law of Averages

Some widely believed information is incorrect because colleges and the college industry love averages. Averages are easy. People like them. They are easy to compute: add, then divide, equals *the answer*. So simple, so easy.

Please keep this traditional—geek, not Greek—fable in your thoughts when looking at seemingly-winning college and career statistics.

A River Story

There once was a statistician who needed to cross a stream. He could not swim. He computed the average depth of the stream before venturing to walk across it. The average was three feet deep. So, he started across the stream—as it was three feet deep on average—and, obviously, drowned. The shallows extended far out—ankle-deep—but the channel in the middle of the stream ran deep, over eight feet.

Please resist the urge to go for the easy averages—or your teen may "drown."

Averages can be right and wrong at the same time. Outliers can throw averages way off. And averages can't be used to calculate complex questions that have many obvious factors and many not-readily-apparent factors that must be accounted for. Complex theorems must be created to account for the factors in their appropriate relationships.

The median is somewhat better—"denoting or relating to a value or quantity lying at the midpoint of a frequency distribution of observed values or quantities, such that there is an equal probability of falling above or below it." I will use those when looking at salaries.

I use research that accounts for more complex factors—for example, accounting for the "un-quantifiables," like maturity, motivation, ambition, executive functioning skills, etc., from research operations and think tanks established for decades, and that have passed extensive academic verification.

Here's an example of the meticulous calculations behind facts and figures in this book:

$$\log (P_{ij}/1-P_{ij}) = a_j + \gamma COLLEGE + B4PRIMARYLEGACY_{ij} + B5SECONDARYLEGACY_{ij} + B6\ EAAPPLICANT_j + B7EAAPPLICANT*PRIMARYLEGACY_{ij} + B_{ij}EAAPPLICANT*SECONDARYLEGACY_{ij}$$

This equation takes into account many factors to calculate legacy advantages for different admissions deadlines.[4]

I will use these complex analyses of successful colleges and successful students later in the book. They are more reliable than the college website attesting "students earn $180,000 on graduation." How many students? Two? "We are ranked number one." Where, in what category, and what was the method to arrive at that ranking? In some rankings, the college president is asked to rank his or her own college. Parents and teens think they have done their research, assuming information is inclusive when it is not, or that the criteria are obvious, when the figure really means something entirely different.

This is why my research takes into account complex factors for specific student groups throughout the book.

Here are your two choices: college degree or a high school diploma? Those are false choices.

In a recent book on college admissions, the choices presented in a "persuasive graph" were college degree or high school diploma. The graph "proved" that the salary of those with a high school diploma fell short of the salary of a college degree holder. Those twenty-five to sixty-five were the study group.

The book isn't lying—it is just not presenting you with a truth that is relevant to a student entering the workforce now or in the next ten years. The book's chart left out the biggest demographic of successful earners—those with some college working full-time. And the data was skewed by using such a wide workforce age demographic.

In today's world, a certificate added to a high school degree changes the salary dramatically for the high schooler or even the college grad. (In fact, most college grads are in jobs requiring a high school or post-high-school certificate only.) Those high school grads with a certification or an associate degree earn more than 60 percent of what those with college degrees earn. But the book omitted salaries for this group.

And the work progression of those aged thirty-five to sixty-five does not provide relevant insight into what today's high school student should plan for in the current and future world of work. The thirty-five- to sixty-five-year-old has had a different work arc.

So, make sure data has relevance to your student before basing their future, and the parent's fortune, on it. The book with the top limited choices was published by a major player for the traditional college status quo. Traditional college has been excellent, and it is still an excellent education, but there may be other educational pathways that can help start a career directly. An educational pathway that can get you into a top career is different than one that will specifically get you into that career. Don't make generalizations from partial data.[5]

Who Can You Trust?

Colleges are not out to con you. College and higher education is a good thing. Learning is a good thing. College "country club" amenities should not be part of this equation. Colleges' multi-million-dollar advertising companies create websites and brochures for the purpose of getting the most applications in order to get more students for the college to reject, to increase their selectivity numbers, which will move the college up in the college rankings. Or to do whatever can make the college seems the most desirable. Do you believe McDonald's or Chick-fil-A when they say they have the best chicken nuggets? Ignore the sell-job advertising and use personal judgement.

On a positive note, you can often trust the college admissions officer for specific data. College websites and brochures are usually created by advertising companies to "drive sales." That is their mandate. Admissions officers, however, really want to find the right-fit students who will thrive at their college. It is the same college, but different administration offices have very different goals, so their presentation of information can be different. An ad company driving students to the college will use a selection of "facts" or selective facts, while the admissions department will try to accept the appropriate students for their college who will thrive, and therefore do well and graduate in four to five years.

Cognitive Biases

Dealing with change is hard. A change in mindset is hard to achieve without personally experiencing failure that prompts a new approach. The goal is to process good information at a deep personal level, to allow oneself to adapt to change—without the failure.

Whether the college price tag is $3,000 a year or $100,000 a year, strive to avoid failure. Bouncing back from a quarter-of-a-million-dollar failure or a five-year failure may teach resilience, but it is a life lesson to avoid, as it can be impossible to overcome. We need to change the old prestige mindset as it is leading to poor outcomes.

We think we are open to change, but it is hard to get rid of old ideas.

Cognitive biases trick our decision-making process, usually returning us to our old beliefs. Even when we do the research for ourselves, we make common mistakes.

- We latch onto the first bit of research that backs up what we already believe.

- We find patterns in incomplete information when nothing is conclusive.

- We choose the easy answer over the more complicated one.

- Information overload drives us back to the old, simple idea.

- Hearing something over and over makes us believe it is true.

- We gravitate toward what we are familiar with.

- The extreme or shocking idea is more attractive or believable than the boring or mundane.[6]

Humans have a natural tendency to cling to tradition, but that will not work in times of real change, like the changes due to disruptions or, more significantly, the transition from the Industrial Age to the Technology Age. Traditional methods will simply not work. Rigorously check your beliefs for the biases we discussed earlier, so you can see if you are clinging to old ideas for the wrong or right reasons.

We all hope everything, including college, will just go back to the way it was ten, twenty, or fifty years ago. Disruption aside, we are post- the last recession; we are now in the Technology Age. Colleges had a successful profit model under the old way. Their dilemma is whether to pretend everything is unchanged and make easier money convincing the "consumer" that all is back to normal or to change with the times—the Technology Age times—which is *not* the easiest, most immediate route to profit. Many colleges are "doubling down" on tradition with accelerated marketing pushes to students. They are touting the virtues of not changing their courses as "tradition," which is supposedly better, higher, and more noble, instead of taking on the more costly innovation of advancing their curriculum, as needed in the Technology Age.

Tradition versus "the future"

How are new fields and new careers being talked about at the college?

- Go deeper when new careers are dismissed as fads. A college-industry spokesman, who I deeply admire and respect, shocked and perplexed me. She cited "nanotechnology" as a fad that has died out and that jumping on the nanotechnology fad, instead of a traditional education, would have been a disaster. Her job mandate is to perpetuate college education. Nanotechnology applications are being developed in medicine, computing systems, sustainability, energy, engineering fields, and manufacturing, according to the American Society of Mechanical Engineers. It is a mainstream approach that has been absorbed within traditional fields. It is far from a "fad"—nanotechnology is not "McDonald's Szechuan Sauce." Many colleges will incorporate cutting-edge technological approaches within traditional departments. To throw doubt on academic change, in order to perpetuate "the tradition," is complicated and should be considered at a deep curriculum level per field. Dismissing new learning demands as fads seems perhaps unintentionally suspect, at best. Liberal arts educations are valuable and can provide many transferable skills that in the long run may be the best four-year education for many careers. But specialization for careers will usually be needed. Technical skills should not be dismissed as "fads" as an excuse not to be career relevant.

- A college administrator dismissed nationally recognized certifications as inappropriate and "working-class" in contrast with the unchanged pure academic approach of her college. So, her answer was that her college would create its own certifications, so their students could say they were certified by doing the traditional course and could get jobs. These certifications were not accepted by business or industry, who have nationally agreed standards and practices. In medicine, business, entrepreneurship, or engineering, "her" degree program could be excellent, but an internal certification, more in name only, would not suffice if the job requires certification by a professional body for employment.

- "We are against internships," I was told by a selective college. So, is the college simply "teacher-driven" in fields that need research experience, or project-based experience, for a reason other than budget limitations? What are they doing to make up for possible omissions?

- For a time, some selective colleges had a traditional, unchanging approach to business studies. Their students always got the top finance jobs—until they didn't. The tradition abhorred "data analysis" as plebian. Then their students found they were no longer getting the top jobs without data analysis, which they were forced to learn after their four-year degree in order to get a job. Now those colleges offer data analysis.

Traditional approaches to some careers are valuable. Traditional approaches can be an invaluable foundation. But be wary if "traditional" is used as an excuse to save money by not investing in developments that are needed for the student to be educated for a career.

Worry

Worry is not bad. Different kinds of worry are useful in powering solutions.

Seeking an advantage in the college race has resulted in excessive competition, from ethical to illegal. It has led to pressuring students into coping with a 120-hour school work week, not including homework time. That equals stress and worry.

The growing perception—however false—that only a small number of places are available at the selective colleges needed to secure the most successful future has driven this feeling of urgency.[7] With cheating, questionable ethics, and uneven admissions advantages, worries have been compounded.

Parents from all economic levels are pressuring teens for academic excellence in the race to whatever level of college they can reach…the pressure, the competition, and the worry continue to ramp up.

Understand Your Worry

The survival of the species has depended on worrying. Awareness of dangers is, basically, worry.

We must understand how "worrying" can impact us.

1. Too much worry triggers "fight or flight" instincts. Test anxiety can be linked to the brain shutting down under stress.

2. Compounding anxiety of one worry piled on the next, and the next, can make a matter seem life-or-death when it is not. An escalating number of trivial annoyances, like a toddler repeatedly spilling pudding, actually can create the "fight or flight" danger response equal to life-and-death anxiety when nothing is really wrong.

3. Illegal actions seem justifiable when worry—whether "fabricated" or real desperation—overwhelms common sense. It can "fool" parents into selling their house to pay tuition for a college when a cheaper college would be the better fit or cutting up a daughter's clothes for several B-pluses on a string of math quizzes, as "worry" only allows for As.

4. Psychologists distinguish two types of worrying: positive- and negative-mood worrying.

    •   Negative-mood worry will propel a person to be more analytical in seeing all the problems from all the angles and solving them—in the short term, that is very good.

    •   Positive-mood worry leads to overarching creative solutions using imagination and the ability to envision the future over statistical analysis.

5. Negative-mood worriers set higher standards, but that can turn into setting standards that can never be met.When one new impossible goal

is met, another replaces it—discounting the last achievement as not yet good enough: Admission to an Ivy becomes nothing because admission to the Ivy med school replaces it. Then that isn't enough until the salary surpasses $300,000, and if that doesn't happen, the negative worrier sees only failure from a string of successes all rendered never enough. Being in a state of perpetual negative worry is not the only way to drive success. Positive motivations, like inspiration, love of "work," and a sense of achievement can drive success. Resilience does not spring from negative worry.

6. Positive-mood worrying leads people to make more creative decisions. This may not be the best for smaller, fact-based problems but is invaluable in future planning, which requires imagination to envision the future.

Section I

College Changes in the Technology Age

Part One

College Success Statistics

Teens have been running their best race for admissions to a great college, backed by their dedicated, supportive parents, willing to pay exorbitant amounts for a college experience. College for all, because college was the Golden Ticket to a high-earning, secure job guaranteeing upward class mobility, is now the guiding belief of almost all Americans. So, each year, a staggering 70 percent of high school graduates head to college; that is over three million well-educated high school graduates. And the remaining young people think they should be in college even if they aren't.[8]

So, looking at pre-pandemic success rates, hopeful freshmen were excited moving into their dorms at the beginning of their college years. They had made it. Has college fulfilled all the promises of success?

- Less than 27 percent of those who start college will graduate.

- Over half will drop out during or just after freshman year.

- Those who do graduate will not finish in four years, with five to eight years being the norm and five-and-a-half years being the median.

  - Over half will change colleges.

  - Only 36 percent who start at elite colleges or flagship universities graduate in four years.

- ° Only 19 percent who start at a state university will finish in four years.

- ° Only 5 percent of students in two-year community college programs finish in two years.

- Over half of college graduates will end up in permanent jobs that only required a certificate. They could have gotten certificates in high school, or with a two-year associate degree. And that associate degree is sometimes attainable in high school. This, rather than the pure academic or "college prep" track, makes the "college-bound" student more attractive to colleges by merging preparation with concrete accomplishments.

- 75 percent of graduates don't have careers in their field of study.

- High school grads with certificates make more than 60 percent of what college grads make.

- Contrary to beliefs, graduates of highly selective colleges have the lowest life and job fulfillment rankings, equal only to students attending fraudulent for-profit universities.

The US has the highest college drop-out rate of any industrialized country in the world.[9]

To me, those figures reveal a little-publicized catastrophe. Even the elite and "selective" college students do not escape these poor outcomes.

Parents are so proud when moving their college freshman into their first dorm room and saying goodbye. Maybe don't cry when you move your teen into that first dorm room. Don't turn their room into a study or guest room too fast—you might be seeing them soon.

They'll be back—either within a year, or when they don't get a job after college, or even when they get a job (over 50 percent of those eighteen to thirty-four live "at home," 34 percent pre-COVID-19). Just an important note: financial considerations are *rarely* the reason for the move back home at *any* stage.

Why does the US have the worst college outcomes in the world?

No, the poor outcome statistics are not skewed by adult students. Adult students have the lowest completion rates, having to juggle college with jobs and families, *but they are not part of those statistics.*

Again, dropping out is rarely from financial hardship.

One toxic and reprehensible argument is that most students are just *not* "college material." Some point out that about 27 percent of college freshmen need remedial courses, but that is not because these students are stupid, but to remedy language differences or disparities in their high school offerings or language challenges. They graduated with sufficient qualifications for college.

More students drop out from immaturity—they too are not stupid. No one would say that they are "not college material"—just inexperienced or "undecided" about life goals. They would be better off postponing college, getting some real-world exposure, or completing some career exploration and planning (at school or offered in this book).

Students are not to blame for college admission priorities, some of which have turned toxic through intense competition at all costs. College admissions tests do not predict college or career success but have taken over as student goals to meet college targets—useful for the college, but not the student.

Colleges and universities are vital to society. Educators are the "good guys." Accepting standards based on rankings, not on educational value for students, colleges' and universities' cartel-like operations allow college profit and falsely perceived "prestige" motives to go unchecked. Reform is needed. Again, educators are the "good guys," but some college marketing operations make the Varsity Blues parent scandal look mild—or worse, normal. One university board member stepped down to accept endowment fees—management fees in the tens of millions—larger than the college's retirement fund, setting up his profit while on the board; or board members or administrators with million-dollar salaries replace permanent professors with low-paid adjunct professors, earning less than an Uber driver, to cut costs. Make sure that what is in the profit interest of the college is in the educational interest of the student.

But There Is Worse News for College Graduates

The economic outcome is worse news.

- 60 percent of those with lesser degrees or certifications earn more than those with bachelor's degrees

- 43 percent of young workers with occupational licenses out-earn the average associate degree holder

- 27 percent with a license out-earn those with a bachelor's degree

- 31 percent with an associate degree out-earn bachelor's-degree holders[10]

This is looking at outcomes in the last ten years. While this is different for the fifty- to sixty-five-year-olds, it is very relevant to those entering the workforce now.

If We Don't "Blame" the Students for Poor Outcomes, Who or What Is to "Blame?"

- Colleges provide an excellent education, but that education is often slightly out of sync with high-earning careers in the Technology Age.

- College preparation has become prepping to meet college admissions requirements. Acing multiple-choice tests is different from the deep learning or applied learning necessary to succeed in the Technology Age. Parents and teens are not at fault—they were following the rules or trying to better the previous year's students with better scores, more APs (Advanced Placement classes), etc.

- Career planning has become "go to college." Great jobs used to be reached by having *any degree*. That has changed.

- College choice is based on an excellence perception generated by rankings that can be easily manipulated. Prestige should not be based on fifty- or seventy-five-year-old "truths," nor manipulated with marketing techniques. Technology Age prestige is different from Industrial Age or pre-Recession prestige—just check out all the current *Forbes* "top" lists to see from where excellence originates. The "prestigious" colleges are absent.

- Students will go on to have seven to eleven completely different careers in their Technology Age working lifetime. Planning that first career needs to start before college. It's a first career. It can be based on the student's passions—gifts and aptitudes that link up with great careers—and not on finding a career and trying to change the student into something he or she is not.

- How can students be the selective buyers in the college choice process? Currently many students are at the mercy of selective colleges who want students to have a high school program that boosts their rankings goals. But college admission requirements are often completely out of line with the best educational preparation for students to actually excel, once in college study.

I am not saying that selective colleges are bad. This book is not entitled "How to feel okay when your teen gets an elite college rejection." The book is about "best colleges" that get the student where they want to be at the end of college—not going into college. I am looking at a variety of ways to increase the probability of more successful outcomes than we are getting now.

Many parents do not want to hear any of this, even when the chance of positive outcomes with the "traditional" ways ranges from disappointing to tragic.

The current future of work is seven to eleven entirely different careers in a lifetime for today's young adult. So why do we think college planning for one lifetime career will work for the new future of work?

Is the Titanic Unsinkable?
Or Do We Get in a Lifeboat?

A leader in the career education field described parents of the selective-college-bound as being the last ones left on the deck of the Titanic, refusing to get into a lifeboat from the belief that the ship is unsinkable, even as it approaches the iceberg—in this case, college and career choice. The parents of the highly-selective-college-bound are described as making the most mistakes.[11]

Parents are amazing people, leading kid-centered lives out of dedication, for no reward, wanting only the best for their children.

But government surveys show that only about 27 percent of parents understand Technology Age career changes and how teens can prepare "better" for college and those new careers.[12] Most parents have missed the memo:

> Gone is the Industrial Age. And in this Technology Age, pathways to careers and upward mobility are being redefined.

The world of work has changed so much and so fast that our young people—although academically almost overprepared and brilliant—emerge, even from the most selective colleges, as poorly equipped for these twenty-first century careers. Turning potential—academic knowledge—into ability means adding application through experience to the kind of great degree that will lead to a great career.[13]

Ignorance of college outcomes and no knowledge of new opportunities are not the parents' or teens' fault. Most information reaching parents originates from the college industry, college testing and ranking companies, and high-end advertising firms hired by colleges and the college industry to "hard sell" their product, but some also comes from public schools, which are dependent on selective college admissions to push for bond issues and funding.

Even the government has "sat" on some statistics about aspects of failure with college-for-all, wanting to encourage college, until new programs and strategies are put in place that could solve the poor outcomes.

This year, the parent-education effort to promote higher education opportunities has shifted into high gear. As of spring 2020, the Colorado Department of Education, backed by the state government, has trained over five thousand teachers, counselors, and professionals to roll out courses, higher education and college planning, and career pathways programs, along with a new look at college goals and choices. Parents will now start hearing about the poor outcomes and the new opportunities in similar efforts being rolled out nationwide.

Fascinating, high-paying careers with advancement opportunities and career longevity are out there. Highly educated, highly intelligent, high-skilled employees are in demand. There is a national shortage. Everyone needs college or some targeted college—higher education—to advance, but the strict four-year model is only one pathway, and that four-year college must combine professional application with the academic instruction, regardless of the college's selectivity, regardless of whether a student is pursuing a STEM or non-STEM major.

A little planning sounds like an easy tweak. But this radical change to new behavior requires acceptance of the new and a change in mindset. Our beliefs about education, college, and careers are entrenched, rarely questioned, even held with cult-like fervor.

Who Knows About These Horrific Statistics?

Your high school counselor knows these dismal outcomes; so does your high school principal; so do the local, state, and national departments of education; legislatures, state and national, all know this. Business and industry know, and they are entering partnerships with high schools and colleges trying to solve this.

When the terrifying outcomes started to come in, national, state, and local departments of education developed *new courses, new planning, and new tools* to stop the "college-for-all" mistakes and failures. College or higher education is vital; it just needs to be approached differently.

One of the nation's leading high school principals described the slowness of the change. "College-for-all took a long time to catch on. Change is slow. By the time everyone finally, firmly believed it was the best route to a great career, huge flaws became known to educators and employers. Change will take a long time, but it is happening. College graduates are coming back with degrees but are unable to get jobs. Others come back with huge debt. Others are unable to finish college. And those returning college graduates see that high school friends, who didn't go to college, are doing well."[14]

Word is filtering back, but change is slow. Many parents won't admit that the dream college was less than perfect. Paying $200,000 for no job result makes parents feel stupid, but it is not their fault—they did what was perceived as "the best." The situation is tragic. But incorrect information slows progress to healthy outcomes.

Four-year college is an invaluable education. Learning is a worthwhile and noble pursuit. But it now takes extra planning for it to line up with the twenty-first-century job market.

Not knowing these statistics is not the parents' fault. Massive parent-education programs are just being rolled out now that solutions have been worked out. These include new course offerings, new pathways to careers—the focus being on high-earning careers with longevity—new teaching and grading methods, old courses rewritten. College is the path, but it looks different—everyone needs some college or a lot of college.

Schools across the nation have plans and pathways that can fix this problem.

College-for-All Community Destruction

Government agencies and initiatives in Washington, DC, are studying the effect of college-for-all on small local and rural communities. But

Washington is not releasing what prove to be highly negative statistics, as it could cause a panic.

In smaller communities, as everywhere, students have been sold on college. The trend is that the student will leave the small town and go to a larger center that has a college. As we saw with the failure rate, many will not finish college, many will have debt, or if they do finish college, none return to their small or rural community. Jobs are rarely available in the small towns, as all the young adults have left, causing failing businesses. The communities they left are failing because of the perceived imperative to go to college when there is no access to higher education in the small communities linked to the jobs there. The government and national think tanks have the information, but it is not published. The thought process for not publicizing the results is that targeting failing communities so directly would probably cause even further damage with growth business becoming reluctant to go to those communities or stay there. So, initiatives are working in the background on solutions to keep youth in the community, to provide more attractive jobs and educational opportunities locally to stop the death of these communities.

Those problems can be stopped with better career planning and career exploration in high school, run in coordination with local businesses who need a skilled, smart workforce. High school courses run with local industry (or using online college, or a combination of both) can keep young adults in their communities with growth jobs in local business and industry, thus providing an exponentially positive result for students and the community.

Careers and education need to be linked more closely—not just for rural and small communities, but everywhere.

So How Can Our Kids Take Part in New Courses and Individualized Planning?

Your children already are. Departments of education, national, state, and local, working with industry and business, have worked to develop new education and career planning programs, and professional and academic courses, in line with the future of work. Parents are the last to know, but you can learn in time for the new changes and challenges. So, when your kids bring home all of those career planning information sheets, don't throw them out thinking that career planning means "college." It does mean college or higher ed but backed by career planning and career exploration.

Most parents saved for a four-year degree—but the four-year degree is taking five to eight years. What parent saved for eight years of bachelor's degree tuition?

Taking six years to graduate (and that's before embarking on a master's degree) can be financially crippling, lasting a lifetime for parents and the college grad. When students (remember, the parents are cosigning) have taken out a loan to pay for college, and then take two more years to graduate than planned, that loan increases by 70 percent. The average student borrower has $37,000 in debt, but that rises to nearly $63,000 with the extra two years. *If a student borrows $100,000 and takes two extra years for college, the debt is nearing $200,000.*

We have come to a point where most college students change majors eight to eleven times. This adds years to degrees. A better solution is to complete the first degree, in the four years, then move on to the higher degree in the other area. Adding one semester for a major that the student is passionate about, with internship opportunities and a high employment chance, could also be a sound decision. Switching majors a year before graduation can end up requiring another year or two of college. And then the student changes his or her mind again and again. This sounds crazy, but it is happening.

If the student decides near the end of the four-year program that he or she hates the major, changing to a new major, adding years to the bachelor's degree, is not a good course, although it is what many students are doing. Even when the hatred is real, finish the "loathed" degree, identify transferable knowledge and skills within that degree that you can use to transfer to a desired field, and move on to advanced training or a master's in that new field. Taking five to eight years for a four-year degree does not present as well as getting the degree, then tailored training to enter the new field.

Part Two

The Technology Age

The Future: Upper-Middle-Class Salaries for the Whole Country

Much of Europe and Asia have already adopted a new model—one to develop growth industries with high-paying careers coordinated with education and higher education. Their goal is to achieve above-middle-class pay for each and every citizen. There, colleges and universities even allow graduates to return to upskill and retrain as needed to keep up with the newer, better careers. This is working: target higher education for all in line with growth industries and business with upskilling and continual higher education training expected and available as part of the strategy. Singapore and Switzerland are excellent examples, although they are smaller countries. Even with the COVID-19 disruption, in the US, high-paying, interesting jobs are going unfilled because people are pursuing old education paths out of line with newly emerging careers.[15]

The Past: College Is the Golden Ticket

We won't even entertain the thought that a top college degree isn't the guaranteed Golden Ticket to a top job. Any college degree used to be that guarantee! But, in this, the Technology Age, many of the old high-paying jobs-for-life reached by the "any degree major" have been replaced by software.

Now, of course, many feel they "totally get" the new Technology Age. They write it off as the impossible dilemma that our youth will be "studying" for careers that haven't been invented yet, so shrug their shoulders, and proceed to approach college as that all-encompassing Golden Ticket. Be aware of your biases.

Crash course in Technology Age work:

1. Technology's exponential destructive innovation means the transformation of work: the rendering of some jobs obsolete and the creation of new jobs, happening faster than we can train for them.

2. The job for life is being replaced with seven to ten completely new jobs during a working life.

3. Companies want short-term specialists to tackle emerging problems, not the traditional full-time staff. In this gig economy, experts are employed for short-term stints, like a musician performing in different clubs weekly. This has replaced full-time, year-round company employment. An engineer may work "gigs" for five or ten different companies in a year, not just one full-time.

4. Agile planning allows for quick innovation and immediate employee evaluation with possible termination or advancement. Five-year and ten-year plans are replaced by five-month plans.

5. Businesses thrive by quick incorporation of new technology and innovation through collaborative groups of experts from many fields.

6. Proven job experience and a mastery of twenty-first-century skills are beating out the college degree in the job market, but having all three is a winning combination.

Careers: A Brief, Complete, Over-Simplified History

In the agrarian economy, before the Industrial Age, skill in farming and local support businesses were a wise planning choice for "education and career."

In the Industrial Age, the work shifted to the factories, with mechanization leading to new ways of working. Training to manually do the work of a combine harvester or automated loom would not be a wise career choice.

Post-World War II, options opened for management, and a college education led to more entering the "executive" class. Any degree, irrespective of major, led to management. The better the college, the better the degree, the better the job.

But we are now in the Technology Age. It isn't just factory workers being replaced by robots, but those high-paying management and office positions being replaced by software. Still, most continue with the belief that any college degree is the ticket to any high-paying job and upward mobility.

Society, and over 70 percent of high school grads yearly, have bought into the concept that college guarantees affluence. It used to! Now it can be important, but there's no guarantee.

The traditional college education is still an excellent education, and every college can provide a great education available with or without all the expensive frills. But for better results, parents and students can take control to make sure courses and the college experience also line up with today's careers.

College Graduates' New "Grey Collar" Destiny

In the past, social classes and economic classes used to match. Now, class signifiers are changing.

Increasingly, a college degree is no longer the definer of economic success. This leads to social classes losing their clear traditional definitions. For those to whom social status is important, it is a new social dilemma when someone without a degree is earning the same or more as the college grad.

Students may get their college degree, but not acquire any practical experience or recognized certification they need to get hired. Half of grads end up working in what is now known as a "gray-collar" job: a career not using their education and not in their field of interest. College is something to be proud of! But it can be like the old royalty, who might have had a title but no wealth. Obviously, having a college degree is more valuable than being an aristocrat with manners but without wealth or abilities. But entrance to great careers is eluding students for lack of proven experience applying that knowledge. Even though most jobs advertised require a college degree, employers are hiring those with national certification or experience in doing the job. This is important knowledge for college-goers to not get complacent that they will get hired automatically simply for having any bachelor's, and for those with the right certification, those who also have proof of success in the specific job are getting hired.

In the past, jobs requiring a bachelor's degree were traditionally seen as "white-collar" jobs. Working-class jobs were "blue-collar"—that meant working with one's hands, doing manual labor, and earning far less. Now most jobs require high skill, in addition to academic learning. The high-paying jobs in growth fields require both professional and academic study. Now, a technical certificate can land what was classified as a "white-collar" job that used to require four years of college. Advanced manufacturing is no longer labor-intensive, but is now knowledge-intensive—like coding or data processing replacing wrenches and oily rags.

The old perceived social definers are not propelling success as the job market for those "white-collar" skills has changed. Social and economic class will no longer be synonymous. Now, a new "collar" system has evolved. Hopefully, this new "diversity" will end the polarized social concepts of "white-collar" and "blue-collar" that stigmatize workers.

"Collars"

White collar: desk jobs and management
Blue collar: jobs requiring manual labor
Pink collar: service industries like retail, waiters
Gold collar: combines high education with high technical skill
and training
Red collar: government work
Grey collar: combining white and blue collar—a job for which the
worker is overqualified
Brown collar: the military
Green collar: environment, ecology, renewable energy
New collar: technology worker trained through nonconventional means
No collar: free-spirited artist types

Just this reclassification of workers is a "working-class" revolution.

The Highest-Paying Careers

True or false: The college grad will make $2.26 million more over a
lifetime rather than those with no degree.—False.

Right now, society believes that college grads earn more. Charts and graphs back
that up. *US News and World Report* said that college grads earn more. The high
school counselor says it. The college websites say it. The College Board website
confirms it—until you notice that the webpage was written sixteen years ago
about data covering a period ten years earlier.

The median salary for a college graduate with a bachelor's degree is
$50,390.00 (2018).

The median salary for Americans is $50,000.44, according to government data
(Department of Social Security, 2018).

That is a total $389.56-a-year earnings boost for the college degree holder.

Some statistics say that, on average, a college grad will earn $400 a week more than someone with no degree. Some statistics say that, on average, the college grad earns $2.26 million more in a lifetime. Other statistics say that, on average, that the college grad earns $1 million more.

A fifty-five-year-old college grad at the height of his career is probably going to make much more than a sixteen-year-old in a part-time job—again we have an apples and oranges comparison. Most low-level jobs are part-time—the yearly part-time income can't be compared with a full-time job, but these are frequently compared, leading to misleading information upon which big decisions are based.[16]

The college grad finance officer earning median $170,000 for a 120-hour work week earns $27 an hour. The aviation mechanic earns $32 an hour starting salary (for a fifty-hour work week) or $85,000 a year. Working a second job or working up to a pilot's license can result in the $170,000 job with a fifty-hour work week. A doctor earns less than a teacher if one looks at the hourly wage.

Salary alone doesn't dictate lifestyle or even affluence. An $85,000 salary (no student debt) where a four-bedroom luxury home with a pool costs $165,000 in a state without income tax like Florida or Washington, is a higher standard of living than $170,000 salary (with high student debt) where a studio apartment costs $600,000 with a high tax rate like New York or California, or even states with moderate state income tax. But the bragging about the $170,000 salary goes on.

Depending on the career and the major, the millions can be off by millions.

Top Ten Majors with Highest Starting Salaries[17]

1. Petroleum engineering
    Median starting salary: $97,000
    College with that median salary: Regional universities (West)

2. Nuclear engineering
    Median starting salary: $75,000
    College with that median salary: MIT

3. Chemical engineering
    Median starting salary: $72,000
    College with that median salary: MIT

4. Computer engineering
    Median starting salary: $70,000
    College with that median salary: University of California (Berkeley)

5. Electrical engineering
    Median starting salary: $69,000
    College with that median salary: Princeton University

6. Aerospace & aeronautical engineering
    Median starting salary: $68,000
    College with that median salary: United States Naval Academy

7. Systems engineering
    Median starting salary: $68,000
    College with that median salary: United States Military Academy

8. Materials engineering
    Median starting salary: $67,000
    College with that median salary: Stanford University

9. Mathematics & computer science
    Median starting salary: $66,000
    College with that median salary: University of Central Florida

10. Mechanical engineering
    Median starting salary: $65,000
    College with that median salary: United States Naval Academy

Please notice that one of the colleges listed is an Ivy, although a few are selective colleges—but not all. They are colleges featuring application over strict pedagogy.

The Formula for Reaching High-Salary Jobs

Train the youth for the highest-paying career. That is obvious—but it is wrong.

Don't blame parents for pushing teens toward certain jobs. Teens often self-censor their own dreams to choices they hear about and think are realistic. And, with the high cost of college education, parents and teens may chose the major that will lead to a money-making career worth the high costs of college. (Remember, having exorbitant college loans to pay off can dictate career "servitude," the taking of a hated job to pay off the debt.)

The traditional approach is not working out happily for the young adult.

Within the first two years of college, 94 percent will change their major. Those entering with firm thoughts (but without real career planning) change their major more frequently—five being the normal number of major changes per student. Parents may have to decide if they will fund college for a career that is no longer the high-earning goal with a future or a career suffering from no planning.

College Majors with Lowest Salaries After Graduation, for Those Aged Twenty-Two to Twenty-Six

Take note, an elite college will not boost the salary of a career that pays poorly. The elite-educated social worker will not make more than the state-college-educated social worker salary. The career, not the college, determines salary.

These college majors have the lowest salaries (but often with high job fulfillment).

Anthropology and Archeology
Unemployment rate: 10.9 percent
Median salary: $28,000

Film, Video, Photography
Unemployment rate: 12.9 percent
Median salary: $30,000

Fine Arts
Unemployment rate: 12.6 percent
Median salary: $30,000

Religious Studies
Unemployment rate: 10.9 percent
Median salary: $30,000

Philosophy and Religious Studies
Unemployment rate: 10.9 percent
Median salary: $30,000

Liberal Arts
Unemployment rate: 9.2 percent
Median salary: $30,000

Music
Unemployment rate: 9.2 percent
Median salary: $30,000

Physical Fitness and Arts and Recreation
Unemployment rate: 8.3 percent
Median salary: $30,000

Commercial Art and Graphic Designer
Unemployment rate: 11.8 percent
Median salary: $32,000

History
Unemployment rate: 10.2 percent
Median salary: $32,000

English Language and Literature
Unemployment rate: 9.2 percent
Median salary: $32,000[18]

These are not close to the median salary of those with bachelor's of $50,000. These may be beloved careers and worth the sacrifice—if the degree holder lands one of the jobs in the field.

Otherwise, if no career position is available, a "grey-collar" job may await.

Again, paying for a selective college with a $350,000 price tag will not transform a low-earning career into a high-earning career.

But it can be the fulfilling career of a lifetime!

What's Going Wrong and How Do We Fix It?

For years, many high schools have been directed to achieve a 100 percent college acceptance rate.

"I didn't question the target to get every student in my high school accepted to college. One year, 100 percent of the students got accepted to college. But no one followed up on the outcomes. Once those became known, I felt bad pushing college for everyone, but it was still my school district's directive," said a high school assistant principal who now works for a nonprofit creating high school apprenticeships in higher-paying growth businesses and industry.

The road to hell can be paved with good intentions.

Episteme Versus *Techne*

The Greek *episteme* meant knowledge, a great goal, but for a different generation. *Techne* is craft, art, or practice. Colleges have been in the "episteme" lane. Harvard condemned "techne," the application and practice of theory, so MIT was created, but was considered inferior by elites. Episteme has been the elite ideal for colleges, but Technology Age careers require both, episteme and techne.

Not Enough Jobs for College Grads

Sixty years ago, 13 percent of high-schoolers went to college. And over 20 percent of the jobs required a bachelor's degree, so there was a real shortage of college grads. So, any college grad with any degree was in demand, with a choice of great jobs.

Now more than 68 percent go on to college. But there are not more jobs for those with a general college education.

Even with a 27 percent graduation rate, not all college graduates will get jobs requiring a college education. Worse, employers may say they want someone with a college degree, *but those with targeted training and experience in the field will be hired with or without the degree.*

An Anesthesiologist or a Nurse Anesthesiologist?

Let's take the idea of prestige further. Does prestige equate to earning power?

Look at the path: **Anesthesiologist.**

Training: BA, pass MCAT test, go to med school for four years, then a four-year residency in anesthesiology.

Anesthesiologists make a median salary of $208,000.[19]

Anesthesiologists make an average salary of $371,000.[20]

Anesthesiology nurse,

Training: Bachelor of Science in Nursing (BSN), a four-year program (with foundation courses that can be taken while still in high school), then a two-to-three-year nurse anesthesiologist course. The student could do foundation courses in high school that lead quickly to an associate degree in nursing (under two years), then take a nursing job and continue to a BSN with tuition reimbursement, then complete the two-to-three-year nurse anesthesiologist course, comprised of fifteen hours a day of extremely hard work, to earn a master's in Nurse Anesthesia.

Anesthesiologist nurses make average salaries of $160,000 to $245,000 depending upon the state.

However, the CRNA (anesthesiologist nurse) often can earn more than anesthesiologists, due to nurses' bonuses and their being able to attend more surgeries in a day. The nurse will be qualified and earning as much as five years earlier than the doctor will.

The doctor has $100,000 to $300,000 in debt, not including the debt from the bachelor's degree. The CRNAs have education costs of $30,000 to $100,000 on average to pay back. Most nurses with MAs pay back their loans in two years.

So, which one are you going to brag about? Society answers, the doctor.

Same work, same salary, one with longer hours and crushing debt, one with shorter hours and no debt. Both are valuable. Society has respected one more than the other. Both are valid paths.

The only moral is that there are different paths to the same work, the same salary. Choose the path that works for you.

New Golden Tickets to Top Jobs

CTE (Career and Technical Education) is considered one way forward to a twenty-first-century career. Cherry Creek School District, outside Denver, has opened an entire CTE high school. Buses from the district's other high schools run students to these professional courses. This public high school offers courses in IT/STEAM, Engineering Physics, Business, Marketing and Entrepreneurship, Medicine, Health, and Wellness, Hospitality and Tourism, Advanced Manufacturing, Automotive and Aviation Transportation, and Criminal Justice and Pre-Law. These are accredited by the state community college system, and many of the courses are dual enrollment (guaranteed college academic credit). Dual-enrollment courses can be pursued to the second-year college level, while few AP course allow that Year Two advanced work.

Depending on the CTE program, high-schoolers can graduate with a high school diploma and be one class short of an associate degree, i.e., a two-year community college degree which they will receive without paying a cent, allowing transfer to a four-year college as a junior, or direct entry to high-paying growth careers. Other CTE programs result in jobs with starting salaries of $40,000 to $110,000 in criminal justice, aviation, etc. A nursing certificate can be the start of a career that will lead to employer-paid further college and post-grad degrees.

Doing CTE, the student is still likely to get into that selective college, is more likely to know what he or she wants to do, and may have a skill to fall back that will earn real money and that could be developed into a job.

But we are stuck in the "only academics" mindset.

Most parents will not even consider any of these courses. CTE means working-class, low-class, dumb, low pay—assumptions which are completely incorrect. But that is the belief.

At one high school of 3,800 students, the selective college meeting overflowed the large lecture hall and parents had to sit and stand in the aisles and at the back, cramming the room. The CTE and career planning information session had eleven people show up. The lecture hall was empty. I am not shaming the college-obsessed parents at the school, but they shouldn't feel "smart" avoiding career planning.

Tragically, the CTE student has been made to feel inferior to the AP student. "It has always been" that technical education in high school is anathema to all parents, from elite to the economically disadvantaged, who see academics as their ticket to a higher economic class. CTE conjures up auto mechanic, short-order cook, hospital aide, HVAC repair, greasy overalls from manufacturing. Less time spent in "institution-based" education equates with the working class, blue-collar work, and low pay. Fewer years of education has come to mean lower-class. So, the young adult with a tech certificate feels inferior to the one at community college, who feels inferior to those at the four-year college. The graduate of Metro Denver feels inferior to the graduate of CU Boulder, who feels inferior to grad of Fordham University, who feels inferior to the U Penn (Ivy) grad, who feels inferior to the Harvard grad, who feels inferior to the Oxford grad, etc. And we accept this.

CTE is Career and Technical Education, but don't think for one second that this means "greasy overall" careers anymore—they are knowledge-intensive, not muscle-intensive, careers and every student in America needs some or a lot of this professional education, just as every student in America needs some or a lot of ongoing academic education. Fields include high finance, IT, medicine (with education paths to $300,000 salaries), entrepreneurship, advanced manufacturing, engineering, teaching, computer science, etc. These can be degrees or certificates, and all have higher education components, stackable courses, internships, and apprenticeships, in high school and after.

The saying goes, "Training is for pets. Education is for people." Get rid of that idea. Success in agile planning and interdisciplinary project work to keep up with innovation ahead of technological change for any field requires *training and education*. Career planning consisting of "just go to college and any degree will get you a great job for life" no longer works.

The Elite Advantage?

We are caught in an abusive relationship with the college admissions industry, once created to help the less advantaged gain access to better learning. But now, unlike fifty years in the past, education standards have improved everywhere. But we still believe the hype of "the best," "the elite." Remember, the elite rule the world… *The Meritocracy Trap*, written by a Harvard professor, writes that the middle and lower classes have no access to quality education, although his overall argument discusses the toxicity of elitism. This is the concept that the educated elite are "the elite" and that only the elite things have worth.

But when we break down the backgrounds of leaders in politics and business, the Fortune 500, the influencers, the creators, the tech geniuses, most did not go to elite colleges. But that is not what society still believes.

Of two astrophysics majors, the New Mexico Tech college graduate makes more than the Harvard grad. The anesthesiologist nurse makes more than the anesthesiologist doctor. An elementary school teacher with a Harvard degree doesn't make any more money than the teacher graduating from UCF (University of Central Florida) or Morningside College in Sioux City, Iowa. A Columbia graduate in finance living in Seattle will not earn what a Columbia graduate in finance living in New York City will, and the finance grad from University of Washington will probably get the Seattle job over the Columbia student, as the UW student will probably have interned in the area and will have a business network in Seattle. And neither may get a finance job without learning a specialty like data analytics, so they can code and can apply machine learning— the academic needs integration with practical technical skills.

"The best" is our education god, our guarantee of surviving and excelling. We need serious de-programming to broaden our concepts of excellence, success, and the real "best." We need to stop living out an old value system.

Talent development that states can implement is supported by legislation like the Workforce Innovation and Opportunities Act. The act calls for business sectors to work with programs for industry-driven career pathways. The Colorado Legislature outlined their commitment: "We know that we must create the trail guide for citizens to follow, align the work of all education, training, and economic development activities in the state, and ultimately get this information into the hands of individuals so they can take charge of their careers."[21]

High Pay, In Demand

"Very highly paid careers with longevity" was the answer given by school counselors at the Colorado School Counselors Association Conference, October 10–11, 2019.[22]

Was the discussion about APs in high school? Selective colleges? No, it was education experts' primary description of the outcome of taking CTE courses.

The question was "What is the first thing that comes to mind when you hear CTE?" (Career and Technical Education courses.) "Very highly paid careers with longevity…in growth fields."

Here are some examples of high-earning jobs for a high school education and basic on-the-job training or a certificate.

1. Air traffic controller
   Median salary: $123,000
   Training salary: $17,000
   Starting salary: $63,000 (New York), $27,000 (lowest starting salary in rural area)

2. Nuclear power reactor operator
   Median salary: $93,000
   Starting salary: $44,000–$64,000

3. Transportation, storage, and distribution managers
   Median salary: $92,000
   Starting salary: $38,000–$64,000

4. First-line supervisors of police and detectives
   Median salary: $89,000 (California—$120,000)
   Starting salary: $64,000

5. Power distributors and dispatchers
    Median salary: $82,000

6. Detectives and criminal investigators
    Median salary: $80,000, federal level: $110,000
    Starting salary (rural-city) $37,000–$67,000

7. Elevator mechanic
    Median salary: $79,000
    Starting salary: $40,000-plus

8. Commercial pilot
    Median salary: $79,000
    Starting salary: $20,000–$40,000 (depending on hours and aircraft type,
    for training period)

9. Power plant operator
    Median salary: $77,000

10. Firefighters
    Median salary: $76,000

These are median salaries of jobs in high demand with job security. These can
be reached through CTE *high school* course work. This contrasts with careers
requiring a college education that, after five years, will have a median salary of
$28,000. That is with a four-year degree and five years of experience. They may be
rewarding jobs, but the four-year degree will not automatically bestow an upper-
middle-class salary.

The lowest-paying college majors with five years of work experience but no
further training, from the 2019 US News Best Colleges' top rankings, can often
be the most rewarding personally, but the least rewarding financially. These have
median starting salaries of roughly $25,000–$35,000, with median salaries at the
five-year point around the $45,000–$55,000 range (except for teaching/education,
which has a career median of $84,000).

Again, though rewarding, these are careers that are low-earning from often high-
cost degrees:

- Child development and psychology
- Work and family studies
- Culinary arts
- Social work
- Theological and ministerial studies
- Gerontology
- Education
- Parks, recreation, and leisure studies
- Animal science
- Biblical studies

The top forty careers that require a certificate or associate degree (two years) have median starting salaries of over $50,000. The degree careers pay $25,000, if there is a job available.

What Employers Really Want

In extensive surveys, employers from 1,001 fields listed *job experience* as the number one factor for hiring the candidate.

Even with job offerings listing a bachelor's as a requirement, over 70 percent of employers said that they would hire a candidate with no college degree, but who had relevant internship or job experience.

What are the key hiring factors?

1. They would take someone with no degree, who has performed the exact job, over someone who has a top degree but no experience.

2. Listed second was a degree with good grades. Good grades show competence, training, education, and perseverance. *Good grades from any college beat weak grades from a prestigious college.*

3. Third was the college major. This varied by profession because, obviously, some careers, primarily STEM jobs, demand specific technical training and education as a prerequisite. But internship or job experience was still usually required to land the job.

4. Prestige of the college or university was rated last in importance. College name isn't an issue except in narrow areas. Those wanting elite grads are specific—New York law firms (after law school), or New York financial establishments (but these companies are now recruiting in the Midwest. J.P. Morgan Chase is recruiting at the high school level and overseeing the training of these bright kids).[2324]

Once the worker has a job, college name almost never comes up for subsequent jobs.

Life Skills Shortage

An IT company assessed that their millennial college grad employees work three hours a day. So now they look to hire managers who have demonstrated "the ability to get the millennials on staff to work." The HR interviewer asks the management candidate to describe strategies and past successes in upping millennial college-grad productivity.

In interviews for this book, HR and executives, from finance to the medical management field, preferred not to hire college graduates.

- No work ethic

- Feeling of superiority: though they are the lowest-level new hire, they feel they have superiority over anyone without a four-year degree

- Limited cultural, world, and "human" awareness

- Lack of social intelligence: no charm, charisma, or skills of persuasion

- Inability to communicate with customers, senior staff

- Negative attitude because of their subordinate status

College grads who have pursued professional courses, internships, or certifications will have the hiring advantage.

Lifelong College for All

Your teen will have a working life of not one career, but seven to eleven completely different careers. Have you saved for your child to go to college seven times for seven new bachelor's degrees? Obviously, that would be ridiculous. But we need to use new planning when we send them to college for that one degree.

College can still set a student up for life. But also know, education will need tweaking and will continue. Jobs and how we train for them are different now than in the past. Most jobs will require a combination of academic and professional—for everyone! Continuing for a lifetime. Foreign universities have adopted the new mindset and are offering many paths to degrees. With academic and professional training being viewed as equal, shorter and longer degree programs, and the ability to retrain, these have even become an option for graduates of some universities.

Self-exploration, career exploration, skills development and career planning are barely touched on.[25] But now, these new courses and planning methods have been adopted and are available at most public schools.

Two paths exist: academic and professional. Neither is best. But some of both is needed for every job.

A whole new curriculum and approach to planning has been developed in an education, industry, and business partnership.

That includes teacher education, setting new standards. Training teachers for new standards of grading, schools are transitioning to new ways to demonstrate a more comprehensive excellence that employers need to fill high-paying jobs with longevity.

No one wants to say "college for all" is a failure because college-for-all is still a good idea. College is vital for all to advance and stay employed in high-paying growth jobs. The Minnesota Department of Education rephrases it as "some college for all." But *this should be rephrased as "continuing college for all," as keeping up with technology in every field means "lifelong learning."*

Reskilling and upskilling will be part of staying employable to respond to fast-changing work.

Businesses must continually transform to keep up. In technology development, the new style of work is called "agile." Five- and ten-year goals do not work to keep pace with technological development accelerating exponentially. Short-term goals, interdisciplinary project groups working together to tackle short-term goals, employee evaluation per project, are necessary to keep up with revolutionary technology, allowing companies to make fast-paced innovations.

Continuing lifelong education, in academic and experiential forms, is how college will work now. That is a complete lifestyle-altering shift.

The Academic Path and the Professional Path

In America, we have two routes to careers—the highly respectable, dignified academic path and the often-stigmatized professional path. But now the professional path leads to high-paying careers with longevity—more so than the strictly academic route.

As a result, the government is moving to create professional "degrees," so that path will be as "respectable." This is becoming common in other countries. Both degrees require intelligence and expertise.

The academic path can be the route to the career *and* so can the professional path.

In fact, those on the academic path now need some professional training, just as those going the professional route need "academic" courses. It can be one or the other, but it should be both.

1:2:7

That is the job/education requirement breakdown:

- *One job out of ten requires a post-graduate degree above a four-year degree*
- *Two jobs out of ten require a four-year degree*
- *Seven jobs out of ten require a certificate or a two-year associate degree*
- *Unskilled manual labor jobs are shrinking to the point of being not a factor.*[26]

Americans believe that they must get a bachelor's degree, but only two out of ten jobs require the four-year degree.

College education for everyone is excellent, the dream, and the goal. *But most actual jobs require different qualifications. These are not jobs for the stupid or unskilled. They are not labor-intensive, but knowledge-intensive.*

These seven out of ten jobs still require intelligence and high skill. These "Category Seven" jobs, as we will call them, are not low-paid, they are not manual work. These are the new Technology Age jobs requiring high skill and intelligence and specific training. Again! These careers are not labor-intensive, but knowledge-intensive.

Right now, half of college graduates get jobs in the seven category. Their college degree isn't going to waste; other skills just need to be added.

Category one jobs are doctors and lawyers, academics, professors, scientists, etc.

Category two jobs require certain types of four-year study. Internship or work experience is important. Certification and technical skills are important. A liberal arts degree can prepare a student brilliantly to adapt and excel in many careers ahead. But actual career entry usually requires specialization.

Some college is essential to almost all careers. Ongoing college and professional higher education are essential. The four-year model of the past may not be the easiest way to start high-earning careers. Four-year degrees provide excellent education, but not automatic career advantages.

Where are the jobs? And where were most jobs lost during the pandemic (up to August 26, 2020)?

Here is a general list of the major businesses and industries in the US, the proportion of Americans employed in those areas, and the percentage of layoffs in 2020 (up to late August).

Major Business and Industry in US	Proportion of Jobs in US	Job Loss Percentage in Field
Govt. & Public Education	15 percent	5 percent
Professional & Business Services	14 percent	11 percent
Wholesale & Retail Services	14 percent	12 percent
Healthcare	14 percent	10 percent
Leisure/Hospitality Services	10 percent	37 percent
Manufacturing	9 percent	6 percent
Financial Services	6 percent	6 percent
Construction	5 percent	5 percent
Transportation & Utilities	4 percent	3 percent
Personal Services	4 percent	6 percent
Information Services	2 percent	1 percent
Private Education Services	2 percent	2 percent
Natural Resources[27]	.5 percent	.2 percent

Part Three

Challenges for Colleges

Shaky Foundations: The Broken Model of Higher Education

College admissions and degree programs have changed little for decades, even though we have left the Industrial Age for the Technology Age, with its exponential rate of change: "In the nineteenth century, we saw more technological change than in the nine centuries preceding it. Then in the first twenty years of the twentieth century, we saw more advancement than in all of the nineteenth century. Now, paradigm shifts occur in only a few years' time... We won't experience a hundred years of progress in the twenty-first century—it will be more like 20,000 years of progress (at today's rate)."[28]

Even before the COVID-19 disruption, society had been clinging to an "old normal," and old traditions, when approaching "college." This traditional approach had stopped bringing sought-after outcomes. Ironically, the disruption has accelerated needed change to our college system.

College needed to change even before the COVID-19 disruption:

- 75 percent of college students never graduate
- Most students who do graduate take five to eight years for a four-year degree
- Less than half of the grads get a job requiring a college education
- High school grads with certificates make more than 60 percent of college graduates[29]

Many college educators say that "the model of higher education is broken."[30]

Nationwide, many college presidents and deans agree with this—that the decades-old model is broken. Many deans and college presidents now admit that high-cost degrees are not worth the amounts paid. But that same economic model has been profitable for most colleges, so there has been no impetus to change. The outcome for the student is far from optimal, but those profiting have not seen that as a reason to change the status quo.

Most college presidents have been pushing for change, implementing it incrementally, often fighting the boards of directors who have financial motivations overriding educational priorities to students, alumni who want the college to remain the same, and professors for whom students' careers were never part of the learning experience.

Accelerated by the COVID-19 impact, colleges are adding modern relevance to the great traditional education. A great education linked to modern careers will profoundly improve life outcomes for their students. So, in addition to being a valuable, enlightening educational experience, college will be "value for money" in terms of salary return on investment.

It Used to Be So Easy

Just get into a top college…

Bookstores have rows of shelves stocked with books devoted to raising chances for admittance to that great college. The traditional plan for a high-earning career was to secure entrance to the "best" college—whether you define the "best" college as an elite college or a community college.

Getting better grades and better scores for that acceptance to the best college has been fully embraced as an "Olympics-level" competition.

College prep for college admissions and college learning success used to be the same. Preparing for college admissions and college learning led to college and career success. Standardized testing was introduced so all students could show expertise—good thing. Course success became test success.

Many "college prep" high school courses, AP, IB, and honors courses, are preferred by college admissions departments, as these courses show the student can handle college material and is willing to challenge himself or herself. These courses were started to expand access to elite colleges by providing higher-level standardized courses nationwide. This was excellent.

But success on the tests became the goal for college admissions.

Test success, however, can be different from course success. College prep curriculum is evaluated with standardized tests, and college admissions tests themselves have grown out of line with deep learning. That standardized test prep has also grown less and less correlated to the in-depth learning and experiential application of theory needed to succeed in college and careers in the Technology Age.[31]

High test scores have become the goal, rather than in-depth learning. Learning for a multiple-choice test calls on short-term memory, forgotten in four to six weeks—a high short-term memory standard. So preparing for college admission has become not highly educative.

Great courses are now often "taught to the test" as achieving the high test score has become the goal. And that can distort what the student should be learning in the course.

Admission to a great college has become the goal. So, test success is all. Exploration and interpretation are all part of these great courses, but when "short-form test success" is the primary goal, in-depth exploration can take too much time and may not lead to test success. So gradually test success became the goal. Test success used to predict college success. But we have reached a point where success on college standardized tests has no correlation with college and career success, because teaching to the test is often an obstacle to learning and exploring the material in-depth.

Even so, society has firmly established college *admission* as the goal of high school learning and college prep. But runaway "competition" turned the good toxic. If a couple of APs are good, why not ten, twenty, or more? Then high school funding often became linked to higher college entrance test scores, APs, and the number of selective college admissions achieved. Schools began "teaching to the test" when score excellence was vital for school improvement. So, "college admissions" has unintentionally become distanced from in-depth learning and the application of knowledge needed for Technology Age college and career success.

To be very clear, today's students are, as many college deans describe, "academically overprepared." These are smart, dedicated students. They are truly excellent, but much time is wasted and undue importance has been given to meticulous study for increasingly superficial evaluations. The affluent have more chances to prep for tests and pay to retake them over and over until perfection is achieved. Perfection, but it doesn't correlate with future success.

Whatever the economic background, those students and their parents with college dreams—which is most students and families—would never consider anything but the "academic" or "college prep" track of honors and AP courses (AP being Advanced Placement college-level courses from the College Board, taught at high schools across the country). All economic levels accept this unquestioningly.

Over 70 percent of parents are oblivious to, or reject, usually recoiling in horror at the thought of anything vulgarly "vocational," and have their students opt for the "academic option." But this leaves most students missing real Technology Age opportunities. We cling with cult-like ferocity to the elitism of fifty years ago when elitism can be shown to not be working even for the "elite."

For example, the "best" path to a finance career was to attend an "elite" college. Now, the path can be a high school apprenticeship with JP Morgan, attending high school while working for a salary of $35,000 yearly. The high school apprentice knows he or she has the job, and will complete college, usually paid for all or in part by the company, while working in the job. Going the college route, the college student may pay for the degree at a college with an $86,000 a year list price, but there is no guarantee upon graduation that he or she will land the JP Morgan job—while the high school apprentice has the career, has a degree paid for, and has six to seven years of corporate experience when the college grad comes applying for an entry position.

$200,000-plus spent or borrowed, a degree that may or may not be fine-tuned to corporate needs, plus no experience—*the former "sure thing" college degree is now the risky path…unless properly planned.*

Options Students Might Be Unaware of

K–12 departments of education partnering with business and industry have worked together to align education to growth fields, which is reflected in new expanded, high-level high school curriculum options:

- Capstone research projects with defense (even some public school systems offer a Capstone project every year from K–12)

- Experiential courses (where some students emerge with their own patents)

- Dual enrollment courses

- Some courses are apprenticeships where students earn $35,000 while going to high school, in companies that will help fund college

- Some courses check the internship box, valid even after college graduation

- Some courses certify students for a medical assistant job, teaching assistantship, marketing, business data analysis—either a career or a great part-time or summer career-growing job

- Some high school courses can make an eighteen-year-old employable in a $65,000–$125,000 a year starting salary on graduation

Pedagogy is essential. So is its application. College planning shouldn't be about "assembling high test scores." Planning is laying out an individualized path made up of relevant learning progress where academics are learned and applied. Credentials show academic learning demonstrated through performance excellence. This approach is more complicated than multiple-choice tests but produces substantive results.

New twenty-first century courses enhance college admissions and outcomes as much as or more than the traditional "academic" or "selective college" track. Private schools, too, are replacing APs with more experiential or deep-dive courses.

But in our laser-focused college admissions fixation, the priority drifts back to "getting in." The "law of the land" has been that tests and scores guarantee getting that acceptance letter to that great college that sets the whole process rolling to success.

Admissions has become the goal, the prize. After that, just "follow the program" to the degree, and the graduate is set for a great career promising a high salary and upward mobility.

The acceptance letter comes with its automatic prize package. The program of study, a five-star college life, the career preparation, the networking, obviously, *must be* "a given." For the price of most colleges, the package should be "all-inclusive." The worth of the "college experience" is rarely questioned.

The COVID-19 Disruption to the College Experience

With the coronavirus disruptions, much of the campus experience—that all-the-frills prize package—was gone, but colleges didn't substantially drop the price. The rite-of-passage campus living experience, the networking, the internships, and the rich learning environment were over or bore little resemblance to what we think is essential about the campus experience. And that experience will be profoundly impacted for a number of years to come—even with a vaccine—as the economic impact of 13 to 85 percent budget cuts affects course offerings, sports, frills, education delivery, and the enriching campus experience.

Now consumers—parents and students—are asking, "What is important about college?" Finally.

The "what's important" question is often prompted by wrong reasoning—"Why should I pay for something my student isn't getting—the campus experience?" The on-campus experience is accepted as the core of the educational experience, although a variety of educational environments of mentors, tutors, advisors, and friends can inspire a life journey from anywhere, by any delivery method.

The reason should have always been, "How is all this money going to lead to a great education that could lead to a great career?"

But, whatever the reason, the college experience, now under scrutiny, is leading to long-overdue, positive changes in what colleges will be delivering educationally in the future to make the fine education college has always offered align with Technology Age careers.

The College Mission: The Degree

Colleges provide teaching and learning for an excellent education. The end goal is the degree, knowledge, enrichment, and development of logic and reasoning. Degrees had nothing to do with careers. It coincided that a degree was the Golden Ticket straight to a high-paying career.

To be crystal clear, for academics at many colleges, the goal of college has been to provide an education resulting in a degree. It was not seen as career preparation or job--focused. It was about education, not education to get a job. This stems from old ideas of the gentleman becoming educated. The idea of it being designed to lead to a job was considered vulgar. College was education for its own sake. Fifty years ago, it was coincidental that any college education led to a good job.

Career preparation was never part of the college mission—bestowing degrees was. A degree represented education, persistence, and competence for careers that required logic and communication, but not necessarily any specific expertise. Traditional degrees met requirements for most jobs. In the past.

Colleges and universities have continued inside this bubble.

But, in the Technology Age, traditional education is no longer aligning to a career entry on graduation. Traditional education is valuable and excellent preparation for life—logic, communication, pedagogy—but now a college degree rarely leads directly to a job. The college degree and top job requirements no longer line up.

For example, most finance jobs require some expertise in data analysis—many colleges would not teach data analysis to finance majors, as it is considered "nonacademic," practical, and therefore vulgar—so on graduation, those finance majors had to enroll in data analysis classes for certification to be employable. After paying $240,000 for an education, more training for certification, and often grad school just for internship, work experience may be needed. Straight academics left these elite, truly excellent grads needing additional education to combine the knowledge and the practical.

Those majoring in marketing are rarely certified in the software needed to be employed—they were very smart grads with great ideas but did not have the skills to perform the job. Again, they must get a master's largely to get an internship, that essential job experience that an employer needs. A non-degree, but certified high school grad with internship experience who has actually performed the job will trump the college degree holder with no certification and no job experience. The college grad has great potential, but today, the employer needs someone who has performed the work.

Simply put, acquiring matching professional skills and experience have to be added to the degree. Some colleges are adding those courses; for others, those courses are considered beneath them. But the grad will still need those skills and experience to add to their academic expertise.

College is perfectly placed to integrate theoretical learning with the new professional practical training and internship experience to create exceptional future job applicants.

Some colleges are rethinking whole programs to add experiential elements. Other colleges are just tweaking their majors, making connections with local growth companies to provide proof of job success. Still other colleges are adding courses for national credentialing where students can demonstrate their application of knowledge. But the move to career relevance will vary greatly from one college to the next. Students can learn how to make their college education employer-friendly.

Education for its own sake is wonderful if you can afford it. But if the student needs to earn a living, then make some tweaks to the genuinely amazing education currently available to increase employment opportunities. This would make college a no-brainer—but academia has been resistant. Pure pedagogy is excellent learning; why change? Change because some people need to get a job...

The Goal of College Has Been to Provide an Education, Not a Career

Relevance to the job market or any concern for the application of that degree was not in the college remit.

Again, that was fine when any degree worked for most jobs.

Now high-paying careers exist, but they require an additional proof of being able to apply theory.

The choice isn't between college as providing an education versus college becoming "trade school." This isn't lessening college, but merging knowledge and expertise. Remember that MIT was created because Harvard found application of scientific theory demeaning—or *episteme* versus *techne*. If one thinks that MIT provides a great education, then there should be no resistance to this concept. Work requirements have changed. It now requires expertise in the application of theory.

Colleges should be perfectly suited for delivering theory merged with high-level application. It wasn't their remit earlier; it is now.

"Colleges failed to make systemic changes during the Recession where they could have adapted to a world of new excellence. They will get left behind if they do not create more interdisciplinary programs in line with the twenty-first century... They need to use real metrics to prove the value of high-cost education which currently is not worth it."[32]

STEM Isn't the Only Answer

Meeting the challenges of the Technology Age does not mean that the student should just study STEM—science, technology engineering and math—in high school and college and their success will be ensured. Over

95 percent of college-goers change their major, and a huge portion are STEM majors. The parent may have had the five-year-old pulled out of kindergarten for Algebra 2 tutoring, but many current academically geared high school STEM courses, not allied to application, seem to lead to burnout, with the students changing majors to music, theatre, or anything but STEM when they reach college. College prep STEM has separated the academic from the practical, practical being shunned as "blue-collar," which is preposterous. All fields are being advanced by the application of STEM principles or techniques—application being the key word. More on this later, but just making your high schooler concentrate on STEM, especially "college prep" pedagogic STEM, is not the easy fix guaranteeing Technology Age career success.

Value for Money

Colleges have been left exposed and "speechless" when asked to demonstrate value for money by parents wanting to know why they should pay huge amounts for "less," although residential colleges are still providing teaching and a learning environment, just without the campus experience.

That lazy river and the food court with Italian, French, Thai, Mexican, Asian Fusion, Pho from five regions, designer teas, gourmet burgers with steak fries, keto, gluten-free, organic, sustainable with twenty-four/seven robot delivery, the concierge rooms with valet options, personalized parking, Greek isle yacht trips to study Homer, ski shuttles, "Patagucci" (expensive, though excellent, hiking gear) in the college bookstore, even an Antarctic campus—the campus experience is often more "country club" or "lifestyles of the rich and famous" than an obvious learning environment. Colleges found they could charge disproportionately more than cost for offering those amazing amenities. These are gone, now and possibly forever. Colleges will no longer be in the luxury food, travel, parking, gym, and valet service businesses.

What is the obvious "cost-effect" proof, shown with real, solid data and analytics, proving that their college provides future possibilities? Job success is a tangible metric that appeals to parents and young people who are now forced to consider career entry more than ever. Now colleges are scrambling to show career value. Previous "job" numbers from colleges are less than accurate.

Heads of colleges are moving to align degrees with career entry, employing real metrics to evaluate. Marketing statistics of amazing student success rates are easily shown to be misleading. The deans and presidents know that they must update aspects of teaching and then show that degrees will lead to careers.

Alumni often want the college to stay as they knew it. Boards usually have no members actually involved in education—theirs are endowment investment goals, research goals, and money-making goals, not educational goals—hence the educational component of many colleges is farmed out to low-paid nonpermanent adjunct professors and graduate students. This has missed the needs and wishes of the students.

College Business Plans

Colleges are actively using "price strategies," just like mattress sales, to make more money. College costs have not risen overall, except for COVID-19 expenses. The profit motive is still a driving force for nonprofits.

Aside from the elite colleges with large endowments (basically huge endowments with colleges attached), most colleges rely on tuition to exist. In 1992, a financial consultancy firm came up with the concept of "financial aid leveraging." The idea was to add country-club-level amenities to colleges, then grossly inflate the tuition and room and board rates, then offer discounts to lure students. The reauthorization of the Higher Education Act in 1992 made it easier to get student loans and changed the way family responsibility was calculated.

The company, Noel-Levitz, came up with "enrollment management" using data analysis for colleges to find the maximum amount families would be willing to pay to attend. The actual cost is irrelevant. Colleges grossly inflated tuition prices, then discounted them differently for each student arriving at the maximum that the family would pay for that student to go to that school. The real college year cost might be $25,000, but the list price would be $62,000; then the college would award the student a $20,000 merit scholarship. Parents would think that their teen was amazing and would pay or get a loan.

With this "enrollment management" practice, colleges saw an average 10 percent rise in profits.

COVID-19 Financial Costs

- Moving to online teaching is expensive and can cost more than in-person classes.

- College budgets may be down from 15 percent (2009 recession levels) to 85 percent.

- Public college and university budgets will be cut from reduced tax revenue.

- Private colleges have restrictions on their endowments, so can't just use endowments to solve COVID-19 problems.

- Some colleges will merge, be purchased by other colleges, or go bankrupt—many were on the verge of bankruptcy already.

- Even empty dorms and classrooms have to be heated and cleaned, and mortgage/taxes/rental still has to be paid by the colleges.

Possible Future Trends

- Colleges will specialize, and not offer "everything."

- Colleges are merging departments.

- Post-COVID, the trend may be to expand enrollment and lower tuition, with some adding a summer "semester" option. Many basic classes will remain online, allowing a larger enrollment, with "on campus" being offered only for a portion of the degree.

- A quicker graduation will be offered with the summer option.

- More university and college places, and cheaper ones, would be positive. At one point, Harvard considered doubling the enrollment but keeping the cost the same.

College Services Exponentially Increase

Noneducational college spending has increased. Parents and students expect state-of-the-art gyms, dining facilities, and mental health support to support "achievement"-obsessed, anxiety-ridden students who have lived programmed lives, and entitled lives, so they lack the maturity of students of thirty years ago.

The increased tuition does not go toward education improvements, but rather to amenities, board member and administration salaries, marketing, and fees for managing the endowments.

"The Best" Education System

"College" is a multi-million-dollar industry, primarily nonprofit, but ambitiously striving for success, which manifests in pursuit of a high profit motive.

Colleges, college testing, and college prep, are a huge industry based on the perceived importance of college-for-all. Profit isn't a dirty word. Neither is college.

The College Board (which runs the SAT, AP tests, etc.) has an annual income of $200 million.

The Independent Education Consultants Organization estimates there are over 14,000 legitimate college consultants who charge between $850 and $40,000 per student—for legal help. SAT and ACT prep courses from reputable companies run about $1,400 for about twenty hours of online or in-person group classes, three to four practice tests, and support material, with discounts for hundred-hour packages.

The college industry will want to "help" your student get the highest grades and scores and try for the "best" colleges. The industry is there to help your student to do his or her best—the best at what they define as the best.

Don't you wish it didn't matter…

Why ACT, SAT, and APs Are Being Phased Out

College entrance tests were created to assess non-elite high school students so they could have a chance they otherwise would not have to get into elite schools.

Advanced Placement courses provided non-elite, non-East Coast public high schools an advanced curriculum, designed to allow students from non-elite schools to learn advanced material and demonstrate excellence.

These were all good things. But they went from being something of value to being something to exploit for runaway competition.

Being a College Freshman for Five Years

APs became useful to show that students are college-ready. College dropouts are a financial problem for the college—the AP student is less likely to drop out from course rigor. One to three APs is what colleges look for if offered at the high school—but again, competition has been runaway: If one AP is good, ten, better, twenty—are twenty enough?

Having your teen spend five years as a college freshman would sound strange. But taking twenty-nine APs is the equivalent of spending nearly five years stuck in the freshman year of college—all those semesters in freshman-level courses, taught by a high school teacher (why is World History so often taught by the football coach with extra credit for attending the game?), not by a professor with a PhD, passionate, having devoted his life to that area of study.

Twenty-nine APs is an impressive feat and demonstrates real discipline and courage for a challenge, as well as academic accomplishment! But other learning experiences are equally or more valuable.

Had the student chosen dual enrollment, he or she could have advanced in courses that interested them—not just a basic introduction to thirty or forty areas. The student could have pursued interests in-depth. They could leave high school with the equivalent of several associate's degrees or beyond. They could have "published"; they could have attained a patent.

Most with thirty APs will go on to colleges that will not accept that work for credit. And because they are basic courses, the student may have to repeat many of the courses because the college wants the student to be taught the basics "their way."

Thirty APs may qualify a student for *Jeopardy* but that wide a spread of knowledge is trivia mastery more than in-depth learning. If the student loved one of the subjects, he or she just dropped it and moved to the next AP. This is not the most sensible use of time if deep learning and understanding is the goal—which it should be.

We Forget AP Courses Are College Courses

AP courses are far from easy! So doing one or forty is an achievement. We should remember that a student needs to be ready for AP courses.

Ninth-graders are being pushed into APUSH (AP US History) to be competitive. They are rarely allowed to struggle or fail. At the first sign of any difficulty, he or she is pushed into hours of tutoring support. There is often no thought of the student working harder on their own, or of switching to a lower-level course and tackling APUSH later. The student is tutored to passing, often giving the teen the impression that they cannot do it on their own or that they are not smart.

Challenge shouldn't be about beating the competition, but about learning.

All the IB students at a private school had straight As. The parents bragged about the wonderful school they were paying for. But about 98 percent of those students failed the national IB exams. The school published grades, not IB scores. But colleges knew. The school "solved" its problem by offering scholarships to high-achieving senior-year IB students, trained elsewhere, who would pass the IB exam and make the school's statistics look better. But that didn't improve the quality of the education—elite colleges still knew and didn't accept the original students, but school enrollment increased, with parents sending their children to this "amazing" school, which then published select IB test scores.

Part Four

Challenges with Admissions

The Desperate Quest for the Golden Ticket

It may start from the belief that college is the Golden Ticket to a high-paying job, as it has always been, and the added perception that the more selective the college, the better—that it is the Platinum Ticket to a happy life, wealth, and security. This has been true for generations.

It may start when a teacher tells the parent how amazing his or her student is and advises the parents to do all they can to help the student get into a prestigious college. It is unbelievably flattering. How could a parent not sign on for developing their child to the highest levels he or she can attain!

It may start from listening to the media portrayal of elite and selective colleges (or even just preaching the necessity of college) as the place for superior beings, or as the exclusive creator of superior beings.

It may start from trying to keep up with what friends are doing for their children.

It may come with the belief that your child is amazing.

"It" is the stress and worry, and in some cases, desperation, that it is vitally important for your teen to get into the best college possible, whatever that means for the student and parent.

Some parents will pay six million dollars to lie, cheat, and bribe their teens into great colleges, leaving other parents wondering how they can help their teens compete against illegal acts and money that can buy an edge in admissions.

Many parents act as if not getting into a selective college means their child is destined to become a derelict living in a tent down by the river.

Making the Best Decisions for Admission to the "Best" College

Acceptance to a great college has been a laudable goal, but distortions have turned what should be an exciting process into a confusing, frantic, and even desperate competition, as evidenced by the criminal actions of some parents. Factors exacerbating this mindset of desire verging on desperation include:

- The perception that selective colleges are the goal, with places at selective colleges being increasingly scarce.

- Any lengths are justified to make admissions happen, from parents cheating to teens on eighteen-hour-a-day schedules.

- College-industry information that appears to be reliable comprehensive statistics but is really just marketing material from the "seller" (including the college admissions industry, colleges, testing companies, rankings companies, and support industries, who employ advertising companies or professionals to "sell" their colleges using the most persuasive methods).

Parents will find themselves thinking, "This is terrible... I wish it weren't like this..."

Is This Avoidable?

Picture a high school counselor's office. "I know you are already stressed. Meeting the academic targets for the selective colleges you like, the application process, tests, prep for tests, more tests, GPA, this will be a stressful year. Acknowledge that it will be stressful, and then put that emotion away in your pocket," said my daughter's high school counselor, opening our "monumental" Junior Year College Conference with my daughter and myself.

This school, like practically every school in the country, public or private, has a vested interest in academic excellence and college acceptance rates to drive increased funding. Standards and funding are necessary. This is an amazing public school that the community supports by passing substantial bond-issue funding.

The counselor talked as fast as a person can talk to check off the list of college planning and application deadlines, helped us target colleges, asked probing questions to elicit ideas for my daughter's college essay, brainstormed topics for the references she and favorite teachers would write for my daughter, and even touched on tricky financial-planning issues. The counselor was honest and spoke to the logistics of getting a good student into a selective college.

Though logistics are stressful, all parents and teens have access to brilliant resources even if they do not have the hand-holding this school provides. Naviance, or wonderful planners like *The College Bound Organizer*, can keep parents and teens on track.

Books with spreadsheets, calendars, and charts dictate something for a parent do every single day, starting in ninth grade, to help the student be the high achiever that will check the boxes for a chance at a top college. Does an extra worry a day for four years—1,450 tasks—sound like a good idea on top of the teen's own "to dos"—classes, prep, studying, sports, community service, and solving poverty in the Third World—that are required of teens today to be "competitive" for the selective college?

Basic Logistics for the College Application Process

- Start saving for college at birth and check out college scholarships for the state and college as soon as possible. The money saved in state education accounts can usually be withdrawn for emergencies.

- *PLEASE REMEMBER*: The statement that most students have $30,000 debt is misleading in many ways. *DEBT DOES NOT MEAN THAT IS WHAT COLLEGE WILL COST A FAMILY. DEBT or resulting LOANS ARE IN ADDITION TO WHAT PARENTS AND TEENS SAVE AND PAY FOR COLLEGE!* Some families save $240,000 per child and still have $34,000 to $100,000 or more in debt.

- Use the planner later in this book to fine-tune the teen's schedule, and academic and career plans.

- If a particular college is too expensive, tell the child as soon as possible. (Sure, apply, but don't be wedded to that college if the student isn't offered a big scholarship.)

- Teens should take SAT and/or ACT college entrance tests at least once, starting in winter of junior year or spring of junior year. Do some free online prep before taking the tests. Some colleges may not use the tests for entrance but are using them as the basis for merit scholarship consideration.

- The student should ask teachers for recommendations in April of junior year so the teachers can write them over the summer.

- Be honest and figure out what college is for. (Use the planner to identify the student's goals.) If the desire that they go to college is because they are passionate to learn—go. If it is because the immature child needs to grow up—no.

- The student should start roughing out essays for colleges at the end of junior year, to be done by Labor Day just before senior year. Tweak the essays when the essay topics are released in late July. Fill out the Common App in early August, so most of the college applications are done before senior year starts.

- Parents, fill out the FAFSA in October, as soon as possible, so the student will be among the first eligible for financial aid—and have your last year's tax return ready.

- Students contact the high school in the second week of senior year with the forms for transcripts they need to send.

- Be ready to click the submit buttons for each college on the first day of EA (Early Admissions—acceptance is not financially binding—or Early Decision—financially binding) or on October 1—free application day—and you are set.

The Basic Truth of College Admissions—It Is Unfair

College is usually one of the biggest investments of a lifetime, so it isn't a surprise that admission to a good college feels like an urgent, crucial undertaking. One college's tuition, room, and board for a four-year degree have passed $400,000. The competition for admission for the privilege of paying nearly a half million dollars is as extravagant as the price tag.

But, how do colleges describe the admissions process? What wise, comforting words do they have to reassure parents and teens? The one word a top admissions director of a wonderful selective college used at a college info weekend, which was backed by other honest admissions officers on the panel, to describe admissions was *"unfair."*

That really did not help the mood of the auditorium filled with anxious parents. There are not enough places for all the great kids: the sports star may get in over the world-class student, or the college already has enough Esports players or choir members, the student didn't sound friendly in the essay, the class needs more diversity, the legacy student may have an edge. It is unfair.

Parents and students can run the perfect race and still lose.

How do you plan for "unfair?"

Birthright Advantages: Big Money and Tradition

The playing field for college admissions is unfair for so many reasons.

Parents worry about the bribery/cheating scandal creating an unfair playing field for admissions competition, but the inequalities and advantages are still about birth and money.

Bribery in the form of huge donations has gone on for centuries, from monetary gifts to entire buildings, even "schools," like entire medical institutions.

It is not just the 400-point SAT bonus that "legacy" students get, those whose parents went to the school. Or special cases, from being famous or being an athlete.

Unfairness characterizes college admissions from birth.

Family Advantages: Parents with Kid-Centered Lives

This generation of teens was the first generation of the helicopter, paranoid, snow plow, stealth bomber, and tiger and dragon parents. These parents lead kid-centered lives. They devote their efforts to their children, their safety, their happiness, their future safety and prosperity. They have or make time and channel resources to their children.

Kid-centered parents provide huge advantages to their kids, "legitimately":

- They move into a top school district.

- They provide early enrichment: museum trips, library visits, books in the home, Starbucks at Barnes and Noble.

- They hire tutors, or take their child to a Kumon, Sylvan, Mathnasium, or homework club to learn new skills early or to help with homework.

- They take European trips or even just vacations out of state.

- They drive their kids to sports (colleges love sports).

- They hire thousand-dollar-a-month sports coaches.

- They know what AP and IB are and enroll their kids.

- They insist their kids to do charity work (colleges love community service).

- They will pay for summer school enrichments at a prestigious college, or at a science, technology, journalism, or political science teen forum.

- They know the process, so they know their teen can take the ACT or SAT more than one time (if they pay for it).

- They can fund test prep.

- They hire someone to coach how to write the college entrance essay ($100–$4,000).

- They will spend $1,000 to $10,000 for a college consultant to help with filling out the Common App, help with essays, advise on colleges, call the college admissions officers.

- They may have their teen write a few general scholarship essays, but the parents will be the ones customizing teen-written essays and sending them to the hundred different scholarship sites.

- They will get their teen to the college interview, will do the college road trip looking at colleges and make sure their teen's interest is shown to the colleges. (Colleges love interest.)

These are considered "fair play," but it certainly does not make for a level playing field amongst students. These kids are getting a greatly enhanced chance of being accepted to perceived top colleges.

Published Acceptance Rates "Lie"

These groups receive extra points when admissions considers their applications.

- Athletes receive 50 percent more points toward admission than the average student applicant.

- Musical students can receive 50 percent more points.

- Legacy students receive 24 percent more points toward admission.

- Diversity students receive 19 percent more points.

- Children of the famous or who are famous themselves will receive 19 percent more points than the average applicant.

So, especially in private colleges dependent on endowments and money from successful sports teams and donors, this results in an admissions breakdown that can look like this for the distribution of places:

- 35 percent legacy students

- 10 percent famous students or students with famous parents

- 18 percent diversity

- 50 percent top athletes or those in award-winning orchestra and arts

Obviously, there is overlap—a legacy student may also play high-level sports or be a diversity student, etc.

The student—perhaps in the top 1 percent for grade point average, even a valedictorian with a perfect SAT math score—without any of those extras will not have the published 10 percent admission chance.

He or she may have a 0.01 percent chance of acceptance because so many places are going to students who bring a monetary advantage, directly or indirectly.

Every year, elite colleges turn down 80 percent of students who had perfect scores on at least one of the SAT tests and were overall in the top 1 percent of the combined SAT score. The student can be academically "perfect"—more perfect than the athletes, or the famous, or the legacy students, and still have only a "lottery" chance of getting accepted.

Legacy Students

Contrary to what many assume, legacy students are usually not slouches who get in because of their rich mom or dad.

The legacy student comes from a family that knows the importance of grades and scores, so the student will work for those targets and would be able to afford more prep and tutors. The legacy student has more contacts for internships and more money for enriching summer programs, working in a hospital in Vietnam or hiking the Silk Road, studying minorities in China. They would be attractive to the elite college anyway, but the legacy status seals the deal.

However, their time at the elite college is not as exemplary. The legacy student's performance at the college shows that most have lower grades, choose the humanities which have a more flexible grading scale, and avoid STEM majors which have more rigorous standards.

Their place at the college might have better gone to a highly motivated non-legacy student, but building on legacy donation history makes financial sense for the college.

Wanting the Best

We want our children to be safe and happy, and we want the best for them.

Definition of **best**

> **1:** excelling all others: the *best* student in the class
> **2:** most productive of good: offering or producing the greatest advantage, utility, or satisfaction What is the *best* thing to do?[33]

"The best" comes up a lot when talking about college: grades, tests, college applications, college choice, choice of major, and career choice. The best may be the teen who is striving to be the first in his or her family to go to any college. The best may be the teen striving for a college that will turn down over 96 percent of its 20,000 perfect applicants.

What is "the best" that you want for your child?

"Best" is leading to cutthroat competition and cheating; it leads to feelings of inferiority and inadequacy; it can motivate financial ruin and mental collapse. Does "best" provide return on investment and sacrifice? If best is best education, your student can go anywhere. If best is about amenities and you are willing to pay for country club facilities and activities, that is different. If best is about being around rich, elite, or super-smart students, maturity will make your student successful. Super-smart students are often highly competitive and their work ethics rarely rub off on the student who isn't motivated. Networking with rich students and their families won't get the student a job unless they have the targeted qualifications.

Focus on the primary definition of "best"—excelling all others—it is the definition chosen by many in the college admission Olympics. That "excelling all others" is the definition believed by many who would go to any lengths for the "selective college." That "Ivy" bestows dominance, it is about winning, it is about excelling all others. But that elite college acceptance letter being waved around is about perception, the perception of dominance, winning, and prestige—but it is what the student does with the experience that has meaning.

I wish the purpose of college could shift to the secondary definition. That second definition of best isn't about prestige or beating classmates.

The secondary definition of best reads:

> **2:** most productive of good: offering AND producing the greatest advantage, utility, AND satisfaction What is the *best* thing to do?

College as the Prize Is a Simple, Clear Goal

College-for-all became a national goal, and now 70 percent of high school graduates head for college. Some statistics say that other 30 percent not going to college immediately want to apply to college, feeling guilty about their "failure."[34]

We are attracted to simplicity.

College admissions is such a clear goal.

Excellence based on test scores is simple.

Career planning based on what jobs are the highest-paying from the best college offering the best prospects is simple.

Standards are important…if the assessment is relevant and the goal purposeful.

PRSD—or PCSD

Of course, there is no Post-Recession Stress Disorder or Post COVID-19 Stress Disorder, but there should be. Real pressure has increased on parents at all economic levels after first the Recession and now COVID-19 and the resulting uncertain economic situation.

- For the elite—and contrary to beliefs, most elite wealth comes from hard work and not huge family wealth that sustained generations—with now nationwide APs and IB programs, the Eastern elite private school student is competing for a limited number of places at "elite" colleges from more qualified candidates outside the elite.

- For the upper middle class, being competitive seems like the way to break into the elite. They think huge college loans will pay off.

- For the middle class, college seems the way to stay in the middle class and reach beyond. Again, college seems like the only sure thing. And they too think that paying large college bills will be worth it.

- College is believed to be the only ticket to the upper classes for the economically disadvantaged. Counselors say that many parents with economic need will not consider their teen doing an internship or an apprenticeship which could help pay for college because it sounds like lower-class vocational training and could divert from the academic goals or brand them as "lower-class." Or they think college is not affordable and choose short courses that don't offer federal funding. College would be paid for; for-profit college and technical school are not.

The Best College and University Rankings Explained

The Times Higher Education World University Rankings are internationally renowned as the gold standard of rankings. Three-quarters of the "best" rank is based on the opinions of scholars primarily looking at the university's research advancements and the quantity of research publications.

Teaching excellence at the bachelor's level isn't the other 25 percent of the ranking—far less—and worse, although the research at these universities is outstanding, these research universities and college do not offer significant research opportunities for undergraduates—research being for professors and grad students. So, the ranking applies little to the bachelor's level student.

That Nobel prize-winning professor is far removed from undergraduates, since graduate students often teach the undergrads.

This ranking is irrelevant to four-year college selection. This is a vitally important ranking for MA/PhD/post-PhD students in the appropriate field of post-degree study, just not for the bachelor's level student.

Six-Million-Dollars Worried

Are you six-million-dollars worried about college? Wealthy parents paying millions to illegally "game" their teens into well-known colleges shows how desperately parents want "the best" for their kids. Parents with ethics want the best for their children too.

Parents have a combination of motives for their student getting into college: for genuine pride in their teens, to boost their teens' future earnings, for doing what society thinks is best, for learning, for the rites-of-passage experience, for maturing, to set their kids up for future, to be around good influences, to get them into the best graduate program, so they can get a great job, for bragging rights. Your child's Harvard acceptance feels like you won the "Parent of the Year" award.

It feels like admission to the "best" college must happen at any cost.

Just one week's headlines read:

> *Wealthy parents are giving up custody of their children to get need-based financial aid from colleges: "It's a scam."[35]*
>
> *Every charge and accusation facing the thirty-three parents in the college admissions scandal: Operation Varsity Blues[36]*
>
> *Behind UCs "admission by exception" side door: sports, money, diversity—and secrecy[37]*
>
> *Admissions for Donor Children*
> *One parent's defense in the admissions scandal is that the University of Southern California encouraged applications from the wealthy—if they would donate.[38]*

How Much Does It Cost to Buy Your Kid's Way into The Best Private Universities?
Wall Street Journal, Financial Samurai

The weird thing is that, if those parents had just donated the money to the college legally, their teens would have gotten in. It's not fair, but that is legal.[39] And donations have tipped the scales for generations.

Outrage...

Parents are rightly furious, angry, resentful, hostile, morally indignant, and feeling helpless and panicked over the cheating parents.

But look at what lengths other parents are going to for their teens to succeed: the mom who cut up her daughter's clothes for a B-plus on a quiz in fifth grade, before "grades count"; the parents who have had their kids transported in handcuffs to therapeutic boarding schools for troubled teens when they started getting B-pluses in AP classes...and what about the hundred-hour-a-week schedules foisted on many teens?

To ease the toxicity, schools are signing up for initiatives like Challenge Success. The Stanford think tank researches the effectiveness of grading systems, homework, and rigor to help schools implement plans to ease pressure while maintaining and raising standards. Less homework leads to higher skills, deeper comprehension, love of the topic, and better grades, with project work building communication skills, negotiation skills, and application of ideas, and allows for interdisciplinary problem-solving—a bit more valuable than extra pages of math problems that the student can or can't already do or topic analysis in a vacuum of the student's own limited knowledge and experience. But parents are outraged, standing in school meetings crying, shouting, "They need more homework. Eight hours a night. Or they won't be competitive. They won't get into a competitive college."

Million-Dollar Cheating Doesn't Justify Low-Level Cheating

Parent behavior has become the subject of a national college initiative advocating "parenting with ethics" as it relates to selective college admissions.

The *Making Caring Common Project* at the Harvard Graduate School of Education has released a manifesto supported by all the Ivy League colleges and hundreds of selective colleges in the US.

Turning the Tide II: How Parents and High Schools Can Cultivate Ethical Character and Reduce Distress in the College Admissions Process, March 2019, discusses the desperation of middle- and upper-class parents that drives them to go to unethical ends, like cheating on college application, over-reporting of activities and awards, help on essay-writing, and faked transcripts. "*At the core of excessive achievement pressure in middle- and upper-class communities is one fundamental myth: Only a small number of highly selective colleges will position students for success.*" (p. 3) Please comprehend this: selective colleges positioning students for success is a *myth*.

Well-meaning, devoted parents, feeling they are evening the playing field, are lying, cheating, breaking the law, or pressuring their children to exhaustion and mental breakdown for the myth that highly selective colleges will position them for success. Pervasive misinformation is misleading good people.

"This Is About Learning the Test, Not Learning..."

That was the opening statement of the SAT test prep tutor to my daughter and a class of students in a general course of SAT test prep.

We'd been advised to do a little prep to learn about how the test is worded—math concepts may be presented differently than they are in the school district—as the teen knows the concept, but it is presented oddly. Or certain concepts will be tested multiple times.

Test prep companies had tried to sell me simple packages costing as much as $7,000; their justification was that this cost (or more) that will get the student a $10,000 a year scholarship for four years is well worth it—if the teen actually gets the scholarship…

Again, the learning needed to pass a multiple-choice test is different from learning in-depth analysis and multi-disciplined experiential examination of problems which leads to higher-level logic, communication, and the development and use of intelligence. The straight academic content our teens now learn is often described as irrelevant, even by Harvard and Stanford think tanks. [40]

Those test-excellent teens are still excellent, but their time learning the test might be better spent.

The University of Chicago just announced that, by 2024, tuition will be $100,000 a year.

So, will you encourage your teen try to be that exceptional student, after a childhood of college prep and a high school college-course and activity workload of 120 hours a week? He or she appears to have a 5.9 percent chance of admission (less than 1 percent if the parent didn't attend or the student isn't a sports star) into one of the country's top-ranking journalism departments, at a school ranked one of the best values in the country. The student will graduate in five-and-a-half years (the new norm), and, five years after graduation, will earn $28,000 a year as a journalist in a career with high levels of unemployment.

That is living the dream at the "dream school" for the dream life, isn't it? It could be the right choice! It is a truly wonderful school and a wonderful program and a noble career!

Is only "the best" the right choice for your teen?

"What Would Be Your Dream College?"

The Princeton Review, the education services company, experts in tutoring, test prep, college admission, and college information, conducted a worries and dreams survey of prospective college parents and teens. 11,900 applicants and parents participated in the survey from all fifty states. The question at the top of their list was, "What would be your dream college…if chance of being accepted and cost were not an issue?"

The schools most named by students as their "dream college" were:

1. Stanford University

2. Harvard College

3. Princeton University

4. New York University

5. University of California—Los Angeles

6. Massachusetts Institute of Technology

7. Columbia University

8. University of Pennsylvania

9. Yale University

10. University of Michigan—Ann Arbor

The parents had almost identical lists, only the colleges were in different order.

So, the message is that the more elite and prestigious the institution, the better—even though only 8 percent said they were choosing a college because it was elite. They listed other reasons besides the prestige factor. But this is the common prestige list.

Parents and teens thought the biggest challenge to admission was:

1.   Getting good scores (37 percent)

2.   Filling out the application and financial aid documents came in second with 33 percent

3.   Choosing the right college ranked in the top 20 percent

4.   10 percent are worried about choosing the right college from those that accept them

99 percent said that college would be worth it for their kids. Half of parents said quality education was the reason and the other half said higher earnings were.

This is a great snapshot of worries and hopes across America. Their perception is that the more elite college the better, that college costs a lot, and that tests like SAT and ACT are important.

Obviously, this survey doesn't say if parents and teens are wrong or right, just what they are thinking.

The survey was offered on the Princeton Review website and to readers of their Best Colleges Guide, so this is not a cross-demographics survey. It is a snapshot of parents who are using rankings guides and resources.

Think Prestige—False

The opportunity to be proud of our teens used to arise only once a year with the holiday letter that accompanied the holiday card. "Jane got into Harvard." "Rob is the first in the family to go to college. We are so proud." But now social media is an ongoing opportunity, every moment of the day, to reach the Christmas card list and beyond.

Bragging is the best way to be remembered and convey acceptability to one's social group. Achievements can raise social standing.[41] So, for social connection, bragging plays a legitimate, even positive role.

Definition of *prestige*
1: standing or estimation in the eyes of people: weight or credit in
general opinion
2: commanding position in people's minds[42]

The most prestigious seems the most desirable. The colleges with the reputation
of educating the best are considered the most elite and prestigious. Those that
are most selective are the most prestigious. These assumptions sound logical, but
they may not be true.

As the dictionary definition says, what is elite and prestigious is based on the
general opinion, "what is in people's minds." Prestige is an opinion, not a fact.

Our teen getting into a perceived "best" college locks in or is thought to advance
our social standing and their future standing.

Becoming a top student is a noble challenge. Being a top student to get a
great education was needed in the past when colleges were not equal. But that
has changed.

Once elite colleges had the monopoly with a top library, top research, top
professors. The internet has become a leveler. Libraries, lectures, research are
online and with more attending college, top professors are common. And in
Chem 101, or Politics 304—all bachelor's level work looks the same—colleges are
even using the same textbooks and tests.

Still, elite, competitive, and selective colleges are now becoming the "must have
or your life is ruined" fashion commodity, just like a teen needing a pair of Ugg
boots or an Apple phone as an essential for their emotional survival.

Parents need to stop acting like preteen girls needing a prize to feel good. Your
teen getting into a great college is not a Best Parent award. Should obsession with
elite colleges be viewed like other fads, nice if you can afford it—but you may look
"kinda stupid" for wasting all that money on a name brand? Or does selectivity
denote true excellence?

How will that elite college prize look when one realizes that the highest-paying careers are attained by grads from non-elite colleges or those with high school diplomas and some certification?

College Rankings

Colleges can be ranked in many ways. Some overall rankings are an averaging of many factors, including academics, admissions exclusivity, team spirit (based on the success of the sports teams), dorm life, activities, clubs, party quality, food courts, gyms, eco-friendliness, vegan/vegetarian food, Greek life, college presidents' rankings of colleges, the college president's ranking of his or her own college, SAT scores, GPAs, staff and student rankings, and surveys. GPAs and scores of applying students may be listed instead of those who actually attend.

Some would not consider ranking colleges that didn't require standardized tests until, mid-COVID, Harvard stopped requiring the tests and the ranking report changed their policy. A thousand excellent colleges that didn't require standardized tests were not worthy of ranking.

Rankings Can Be Misleading

A college with great academics but no Division One sports teams (or any teams) can have a low rating. Or, if some grads don't return the survey forms, it can drop the college's rankings.

College of Notre Dame was a top-tier Catholic institution. Then it changed its name to Notre Dame de Namur University. It dropped from top-tier to bottom-tier because no one recognized it.

Another problem with rankings is that colleges can choose to exclude groups of students applying or attending their college from their statistics. Often, career earnings stats only track the information from higher-income students. For other rankings, like test scores, the college might exclude public-school-educated students. Colleges also just lie, like Tulane, which actually had no reason to lie.

Tulane sent false information for two years to *US News and World Report* for their college rankings. But so did George Washington University, Emory, and Clairemont McKenna College.[43]

Exclusive Colleges

As mentioned earlier, colleges that reject a large percentage of applicants are called exclusive, elite, selective, or competitive colleges. These have become desirable, as it implies that colleges that turn away the most students must be most desirable.

Turning away many students does not improve the curriculum, facilities, or education.

Impressive marketing campaigns are a cheaper way to show "exclusivity and prestige" than building better facilities, more buildings, or hiring more expensive top professors.

UPenn sent out free college applications to targeted students who were less than a "perfect fit"—those with lower grades, test scores, and curriculum rigor than those they usually accept. That can be seen as encouraging diversity, but there was another economic impact for UPenn. UPenn has about a 10 percent acceptance rate. Other Ivies are near a 2 to 3 percent acceptance rate, so are perceived as better Ivies than UPenn. UPenn decided to find more applicants to reject to appear more exclusive. 10,000 more applications will drop them to about an 8 percent acceptance rate. So they are offering free applications. They just wanted more students to turn down to appear more in demand.[44]

One excellent student and his parents tried to "buy" more lottery tickets to the top selective colleges. The boy applied to over 150 colleges. He spent over $10,000 on application fees. He got into five. The Common App has made it easy to apply to many schools, but it works against those who really want to go to a particular college. Make it very clear to the college that they are the number one choice if that is your dream college. Especially make it clear if it is a good "match" school or a "safe" school that you really love—the college may think it is your safe school and just a back-up, so will reject you even if you are qualified or overqualified.

Warning

Be very wary of colleges that barrage your teen, appearing to court them! It could be real. But it could also be to up their selectivity rankings. Or, increasingly, it could be because many colleges are due to go bankrupt in the next few years and desperately need students.

If marketing information from rather obscure colleges is stuffing your mailbox, before your teen applies, research the college's financials, and its retention rate (how many students go back after the first year) and its dropout rate.

Smaller colleges are going out of business or, if lucky, they are being bought up by larger colleges. Check the balance sheet of the college before enrolling, especially if it is lesser-known.[45]

What does Best Value College mean?

The formula was the best education—career and grad school outcome on graduation—for the amount paid.

"Best Value" college guides are bestsellers. These guides frequently change their criteria for "best value."

Some ranking companies changed their best value to reflect colleges which give the most aid to disadvantaged students (tuition, room, board, fees, travel, book allowance, entertainment allowance, etc.). Teens with financial need absolutely need to find out what college will give them the most money! For years, that information was near impossible to find.

These teens often chose educational options that led to crippling debt. Best Value means these students will know which great colleges will give them extra money to cover all expenses.

The problem is that most parents and teens don't know this new meaning.

Parents assume that the $80,000-a-year elite colleges, which are ranked best value because they pay all expenses for Pell grant students, mean that if the student attends that college, they will easily make a return on investment immediately. They assume that paying $320,000 for an elite education will be worth catastrophic loans, selling the family home, or giving up the retirement fund.

That is often not the meaning of best value anymore. Best Value often doesn't apply to the middle- and upper-class student.

Elite College Graduates Make More Than A Middle- Or Low-Tier College Graduates: True or False

The *Washington Post*[46] drew this analysis: "The median annual earnings for an Ivy League graduate ten years after starting amount to well over $70,000 a year. For graduates of all other schools, the median is around $34,000. But things get really interesting at the top end of the income spectrum. The top 10 percent of Ivy League grads are earning $200,000 or more ten years after starting school. The top earners of other schools, on the other hand, are making just a hair under $70,000."

The information came from US Department of Education data, so it must be true. This is the belief held by society, publicized by the college industry.

Our kids must go to an elite school or they are doomed!!!!

No! This is comparing apples and oranges. Compare students with similar majors and academic aptitude. The earnings ten years on are the same regardless of what college they attend!

Comparing an honors college with 8,000 undergraduates with a state university with 45,000 students, some honors, most not, is a false comparison. A state university looks inferior until one compares honors students with honors students, or students with the same major.

Compare the honors physics student with the elite honors physics student and their outcomes are similar—although the bachelor of science from the state university or tech college may carry more industry weight than the BA in Physics from the elite college. So, the less elite college may be "better."

But comparing incomes a year after graduation between a nursing student and an elite finance student is comparing apples and oranges. But if that nurse gets a master's, she may earn nearly double the finance expert's $150,000 salary. But the nurse will not have the prestige of wearing an elite college sweatshirt at the gym or grocery shopping.

State colleges will educate more teachers or social workers than an elite college, and these are low-salaried jobs. So this skews state colleges to look like poor-earning, "less prestigious" schools.

City plumbers can make the same as Ivy grads, or more, for fewer hours of work and usually less debt. Both are smart.

The Quality of the Student

Excelling in an Ivy League or elite college takes brains, rigor, discipline, and motivation, and they can be the perfect place for the right student. But great students thrive in any environment.

The career not the college, the student not the school, determine success. An elite education isn't a lifetime guarantee of wealth and happiness for any of its graduates. More on these concepts later.

"I wish there was a way to go back before the *US News and World Report* rankings, when one could read about a college and see what kind of a place it was and if it was right for the student who wanted to go."[47]

Part Five

Issues with College Choices

College Planning True-or-False Quiz	True or False
The bachelor's degree is a Golden Ticket to a secure, highly-paid job.	
College-for-all is a win-win for the job market and the student.	
College graduates earn one to three million dollars more (lifetime) than non-college.	
The college grad will make $2.26 million more over a lifetime than those with no degree.	
College is a great place to find oneself, and once in college, the path will become clear.	
Think prestige and elite when you think college.	
College is the ticket to the upper classes.	
Tech certificates and associate degrees lead to blue-collar work, the "lower classes," and lower incomes.	
"The best," "prestige," "selective," and "elite" are key concepts to associate with all aspects of college preparation, application, and student admission goals.	
Elite college graduates make more than middle- or low-tier college graduates.	

A student will finish a bachelor's degree program in four years and an associate degree is two years.	
Most students who start college will get a degree.	
As more college graduates are created through the college-for-all ethos, there will be more jobs requiring the bachelor's degrees as our nation's prospects increase with more educated workers.	
The goal is to get the highest grades and the highest scores to get into the best college possible.	
High schools being geared for college-for-all means an increasingly even playing field with a focus on academics nationally.	
Prep is valuable to get the scores and grades to get into the best colleges.	
Prep and tutoring for classes and standardized tests will strengthen the student.	
The goal in high school is to create the ideal candidate for the college/career of choice.	
The listed tuition, room, and board are the cost of the college.	
The average loan of $35,000 is how much a four-year college usually costs.	
Loans are paid back at the end of the degree program.	
The best route to a job for the underprivileged student is get a technical certificate or attend community college.	
Those with technical certificates and associate degrees are marked as working-class, not middle-class.	
Students at technical colleges and "academic" colleges are eligible for federal aid.	
If my child works hard and gets straight As, he or she will get a full merit scholarship or substantial merit money for the immense effort and achieved excellence.	
Colleges want the well-rounded student.	
The tried-and-true "road to college" trip to a great career, going from high school straight to a great college, then straight into a job—no breaks, no detours—is the plan that has always worked.	
The quality of the college is crucial to the student's future success.	

These were all true in the past! Which are true now?

The answer to every question is FALSE.

Paying for Colleges

High-, middle-, and low-income families are all following wrong information.

Low-income families should do four-year college, as it could be completely paid for with financial needs being met. Looking at the published sticker price makes for-profit colleges look cheaper. The federal government does not provide aid to these colleges, so they are in fact much more expensive than the seemingly high-priced nonprofit college, where the student will be eligible for federal aid and where there may be additional funding from the college—funding that does not have to be paid back.

Middle-income families should go wherever is cheapest that fits the student's learning style and interests, but the tendency for middle-income students is to select the most elite college, thinking its degree will lead to an increase in social and earning levels, so these students also have a tendency to accrue high levels of debt.

High-income—elite colleges do not offer advantages in some majors. Traditional elite occupations often require 80- to 120-hour work weeks—earning the same or only slightly more per hour than hourly wage as a fast-food worker.

Is Debt Worth It?

Data shows that students choose rankings and prestige when choosing a college, disregarding high levels of debt, thinking the prestigious BA will increase the salary exponentially.

Top college career advisors forcefully try to suggest the "cheapest" undergraduate school, not to choose to be "strangled by debt." The graduate may be forced into a second-choice career, or worse, because he or she will be "tied to ten years of loan repayment." The education offered is almost always not worth that burden of high debt and years of sacrifice to pay it off. The graduating student may have to take the first job available to start paying off the loan, not the desired job that may take longer to get.

Their advice is to go to the college or grad school that will offer the student the most money in scholarships—that will be the cheapest. That can even apply to law school or med school, although attending the best reasonably-affordable grad school with the student's specialty is the goal.[48]

The Published Tuition, Room and Board, and Expenses Is the Fixed Cost—False

Any college dean will tell you, "The sticker price is never the actual price." What they won't say is that *the family will be asked to pay as much as the college thinks the family will pay*: they have hired companies to determine what parents of different profiles will think is a good deal. What the family pays can be bargained, like the price of a scarf in a street market.

The cost of college education has gone up seventeen times more than inflation and earnings in twenty-five years.

$10,000 Deposits Coming—After the Covid Disruption

Starting in 2020, competition to poach top students from other colleges is allowed and college acceptances are like the Wild, Wild West—where colleges can offer money to students to poach them from other colleges after they have paid their deposits. To guarantee students won't change their minds, college acceptance fees may rocket to $5,000 or even $15,000, not the $25 to $200 norm for the past few years, to discourage students being poached or changing their minds late in the process.

With COVID, some colleges waived deposits, and some families are depositing small amounts for two colleges, trying to decide at the last minute where to go in fall. But, once back to "normal," deposits are set to soar to discourage students from abandoning a college where they had deposited.

Graduation Earnings Metrics

Currently colleges use very "interesting" metrics in reporting graduates' job success. They are all "true" to their metrics—but the metrics used are probably not what parents and students assume. These statistics rarely represent the entire student body. Colleges are adapting statistics for marketing purposes. They publish the criteria, but few click through pages and pages on the internet to find them.

- Some only count those graduating with 3.5 GPAs and above.

- Some may only count those whose families are in the top 10 percent earning bracket.

- Some use averages which skew the salary higher than it really is—the one student going to work for dad at $250,000 a year skews the figure away from all those earning $35,000.

- Some only count the one who got the $125,000 salary—you could have that potential salary by going to the college…even if only one or two students have reached that salary.

Don't let manipulated marketing statistics be your sole source of information. And use some common sense—careers and majors matter, making generalized "salary facts" meaningless. For example, a church youth leader will not earn the same amount as a nuclear engineer, regardless of the college attended.

Scholarships Are Given for Excellence—Mostly False

Your top student will get a full-ride merit scholarship, no.

- A full scholarship may be possible if the parents' combined income is under approximately $45,000. Federal Pell grants are up to approximately $6,000, but colleges may have other sources to supplement.

- The world-class students may get full merit money.

- A lesser-known college may offer a good-to-great student a merit scholarship, especially if they are developing a department.

- Parents need to be prepared to haggle for the best price.

- Sports scholarships are a path, but one injury and scholarship money is gone.

- If offered a sports scholarship, ask if it can be delivered as an "academic" scholarship, keeping the money safe from injury.

- Most scholarships are tied to a grade point average. Don't choose that college if your teen can't keep that GPA, which might be 3.87. Those scholarships are easy to lose and parents will then have to pay.

Colleges will calculate what they believe the family will pay and offer some scholarship money.

It's Cheapest to Choose a Technical Certificate, or Short Community College Course, to Start Their Education—False

Make sure any program or college offers aid based on the FAFSA. Federal Pell grants and federal money are currently only offered for college degrees, not professional and technical programs. This is different in most of the rest of the world and may change soon in the US.

Start certification in high school. Or begin associate degrees in high school. Many technical certificates up to and including associate degrees may be available for free if taken while still in public high schools. Washington legislators are introducing a bill to change this and it has bipartisan support. But as yet, making Pell grants available for certifications is not in place. Hopefully it will be by the end of 2021.

Student Debt Is the Biggest Factor Depressing Future Happiness

Where teens think they would like to go should depend on how much parent and student are willing and able to pay.

Don't sell your student on an Ivy League school if you can't afford $70,000-plus a year when the student isn't eligible for aid because your house's value has gone up and your ability to pay is seen, however erroneously, as increasing. Many selective colleges will expect you to remortgage, take out a loan, or even sell that house.

The student will have high expectations and may work to exhaustion, get in, and blame you, the parent, for ruining his or her dreams if you genuinely cannot pay for the college.

Need-Blind Colleges Versus Need-Aware

Colleges and universities used to accept students "need-blind" so students got accepted based on their fit with the college. College admissions couldn't know if the applicant came from a wealthy or poor family. The student was selected on merit. Of course, admissions officers could tell a great deal about the possible ability to pay for a school based on the essays, on home street address, on the profile of the high school, interviews, and by the kinds of extracurriculars the student did. But this was a step toward fairness.

But it led to a problem with students being accepted, not being offered merit scholarships, and being expected to pay a large proportion of the tuition, room, board, and expenses. So, the student might be accepted to one of the many schools costing up to $90,000 but receive virtually no aid and no scholarships. Because of society's preoccupation with prestige, these families and students would run up huge debts to go to this dream school—the family feeling compelled to raise up to $300,000 or more.

Even the colleges knew that price tag on any basic bachelor's degree was not worth that unless one could easily afford it.

Now, many colleges are listed as "need-aware." The college will turn down the students who do not qualify for substantial merit scholarships and do not have the wealth to pay. This is when they are not "perfect fits," for whom other schools would be equally good or even better fits but affordable—so the teen and family won't be tempted into ruinous debt. Debt rarely outweighs advantages, at the bachelor's level.

It is like a store having the conscience to refuse to sell a designer suit that doesn't even fit to someone who can't possibly afford it—the buyer thinking the name brand will make them irresistible. Of course, too often the student and family found that the high cost was too much and the student dropped out. That damages the school's retention rate (and their prestige), so it is in the college's interest to turn down students who can't pay enough.

Loans Are Paid Back at the End of the Degree Program—False

Repayment on federal student loans starts six months after graduation—unless the student stops studying; for example, if the student drops out, then loan payments start immediately.

So, for the 50 percent who leave college during or after freshman year, payback starts immediately.

Worse, if the dropout defaults on any payments, he or she will be blocked from returning to college or getting further loans until six months of consecutive loan payments are made. The youth may be stuck in a low-paying job, unable to fund training that would lead to a better job.

Average student loans range between $18,000 in Utah and $38,000 in Connecticut. But averages are misleading, as the figure includes those who never finished (so only borrowed for a year or so), and the fifty-year-old who has paid down their loan for years. This causes the average loan amount to appear far lower than it really is.[49]

Most parents are far off in calculating costs.

$25,000 is considered a manageable loan for a graduate going into a job paying $40,000 a year, paying $150 a month for *sixteen to seventeen years.*[50]

Students may be offered as much as $6,000 a year in federally supported loans. But for additional federal or any bank loans, parents will have to cosign and parents will be responsible.

The Best College Solved

This has not been the most optimistic fact picture of our teens' future.

No, this book is not *The Loser's Guide to Feeling Better about Settling for a Non-Ivy College*. Nor is it *The Winners' Guide to Creating the Top Student No College Could Ever Reject*.

Remember when I kept writing, "Don't you wish it didn't matter…"? All those worries, all the pressuring of our students, all the tricks, ploys, and genuine advantages we try to give our students to get into that "best" college.

Twenty years of continuing, extensive research, including research from Ivy League think tanks, concludes:

> *Your teen will do the "best" at the right college—the right learning environment, the most affordable price, the right location.*
>
> *And it is the quality of the young person and not the perceived quality of the college that matters for undergraduate degrees.*

Any College Can Be the Best College

At a bachelor's level, college education quality hardly differs.

- More trained professors means more talented teachers at all levels of college, from community college and online college to state flagship universities and Ivies.

- The internet has meant access to information. At one time, the quality of the library mattered; now the libraries are online.

- An Ivy may use the same textbook as the community college—only, at the community college, the student will be taught by a professor, while the Ivy student may be taught by a grad student (their professors are there for research).

- Adjunct professors are being hired to replace full-time professors. They receive no benefits and can be paid far less than the salaried professor; however, they have a degree, teaching experience, career experience, and usually a love for teaching. This can make the adjunct preferable to the grad student teaching the class.

The right environment, with the right learning style, and in keeping with the student's interests, offering real-world certifications or work experience, with professors who mentor, is the best.

Who will be teaching and mentoring your student?

While voting themselves six-figure salaries, some "elite" university boards are discussing phasing out full-salaried professors and hiring adjuncts to make savings. Adjuncts are excellent professors, but the pay can be less than minimum wage when hours are factored in. And the college saves on benefits and retirement and has no health insurance obligations. However, course programs created by a team of professors can suffer when largely part-time adjunct faculty, though dedicated, are allowed no program input. Alternatively, the adjunct may be asked to create his or her own course plan to be approved by the university—but without a collaborative, unified program approach.

Worse, some students are speaking out, wrongly, about adjuncts. "Why should I take seriously any professor who makes less than my Uber driver?" This is completely incorrect. These are full professors.

Nobel prize-winning professors may be at the college, but they may only be doing their research and have no undergraduate contact whatsoever. Parents believe they are paying for full professors when their student only has regular contact with a grad student; perhaps, the professor may be required to give one student-attended lecture a year. Grad students may have contact with the professor, and they are certainly smart. But they are not degree-holding professors with the experience that most adjunct professors have. Adjuncts may be semi-retired professors or professors with careers in writing or working within corporations or for the government. Full-time professors and adjuncts are currently trying to work for a better arrangement for all, but COVID-19 economic pressures may slow progress to fair pay and increased educational benefits for students.

But it is all far more complicated. A parent should realize that their undergrad student is not on a level to comprehend the Nobel prize winner's forty years of work. Or a full-time professor who has taught a class every year for six or ten years may be teaching it on autopilot. Or, although the adjunct is excellent, he or she may or may not be integrated into the department's program and the grad student, though inexperienced, may have been in that program for several years and understands what the department thinks is the most important to learn.

Research Shows That It Isn't Who Is Teaching but Who Is Learning

Those with similar SAT scores have similar salaries ten years on. Similar grades in similar courses show similar salaries ten years on *regardless of what college they attend.*

An engaged student will thrive. The immature student will need to mature. The quality, discipline, maturity, and drive of the student determine success. The student is the key factor for success, not the college. Quality of the student doesn't mean the quality of the hothousing or the number of test prep hours, but "qualities" the student possesses—resilience, passion, perseverance, empathy, "charm," discipline, and curiosity, as well as education.

The seminal work in the field by Dale and Kruger suggests that students with similar SAT scores do the same at any college.[51] "Students with similar SATs have the same future earnings regardless of whether or not they attend an Ivy or an elite college or a flagship state university or a private school or a college with no prestige."

This is research verified over twenty years; other researchers have had the same results using GPAs and other aptitude tests factoring in "undefinables" like maturity, drive, risk-taking, and resilience.

So, choose a college where the student would love learning, that isn't going to bankrupt the family.

Dale and Kruger identify two possible exceptions. "Possible Exception One: 90 percent of Ivy students from poor families make it to the top 10 percent of earners, and 10 percent into the top 1 percent." That is possibly true. But the reason is disheartening. With poor minorities, the suggestion is that prejudice is still something to fight, and the Ivy or elite degree can serve as a character reference for a minority student. "Possible Exception Two: Women Ivy grads do better than non-Ivy—maybe." Ivy women tend to work longer, but that may be motivated by higher levels of debt. Highly educated women with less debt often seem to leave the career ladder earlier to have families.

Don't Make the Student Fit the School—Find the School That Fits the Student

In a sane world of values, choosing a college that fits the student's learning and living style would be the major focus. For example, a faith-driven student might thrive at a college that has those faith values; the high school varsity football quarterback keen on playing football at college would not be happy at a college with just recreational sport options; a budding film director probably shouldn't choose a college with an under-developed film department, etc. Someone who has trouble with homework but aces every exam would do better with a college that does evaluations.

There are thousands of great colleges and universities to choose from:

- the party school

- the small school

- the college with no grades but evaluations

- the college that doesn't look at scores

- the big team spirit colleges

- the college with no division sports at all (but with yoga on the beach and parachuting)

- the rigorous core college

- the create-your-own-major college

- the urban college

- beach college

- rural college

- the religiously affiliated college which is often an open-minded, accepting, inquiring institution

Find an engaging, serious, but pleasant learning environment.

Going to the best college in the field for grad work is important! Undergrad, the individualized right learning environment matters.

Part Six

Personality Problems

Inferiority Complexes, Failure Paradox, Cult of Meritocracy,
Teen Infantilization, Class Snobbery

Infantilizing Our Teens: The Help That Hurts

A Full Schedule

Swim practice starts as five thirty in the morning, the class schedule allows for no "offs" (off periods or study halls) in order to fit in a challenging curriculum, math tutoring because math is hard for the student, SAT prep online group classes seven to nine in the evening twice a week, then three to four hours of homework. This packed schedule is common but usually also includes community service, debate or academic competitions on weekends, clubs, etc. And college applications, road trips, interviews. Even if the teen loves every moment, this level of activities causes stress.

All this activity is usually coordinated by the parent, at least until the teen can drive.

What an amazing life. What opportunities. And many kids do appreciate it. Or they don't think about it, as it has always been the norm.

Parent Scheduling Takes Away Life-Skill Competence

Highly programmed high school students often do not do well at college when they have to decide their courses, plan their days, choose for themselves.

A private girl's high school in London had the most girls accepted in Oxford and Cambridge, the top universities in the UK. The school scheduled the girls for homework time, extracurriculars, sports practice, matches, debate tournaments, sleep time. The girls were amazing, excelling in academics, sports, music, etc. One would think they would become the top students at Oxbridge with all those skills. But the girl's school had an over 80 percent dropout rate in the first year of college. The girls had no idea how to schedule what they needed to do, they didn't know how to prioritize or organize what they were studying or what they were doing, they were burnt out from having to excel, and they were not able to keep up that pressure on themselves.

Tutors to the Rescue

Extensive test prep and tutoring can genuinely help the student. But it can also sap confidence, take away the chance to fail, conquer, and learn resilience. "Help" can take away vital self-esteem. It can turn a bright, successful student into someone who perceives himself or herself as a failure who can't cope on his or her own.

Over-Parenting: A Cause of Teen Depression and Anxiety

Teens with parents who are involved in the college process show heightened success in admissions. But teens with parents who "over-parent" can have anxiety, depression, and entitlement issues that will cripple their future success.

Parents are in a no-win situation. Parents mean well!

Depression and anxiety among the student population have increased exponentially. New studies show teen depression and anxiety resulting from overly involved parents.

Doing things for your child when it is developmentally inappropriate sends them the message that they are stupid or can't do things for themselves. In a study of teens ridden with anxiety and depression, a frequent common factor was over-involved parents. As the over-parenting continues:

- Violation of autonomy

- Violation of competence

- Depression

- Anxiety

- Lack of confidence (parents doing things sends the message that the child is incapable)

- Lack of self-esteem

- Self-entitlement

- Denied reward from overcoming challenges of hard work

- Denied the opportunity to problem-solve by learning from mistakes

- The flawed expectation that the world will wait on them, that they deserve an executive job without working their way up to privilege

- Unrealistic views of the world

- Dissatisfaction in later life[52]

A new "secrets" to selective college admissions book seriously suggests parents hire a professional mental health team just for surviving the admissions process—a therapist for you, one for your child, and a group therapist for the family.[53]

That would probably be in addition to the psychiatrist for ADHD meds to help focus, the psychiatrist to request extra time on class and college entrance tests, the psychologist and therapists for depression and anxiety from the "never-enough" rigor, not to mention the education consultant, the course tutors and test tutors, and sports specialists like the swing coach, the sports psychologist, and the videographer team to capture all the excellence. The author suggests that the therapists might even be covered by your insurance.

Mental health needs to be taken seriously and appropriately. Suicide in school years comes not "just" from bullying but also from inability to cope with pressure and perceived failure, especially with overworked teens. Teens whose grades suddenly drop from straight As to B-pluses are not troubled teens who need intervention or to be sent to therapeutic boarding schools meant for emotionally traumatized teens, those with addictions, those who suffered abuse, those who have serious issues and need urgent help.

The point is that going to extremes is playing with our teens' mental health. Additionally, college admissions success should not be about the excellence of the student's admissions entourage.

Give your teen the right support, but that does not include sending a "tutor" with them to college—yes, this is a real thing, a really bad thing.

Fitness for College

College Is a Great Place to Find Oneself and Mature and, Once in College, the Path Will Become Clear—False

Ask colleges their main concern about the students they want to admit. Their answers are "immaturity" or "no life skills." Colleges will tell you that the teens arrive almost overprepared, academically. However, they complain that students have no life skills.[54]

Many teens are missing life skills—staying overnight somewhere, riding a bus, boiling an egg, doing laundry, making a schedule, reading a campus map, etc. These life skills problems are products of current parenting methods. Driving teachers commonly complain that teens arrive for their first driving lesson having never having crossed a street without a crossing guard or without Mom. Some teens have never had a sleepover away, not even with the grandparents, because of protective parents, or parents who want to be in control.

Safe Beats Happy

Many parents, especially today's hyper-involved parents, feel that, if they can control everything, they can keep their children safe. "Safe" beats happy. Happiness takes a distant second to safe and secure.

So we infantilize our children. Comedians make endless jokes about the helplessness of today's "snowflake" generation, ridiculing young adults as being as helpless as infants. But society is conspiring to keep them that way.

This is not the teens' basic inability to function, but that parents and society are curtailing their maturing. Many parents are still in "toddler-protecting" mode. Indeed, some toddlers are given more freedom than teens.

Parents impose curfews, dress codes, rules to keep the teen's room clean—with punishments usually not in proportion to the "crime," like grounding and taking away electronics, car, and the phone. Dressing their own way or using slang can cost them the use of the car the teen even bought with their own money from a job.

Society enforces infantilizing teens. Schools impose conduct codes, dress codes, language codes, attendance codes, even cell phone use in the halls is punished, often with two weeks' detention—when often the over-parented teen is just phoning the parents about a change in pick-up time for debate club.

Society will allow the teen to work but not to have a personal private bank account, to buy auto insurance, rent a room or apartment, etc.

We infantilize teens just before they become legal adults at eighteen, just when they need to be given more, if not total, freedom to make mistakes and learn while they still have parental back-up.

Inadvertently, parents send colleges very immature teens who have had insufficient opportunity to learn life skills like resilience, self-scheduling, self-discipline, decision-making, the ability to speak to adults, empathy, self-control in risk-taking, knowledge of safe limits, and the ability to "negotiate."

So how are colleges dealing with this lack of real-world connection?

1.   Many colleges give extra admissions preference to students who have had "real" jobs.

2.   Colleges will pay the student to stay away for a year and grow up. Colleges are encouraging the gap year, even offering merit scholarships to anyone who will take a year before starting college. (See Appendix.)

3.   Colleges "toddler-proof" the college experience as a medical requirement to protect mental health. There are "safe zones" where the student cannot be disagreed with, stricter rules, required finance courses to address that complete lack of experience, more supervision, tutoring centers to keep up the tutoring many have become accustomed to, and valets for five-star care.

College is not the place to make mistakes, as it once was. It is no longer the place to grow up, because many are leaving just about as coddled as they entered.

The Coddling Continues

College Is No Longer a Place to Learn Independence and Face Challenges

Colleges added high-end luxuries that are relatively easy and cheap to implement. These put many parents' minds at ease. And, so, the coddling continues.

Colleges are being asked to create "safe zones" for students who feel emotional stress when encountering ideas different from their own. This fragility and helplessness is classed as a medical condition, so the college must provide the areas. The teens are not able to cope with an environment where they will be contradicted and challenged—which was one of the best parts of the college experience.

College, twenty years ago, was more of a "sink or swim" culture without all the support. Support was still available and probably should have been accessed more. But with the new levels of pampering, the college experience is no longer the place to grow up, as it was before.

So, parents rent apartments to be near their college student.

Other parents send tutors to college with their teens who arrive in the dorm room after class and study with the student until all the course work is done for the day.

The campus experience that has been interrupted by COVID is not the campus experience of challenging ideas, embracing new thoughts, exercising freedom. It had become more sheltering.

And just a question for reflection: Do you really want your teen to live a five-star country-club lifestyle in college, where they can choose not to be challenged, where someone rewrites every paper, and where their personal needs are taken care of by a valet? Do you want to support them in this lifestyle for years to come, until they can grow up?

My Baby Is Too Young to Think About a Career

From parent interviews, I hear, repeatedly, "My baby is too young to think about a career." The baby is a college sophomore or older—the thought being, I want to keep my baby safe forever. "He will choose a career senior year (of college)"—the thought being that the student isn't capable of big decisions. Or "She will be able to choose whatever job she wants when she graduates"—the thought being that the college degree will guarantee any great job the student wants. That was true twenty years ago; again, those jobs are gone.

Wrong Assumptions

The mindset is to protect our teens from "bad" adult things—which means real career planning is avoided to not worry or pressure the student (while, at the same time, over-pressuring them to extreme goals to impress colleges—another method of parental control).

Essential Information

Educators and employers pinpoint lack of career discussions as a big factor in the college failures listed earlier in this book. New "career discussions" started in middle school through high school are showing amazing success.

Departments of education have run studies of the mental health impact of ninth- to twelfth-grade career planning. Students who have done the new career discussion program show:

- Mental health issues were reduced because the teens started focusing on the future—not the daily petty/serious intrigues of high school.

- The teens felt empowered as they were shown how to take some control over the ominous unknown that is the rest of their life.

- Those who did the career discussion program had fewer pregnancies.

- There were more high school completions.

- There were more college completions in four years.

- More went on to get highly paid jobs.[55]

Will you support your teen majoring in "undecided"? "Undecided" is a new major being offered. Or will you still pay when your young adult changes majors for the fifth time (the average), meaning years of college more to finish the newest major? Are you one of the parents who say they will support their young adult until they reach thirty? Or would you consider letting them work at something they love that they do well, for that "starter career" in this lifetime of seven to ten careers?

Other detrimental biases to consider—just to keep an open mind about—include the bias against incorporating "vocational" courses, biases for "prestige colleges," biases toward high-paying careers over passion careers, and many more. These need to be put into Technology Age context before parents and teens can make objective decisions about the future.

The Nation's Failure Mentality

A sense of failure accompanies the explanation that the teen is going to a perceived "lesser" college. "I didn't get into the Ivy, I only got into a top twenty-five." "I'm only going to Metro…I am only going to North _____ State University… I'm going to work and go to the community college first, but then I will transfer to a great school" speak to the inferiority that is felt, whatever the level.

"Maybe you can transfer later…I am so, so sorry…" is too often the response.

Condolences are offered for not attending the prestigious college or choosing a different path. "Law was too much for her, so she went to plumbing school." Oh, the disgrace! The disgrace of leaving the 120-hour-a-week job, earning $180,000, for the 50-hour-a-week job earning—granted, she works nights and weekends— only $200,000. But "what a failure. How low-class."

College signals class and intelligence. The better the college, the higher the class and intelligence it signals. So many act as though that is the ultimate definer of worth.

Wow, I was so impressed by the guy in the Ivy sweatshirt buying on-sale last-sell-by date chicken thighs at King Soopers in a Denver suburb—that sweatshirt says class, it denotes intelligence, it means a $150,000 debt, the location doesn't denote a $250,000 NYC salary. He isn't a failure! "Prestige" may not guarantee all we think it does.

"She is taking time off…" sparks pity. "She was such a bright girl. I am so sorry."

She didn't die!

If it isn't straight to college, then something is wrong somewhere, which is why over 70 percent of high school graduates head to college, often colleges beyond their price range, with the rest thinking that they should go to college.

Then there is the "never-enough" failure. The student gets into an Ivy, but that is not celebrated because there's a new goal. The teen must be top of his or her class. That happens, but the next goal, the top law school, has to be reached, so the Magna Cum Laude becomes irrelevant. Then the top law school acceptance happens, but that isn't celebrated because the young adult needs to graduate and make a top law firm, but that isn't enough when it happens because there is a new goal, a salary, a house, etc. These are real cases of great success that are experienced as failure. The goal posts move, and the student can never win. No wonder the Depression Olympics, as psychologists name it, grip our high achievers through middle school, to high school, college, and beyond.

So, we embrace the college application frenzy to escape humiliation and doom. And we buy into the never-enough failure mindset. Everyone fails.[56]

Elitism

Prestigious careers with high salaries may not be the "dream life" one imagined:

- These are careers—law, finance, medicine—that come with 80- to 120-hour work weeks.

- Often, getting these prestigious jobs means higher levels of debt.

- That $150,000 a year finance salary translates to twenty-four dollars an hour, with less than seven hours a day not spent working, sleeping at the office, and working weekends.

- The high pay means metropolitan areas with high costs of living and high taxes.

- Some doctors, working eighty-hour weeks, taking salary cuts for elective surgery losses during COVID-19, love their jobs and are saving lives, but they are making eight to eleven dollars an hour.

The Accepted Students' Day Celebration

It was May 2016, and one of the "top" forty big-name colleges in the country had its Accepted Students' Day.

The passionate professors and administration spoke with pride of their amazing institution. Most parents were excited and proud of their student's acceptance by this amazing place with its long history of notable graduates.

But the students were a tough crowd. Why? One presenter, talking about the outside attractions, ten-dollar show tickets, cheap movie tickets, free gallery passes, and five-dollar concerts, added "and your school ID gets you into any lecture at _____(the Ivy League college) nearby." Some kids burst into tears, others had the single tear roll down the cheek, many put their heads down into their folded arms on the tables, some left the room sobbing.

The nearby Ivy had been their first-choice school, and they had the all the qualifications to attend the Ivy that only took about two thousand. They had lost the academic lottery. But these amazing students, accepted to this, one of the top colleges in the world, wrote themselves off as failures.

Do you feel like a personal failure because your grocery store scratch card was a dud? The academic lottery is luck. All the applicants were qualified for the more elite college, but there are just not enough spots.

After the presentation, the campus student guide started her introduction. "My parents had to physically drag me to the car freshman year. I didn't get into my dream college and I was stuck going here. Then I saw I could do their five-year law degree program, so I will be a fashion industry lawyer in one more year. I went to Paris and worked in a fashion house in an internship the college set up. If I'd gone where I wanted, I would have to apply to law school, I would have been overloaded with busy work and not gone to Paris, and not worked part-time at Givenchy like I do now."

My daughter attended the college, grief-stricken for the first months, but then saw that her Ivy friends had the same course books and had grad students teaching, not the famous committed professors she had. Both sets of students mastered the exact same material, same exam. But she had time for an internship to apply political journalism theories that her professor put her up for.

Self-esteem is sapped from many high-performing youths. 95 percent who apply to "dream" elite colleges do not get accepted, even though they were qualified. There just aren't enough places.

An Ivy won't guarantee acceptance to the Ivy grad, law, or med school. Harvard chooses non-Ivy students for their medical PhD program, which is tuition-paid, $31,000 salary. They come from schools across America where they as undergraduates were able to work with professors and get their names on research, where they could work in labs not reserved for grad students, etc.

But still, many of these "brainwashed" meritocracy cult members will go on to feel that elite school rejection for a lifetime.

Hiring an Educational Consultant to get into Ivies?

Application time was approaching and a mom who could afford it hired an educational consultant costing far more than $6,000 to work with her smart son. He only wanted an Ivy. But the consultant would only take on even this brightest of students, however much they would pay, if the student would not apply to an Ivy. The son was furious, but his parents forced him to comply. The EC believed there were better colleges than Ivies. The right college would be better than an Ivy.

The educational consultant learned the boy was interested in business and had tech company start-up aspirations. The EC knew a professor at a small college's business school with links to company internships.

The student, still against the idea, got in, attended, and within two years had interned at a company who liked the student's ideas so much that they gave him start-up capital. He was running his own tech start-up even before he graduated. Even if his initiative hadn't led to this level of success, the school had advanced data analytics and internships, which were exceptional preparation for a NYC finance career.

Anyone can find mentors and great programs easier than undertaking the thousand-must-do list to be competitive at an elite school where there isn't a lottery's hope of getting in. Find the great program. Find the mentor. Find the place that has opportunities. Parents do not have to pay $20,000 for a consultant. Look at programs on the website, do a virtual tour, watch a video about the department, visit if possible, and have the teen talk to students in the department on Zoom or in-person. See if the student can talk to a professor or check out internship.

Find the right place...but for some, prestige is all that matters.

The Ivy might be the right place for some, but it isn't the "one-size-fits-all" ticket to success.

I Bought This Book to Get My Teen into an Elite College

For those who want to ignore that better advice of finding a school where your teen will love to spend time learning, here's my best tip. For those who want a quick fix for admission to a selective college…

Give the school something they want.

The big donation always works, but that may not be your "style" or in your budget—but there is a trick: *Develop an extracurricular expertise that fills a specific targeted need at the dream college.*

Like being the sports star, it can be as a virtuoso musician for their orchestra or a Minecraft player.

Get on the college club social media. The trivia contest star who takes a junior year abroad must be replaced. The frisbee champ takes an internship, leaving this college short for their team. The radio host or school sports videographer may be graduating. Fill the spot of an essential student.

- Check the college chat groups.
- Check the school newspaper.
- Research clubs.
- Talk to organizations on campus to get a feel for their upcoming needs—and be sure to mention your expertise to your college admissions counselor.
- Just ask if the college is short on some needed talent.

My brilliant daughter was rejected by an Ivy at age fifteen. But in the meeting, the school officer took my arm and pulled me aside, whispering, "Does she play the viola? There is a place for her now if she can play the viola." I said no. Should I have said yes and had her spend the summer in intensive viola training?

One top IB student applied to only one elite college. His parents were horrified, but he was adamant that he only wanted to go there and nowhere else. He applied to the college and got accepted.

Not just smart, but clever, he researched the college's award-winning orchestra. Following the orchestra chat group, he learned bassoon players were always needed, like some colleges need a star quarterback. So, he spent his spare time learning the bassoon, triangle, and piccolo to cover his bases. He kept the college club and admissions officer informed. He got accepted as the bassoon player.

A prestigious college had accepted the daughter, with a small scholarship. Her mom made an appointment with financial aid. That day, the college choir soprano had decided to study abroad at the last minute, leaving the choir short of a top soprano. The daughter had played down her professional singing theme park job to look more "academic," but now the mother was able to show the opera footage on her phone. The mother walked out with a full scholarship for the girl if she sang in the choir.

Before you push your teen out of the airplane at ten thousand feet...yes, some colleges want to build up their sky-diving teams. Please use some restraint as to what the teen wants to learn—this strategy is not a guarantee.

The Student No College Would Ever Turn Down

The world-class student: here is what "soaring above your peers" looks like:

Basic requirements

- 4.87 weighted grade point average or higher (GPA)
- Perfect ACT or SAT scores (that is approximately 1,900 students with perfect ACTs—0.1 percent—and 300 earning the perfect SAT of 1600, from 2019 data)

- An IB diploma or AP scholar

- National academic tournament finalist or winner (debate, math, history, etc.)

- 100 to 1,500 hours of community service

And at least one of the following:

- Inventor with patented invention or app that has changed the lives of countless people

- Researcher with articles published in "grown-up" professional academic journals or science institute reviews

- Founder of a nationally recognized charity

- Founder of an industry-recognized company

These are world-class students, and it is thought there are about two thousand applying to colleges in the US this year.

These kids, on their own, in their rooms, invented devices revolutionizing medicine, the environment, infrastructure, imaging, AI, apps, etc. Or started a charity that has impacted the world. These teens are usually fiercely self-motivated.

It is important to know that a truly exceptional group do exist. We believe our children are the "best." All of our teens are simply wonderful. But keep admissions expectations in appropriate check.

Granted, one world-class student inventor reportedly got into Yale with about a 410 SAT, not 1600. World-class creativity and contribution can beat the perfect GPA and perfect scores.

But don't give up on future ambitions and aspirations if your child isn't "world-class." That your straight-A, fifteen-AP teen won't get a full-ride scholarship, or even get into Harvard, does not mean he or she is a loser! That your 3.0 GPA student doesn't get into an Ivy doesn't set their fate or make them a loser.

The point is that "world-class" students are out there. That doesn't take away from how wonderful your teen is. But it is necessary to know about these students to have realistic expectations in selective college admissions. (Many world-class students get into selective colleges but opt to attend elsewhere.)

The Elementary School Science Fair

World-class students are often *the kid who does the science fair project himself or herself.* Science fairs have been canceled at some grade schools because the parents did the kids' projects for them. My triplets won the "Best Project by the Student" awards, but there was an overall winner: an architecture project done by the architect dad—the child just said, "I don't understand it. My dad did it."

Being world-class is rarely the kid hothoused from age two, fourteen years of evenings at a tutoring center until ten o'clock nightly, two years of daily SAT prep courses, a dozen APs with tutoring help, or having an admissions entourage. The motivation and passion for learning comes from within. These are rarely parent-pushed prodigies, who are still amazing, wonderful kids.

The trick for parents is nurturing and making opportunities for the passionate, self-motivated, driven, self-created genius. It is hard to let our child thoroughly do his or her own thing when we are intent that they live up to college admissions industry published "ideals" that center on perfect scores, perfect grades, specific college prep courses, and varsity sports success.

The Academic Lottery

When aiming for an Ivy, all else seems like a failure. Are you a failure if you buy a lottery ticket and don't win? Applying to an elite college is playing the academic lottery.

As one principal put it, "Every year I have a dozen top students come to my office, in tears or distraught, holding their elite college rejection letters. There is no reason they shouldn't be at an elite, there just are not enough places. I told them it is called the academic lottery, but most parents and teens don't listen to my warning."[57]

Story Comes from Varsity Blues

In the Varsity Blues college admissions scandal, ironically, some teens of the cheating parents epitomized the twenty-first century career success story.

The girls were successful social media influencers. A social media influencer must be a master marketer, must craft and hone a compelling image, must be an effective communicator, must network, must work with companies for deals to promote the company's products. Good influencers make from $26,000 to $26 million.

Following the tradition of four years at an elite college was considered "socially acceptable."

What these girls were doing was the "new socially acceptable."

If that career died down, or when they decided to move on, colleges are still there.

Youth who don't want to be in college shouldn't be. And they shouldn't be in a college that they are not ready for, that they don't need, or that is not a good fit.

What Is the Most Important Factor for Admission to a College?

The admissions dean of a selective college said he would be totally honest in the order of importance of factors in acceptance.

What are the top three factors you think colleges will use in selecting your student? Scores, grades, difficulty of the curriculum, activities, sports, recommendations?

His truthful response was this:

1. How much money the family would be willing to pay.

2. Demonstrated interest in the college—visits to the website, to the campus (physically or virtually), contact with admissions. The college doesn't want to offer a spot to someone who doesn't want to go.

3. The student's academic quality (based on transcript, GPA, difficulty of classes, test scores if used by that college, essay, jobs and activities, letters of recommendation, usually in that order).[58]

When college budgets are tight, the college needs a certain percentage of students who are paying near-full list price.

They want committed teens who can and will finish what they start. If the merit or sports scholarship is lost, will the parents have the ability to pay full tuition? There will be some (but less since COVID) money for the few perfect-fit students. But most will need to pay without huge discounts.

Even Perfect Students Can't Do It All

Two teens had perfect ACT scores, top SAT scores, and more than a dozen APs. They were debate captains and national debate finalists. They were national academic Olympiad finalists. They did hours of community service. They had straight As. *But*, to have time to do all that, something had to give. So, they cut class. They'd arrive on test days, turn in their homework, take any tests, but otherwise they did not attend class. They missed too many school days to graduate, although they were the top two students in the high school, tied for valedictorian in a ruthlessly tough high school. The high school refused to award them diplomas. Without diplomas, no college. No one can break the rules.

So, they took the GED. Now, they are great students at Harvard and Stanford, the right schools for these students and their majors.

Defining Excellence

"If you aren't failing, you are not challenging yourself enough."

Some cultures believe real challenge begins with not knowing, struggling, persevering, and then mastery. That pattern is not the American approach. That rarely translates into straight As on every assignment and every test. And colleges want to see consistent application and excellence.

Few US teachers, counselors, admissions' officers, or parents say, "You got a C, awesome." The student can get a C but master the material in the end. Even a D can still end in mastery and is far more productive than the easy A, or a grade maintained with the help of a tutor.

Mastery should be the goal, not As. One needs standards, but grading at odds with learning is not a perfect system.

Don't you wish it weren't this way?

Tutors

In spite of what I have said earlier in this book, tutors are not all bad. A student may need instruction delivered differently than the teacher's instructional approach, or just more explanation. But a tutor needed for every subject, every day, probably means the course is too difficult. Turning in homework done more by the tutor than the student, and the student failing the tests, can still get the student a C at some schools—the student has learned nothing.

Equally, the brilliant student who gets As on projects and tests, voraciously studying in-depth, but not turning in the brain-numbingly-easy busy-work homework, can end up with a D in a class where he or she excels.

The Well-Rounded Student

Colleges want the well-rounded student—the whole package. Your teen must check all the boxes—sports, art, grades, music. —False

The Checklist

Parents and teens look at the profile averages of students for each college, usually posted on the college website. Here's a representative example.

- 75 percent had scores over 1325 specializing in reading
- 78 percent had scores over 1395 specializing in math
- 80 percent had GPAs of 3.8 weighted
- 98 percent had won academic awards
- 68 percent had been in student government
- 95 percent had been involved in school clubs
- 82 percent competed on a school team, math, history, science, robotics, art, debate
- 62 percent had jobs
- 92 percent participated in community service
- 65 percent had done summer enrichment programs
- 52 percent did sports at a high level
- 78 percent played sports above a recreational level
- 52 percent played a musical instrument
- 58 percent had their own company or own charity
- 68 percent excelled in art, theatre, and dance

So, parents and teens think that if their teen has those scores and grades, learns several sports, plays an instrument, does charity work, paints, acts in the school play, is president of a school club, joins student government, works part-time, spends a summer either at a prestigious college or building houses for the poor in Nepal, and does a jazz dance class—then they ticked all the boxes. They think that their child will be accepted.

But the list is not what each student does, but what someone in the entering class did. Sometimes, that isn't even the list of students who attend the college, but of the students who *applied*. (When a college is a "safe" school for Ivy candidates, the applicant pool can be higher-qualified than those who end up attending.)

Colleges want the well-rounded class, not the well-rounded student.

Each college will have a target level of academic competency. But beyond that, they want to have amazing individuals with unique interests to share with the other unique freshmen. They want someone who can contribute something special. They want inspiring kids to inspire other kids.

Checking every box on that high-achievers list makes the teen look average.

Colleges are not stupid either. Tennis star, concert pianist, ballerina, Harry Potter fan-fiction writer, weekend hospital volunteer, and patented biochemist, and just seventeen years old? Any of those activities take six hours of practice a day…one hour spent on each means familiarity, but no depth of skill or passion.

"I did everything accepted students did and I didn't get in" …but you weren't you.

Why do we believe being one's "best self" to be a loser's strategy?

Being "the best" has taken over from the concept of being one's best self, which has taken on negative connotations.

How Your Student Can Become One of the Most Successful College Graduates

One college group stands out as more successful:

- High GPA in college: 3.7 median

- Doesn't change colleges

- Passionate about his or her course major

- Finishes in 3.5 years, not the more normal five or six years

- Has less debt

- 97 percent graduation rate

- Has higher salaries in their field

- Double the "happy and fulfilled" at work statistic after ten years compared to other college graduates

Any student can "enter" this group. It has nothing to do with GPA, scores, college choice, family background, economic background, or high school course choice.

These are the kids who take a gap year—a year off between high school and college.

The Gap Year

A gap year is a break, not necessarily a year, usually taken between high school and college.

So, which gap year programs turn students into super students? It doesn't matter; it is the time off.

This time can be spent

- Having a job—but a job related to interest works better than a food service or menial job. Try to explore careers. If the student cannot get a career-related job, volunteer in something career-related. Ask to job-shadow for an hour or day.

- Traveling.

- Volunteering.

- Taking a break in some way from "senior burnout."

- An expensive gap year program (working in a South African law office).

- A medium-priced gap year (helping the poor in Mongolia).

- A cheap gap year program (working in a hospital in Africa or the Far East).

- A high-earning gap year program (like shearing sheep on an Australian sheep ranch).

- Doing "nothing" or playing video games in Mom and Dad's basement (better than playing video games in your dorm room and failing out of freshmen year—this happens as a retreat from high college anxiety).

- Virtual internships are a new and valuable thing. Working remotely all over the world, from your home. The work is still enthralling and valuable.

The idea of the gap year started in Europe in the 1960s and has caught on as a normal part of the road to college and career for European students.

Most US colleges prefer students who take a gap year and may award merit money for anyone going on a gap year program. One offers a five-thousand-dollar merit-based scholarship or more.

Less pressure, recovery from burnout, often exposure to a different location, culture, or living standard, and time to experiment help nurture creativity, originality, and passions. The payoff is big.

Statistically, doing absolutely nothing yields the same results as an expensive internship.

Gap Year Rules

1. Apply to college early in the high school senior year and get accepted.

2. Ask the college's gap year policy commitment and pay the deposit.

3. *Get college approval for the gap year! The college must approve the gap year!*

4. Check with the college whether taking courses during the gap year will make you ineligible for the college (you become a transfer student and lose your scholarship) or whether that credit, if allowed, can be put on the transcript.

5. Working should not be in a menial job to "scare" the teen into studying harder at college. If money isn't the issue, try for career exploration, unpaid or not. Writing scholarship applications makes more money usually than a menial job—the scholarship may be only two hundred dollars but takes less than an hour to apply. Applying for even small scholarships is usually time well spent.

Warning:

Again, be wary of doing college credit courses during a gap year. Get college approval in writing. College credits can turn the student into a "transfer student" and the admission and scholarships will be withdrawn.

Conclusion: Most Worries Do Not Matter

It doesn't matter…the crazy competition, the sweating blood and having a nervous breakdown to get the best grades and the best scores; the competitive student doesn't have to solve the clean water problem in Africa (unless that is their thing). The parent doesn't have to make sure the teen has given a speech at a national cause rally (or fake it by inviting a bunch of people to the steps of the state capitol during an LGBT rally and video them giving a speech to the fake crowd). The time spent in a two-year twice a week SAT prep program is better spent doing other things.

I hope parents will see that the whole current process is completely unfair,[59] that college selectivity can be faked, that rankings are all questionable, and that perfect grades and scores don't guarantee admissions at many selective colleges— admission chances being an academic lottery; nor is test prep time well spent as test content is not particularly useful for in-depth learning needed for college and career success.

There are thousands of "best" colleges out there.

Go where your child will thrive. Access to great professors, internships, and experiential opportunities, in what is the student's preferred environment from ivy-covered to ultra-modern, with or without lazy rivers, climbing walls, ice rinks, valet dorm rooms to apartment suites, with smart students (smart does not rub off), party students, pious students, liberal students, students that seem interesting—it is a matter of personal choice. It can be the elite school if you can afford it easily; it may not be the elite school if you want a twenty-first century education merging the highly academic with knowledge in practice. Country club amenities are amazing but don't get you a job. Active intellectual conversations with other passionate students don't require a lazy river or valet. The name of the college will not be enough to get the job at the undergraduate level if you don't have a targeted education and experience to do the work.

Section II

Be Your Student's Own Educational Consultant

Part Seven

Planning

The High School to Career Planner

Nonexistent career and education planning have led to the highest college dropout rate in the world, four-year degrees taking eight years, and college grads so poorly prepared they take jobs that require only six weeks to two years of college.

This how-to planner is an individualized career and academic guide to explain new programs and planning devised by and endorsed by schools, colleges, and business and industry.

College by Default

Default: *revert to a preselected option*

Many students end up in college by "default." Instead of thinking through plans, they revert to society's preselected option: go to college. They arrive there not really knowing what they are doing there—except they are "supposed to go to college." They are not passionate about majors that seemed "sensible" but which they hate, so they never own their learning. They are excited about the campus experience, but that has nothing to do with passionately pursuing their interests— as they haven't worked those out or been allowed to follow what they love.

We haven't embraced "career exploration" in high school beyond "go to college" or "do STEM" as the career plan. "Undecided" is the new favorite college major, but experts (and statistics) show that is a disastrous approach. "College is the worst place to try to find a career."[60]

A little thought about who they are would go a long way to make college meaningful. If students were more passionate about learning than socializing, then the attitude toward learning through the pandemic would have been more positive. (The campus experience is amazing, but what is more important? The amazing learning experience or a really cool sleep-away camp where you can drink and stay out all night?)

ICAP—Individualized Career and Academic Planning

ICAP is the official name for education planning devised by schools with business and industry.

Every high school plan needs to combine graduation requirements and further education plans with career aspirations.

Identify:

- The student's strengths and weaknesses
- The student's interests, abilities, and values

New, expanded high school options that connect to careers:

- Career exploration classes
- College credit classes (AP, IB, dual enrollment)

- Internships
- Apprenticeships

Educate the student and the family about:

- New education opportunities: college and professional paths
- Stackable credits to get into a career early and add credentials and degrees fine-tuned to specific career growth and in a way to minimize excess spending.
- Pathways to careers: training, certificates, licenses, college courses[61]

Being Your Teen's Educational Consultant

We set high standards for our teens, be it going to an Ivy, selective college, our alma mater, community college, or a job.

Grading scale:
A = Average
B = Bad
C = Catastrophic
D = Disowned
F = Forgotten Forever

The grading system is changing. Not to the meme above.

What is the new grading?

- New performance assessment
- Group projects with detailed grading rubrics
- Portfolio defense
- Capstone presentation evaluations

These move beyond short-term memory testing to evaluate student understanding and application of knowledge in real-world problem-solving.

Parents wonder, "Are these courses available in high school and college?" They are on offer in most every high school in America. But parents and teens, focused on old academic courses, miss scheduling them entirely.

Individually focused planning is yielding better college outcomes, career success, higher salaries, and life fulfillment.

Planning needs to shift from choosing life from the outside, to building on strengths and interests to propel passionate learning and accomplishment. Following someone else's path, pretending to be someone else, is not as successful as doing what one is best at.

> *"Trying to balance? Don't look left or right. You will fall over. Focus on your center. Your core."*
> —MARKESIHA MINER, J.D., DEAN OF STUDENTS, CORNELL LAW SCHOOL

> *The Future Comes from Within*
> —MOTTO, INSTITUTE OF TECHNICAL EDUCATION, SINGAPORE

> *"I guess you've just gotta find something you love to do and then...do it for the rest of your life."*
> —THE MOVIE *RUSHMORE*, WES ANDERSON

This planner could end here with your teen's answer to one simple question:

"If you could have any job, what would it be?"

It isn't "How do we get you into the most prestigious college in America?" Or "What is the highest-paid job in America?"

Why do we want a career the student will love? Leave aside personal fulfillment, the joy of a job well done, a career the student is passionate about, or happiness...

Love of job is where the money is.

We all have things that we would do even if we weren't paid. We have activities where we lose ourselves and all sense of time. But those who love their work get paid more. This book is about statistics, and statistics, studies, surveys for twenty years show that if we love what we do, we get paid more, we get promoted more, and we are more fulfilled.

Why Passion Pays...When We Love Our Work
We don't try, we do.
We persevere more easily through challenges and failures, seeing them as opportunities to learn.
We enjoy striving to know everything about our passion.
We problem-solve happily to learn more and become experts.
Becoming an expert is easier when you love the subject.
As experts, we understand faults and have the ultimate knowledge to correct them.
Innovation is easier when you understand the subject thoroughly.
Work is play.

So, within any career, the top earners are those who love their work.

We all need to do things we don't like, but being forced into an ill-fitting career goes against the way human nature works. If we deeply love what we do, then that passion gets us through obstacles, busy work, challenging work, and even defeat.

Some careers are low-paying, but loving the job usually brings salaries in the highest range within that career. Hating a job usually brings salaries at the low end of that career's scale.

The CG animator will work a month, on three hours of sleep a night, through computer crashes, software glitches, when the motion-capture data was reversed, when blue screen was used instead of green screen, having to recreate the project when Save File doesn't work, and doing it over completely when the director makes changes…because the animator adores the work, even in the face of everything going wrong.

Doctors will put in 120 hours a week, or forty-eight-hour shifts, because they love the profession.

Genius is said to be 98 percent perspiration and 2 percent inspiration. Loving the work drives the perspiration to genius level.

Repetitive training can create a great tennis player. But the tennis player who loves tennis is more likely to be a champion.

So why do we try to check all the boxes to make our student into some other ideal person to learn whatever it takes, regardless of interest, to get a high-paying job on the Pay Scale website?

To be practical, if you want success you can boast about, if you want your student to become recognized in his workplace or field, if you want your student to be an innovator, then help them find what they love, if they don't already know it. It is a good start, a foundation.

Fulfillment in productive work is rarely talked about as a life goal, but that is the way happiness lies—and can be more profitable, for those parents who are worried about those practicalities.

Self-exploration, a fundamental key to success and fulfillment, is shunned. Surveys show that taking the job that pays the bills, but doesn't engage the worker, leads to bitter disappointment. 80,000 hours, a working life, is a long time to be miserable.[62]

Your teen has natural genius, skills, and drive. Work with them and not against them.

Students still need to show excellence, but that should be easier, less stressful, and more fun if the teen can build on what he or she loves to do.

So, the highest paid accountants have an average salary of $122,000 while the lowest $43,000. That is an enormous difference.

An entry-level music teacher makes $36,000 (and has summers off) while a top-tier music teacher earns $71,000–$121,000. Music as a major can seem like a very bad idea compared to other careers. But being a happy music teacher at $71,000 is earning more than the 53 percent of accountants who earn under $71,000.

I am not saying to refuse to do anything you don't love. But look at what you love and what about it matches jobs that are out there.

UK billionaire Sir Richard Branson has two suggestions to find your career. Write down what you like. Write down what you don't like. But the "hate" list can be the most important. If you hate it, then probably others hate it too. And that is the starting point for a problem you can solve. Branson says most of the start-ups he invests in are solving what people hate.

Knowing what you like and knowing what you hate really are the keys to success.

Personality	Skills	Interests		
Home	School	Work	Play	Volunteering
Friends	Family	Strangers	Teachers	Authority
Where and with whom does your teen shine and where and from whom do they shy away?				

Above, try to determine what social settings bring out the best and worst aspects of the student's personality and abilities.

For example, one student is enthusiastic, a leader in the best sense, socially engaged amongst his sports and school friends, but around adults, strangers, and teachers he goes into a shell—even giggling and rolling his eyes. But put him in a volunteering role, he will be courteous and excel.

Another student, a great student, loved by teachers, able to speak with confidence to any adult, is almost beligerent to her boss who treats her like she knows nothing in her part-time retail job.

Those are realities that can be maximized or improved. One student had the choice of a large university or a very small one. He felt more comfortable at the small one but plans to transfer after he masters more social skills and gets solidly into his major. One girl, highly motivated, opted for a big university where basic courses were online. She could breeze through basic work with speed without busy work and daily class meetings.

Parent Detective Worksheet

What is your teen doing when he or she won't come when you call them for dinner?

And being on Instagram and social media is an appropriate answer.

What is your teen doing when he or she won't come when you call them for dinner?
Hobbies
Spare-time activities
Favorite movies and television
Favorite sports
Obsessions
When the teen talks to you, what does the teen talk about?
Does the teen talk about a favorite subject (not teacher)?

Does the teen hate a particular subject (not teacher)?
Does the teen have tutors in any subjects?

In what ways does this describe a different student than the one in the Naviance or college organizer notes for the college essay? This description shouldn't be some idealized student who checks other people's boxes.

The goal is to appreciate your teen for what he or she does and loves, not just for getting an A. Getting As shows a great work ethic and learning. But for now, stop comparing with other students. Also, it isn't about the failures, not being on the winning soccer team, missing the high honor roll, or hating school.

Put external goals aside and look at the kid.

Personality Clues
Organized or messy
Late or on time
Can't read a map
Responsible
Helpful
Talks back or is talkative
What adults do they like?
Who is their favorite teacher and why?

Twenty-First Century Skills Assessment

Be honest. Rank the student's skills. You can print three copies, one for the student, one for the parent to self-evaluate, and one for the parent to evaluate the student.

Parents don't have to share their assessment of their teen with the teen.

Twenty-First Century Skill	Novice	Learner	Proficient	Expert	Example
Collaboration					
Charm: Leading by influence					
Communication					
Agility					
Adaptability					
Initiative					
Entrepreneurship					
Effective speaker					
Persuasive writer					
Access information					
Curiosity					
Imagination					
Self-direction					
Civic responsibility					
Work ethic					
Find and use information					

Understand information technology					
Invention/innovation					
Creativity					
Critical thinking					
Problem-solving					
Cultural awareness					
Global awareness					

"School Personality Tests are Dumb" ...Yes, and No...

Most schools in America use planning tools, like Naviance, that allow free access to aptitude tests, personality tests, learning style tests, career-preferences tests. One can purchase access, but usually schools have access for free or can arrange it.

Your student has most likely been given a series of tests to help him or her plan their future career path. These tests include the Meyers-Briggs and the color test—ask your teen, "Are you an Orange, a Blue, a Green, or a Gold?" You'll be surprised. They have done this.

To unfairly oversimplify the color test, oranges are impulsive and bold, high achievers drawn to crises; green is the logical perfectionist innovator; golds are committed, responsible, organized team players but can aspire to authority; and blues are nurturing emotional artistic idealists.

Again, this is a gross oversimplification. There are many versions of the color test online, some are free, some cost money. None are the same.

The parent and teen may want the results, so ask the teen's counselor.

These tests are old, and range from amusing to a life-sucking black-hole hour for most teens. Others are useful, especially for those who have no idea what they want to do in the future. In other words, they haven't connected what they love and are good at with possible careers. Great educators are working to rewrite these.

Ask your teen what they thought of the tests. My triplets came home and said "Ms. _____ gave me a dumb test. My work in a hospital in Vietnam last summer was converted into 'likes traveling' and said I should change my career to work in tourism. I am not changing from medicine to become a tour guide so I can travel. That took time I was going to use to study for the trig quiz. Dumb." These tests are not dumb, but great educators are working to rewrite them.

Instead, you can ask your teen which house they got into with the official Hogwarts quiz. A login and password are needed, but your teen probably already has one.[63]

Or ask them which Marvel superhero they are. There are many quizzes online.

Our teens love those quizzes, and they can provoke real, more revealing personality discussions than a clinical test.

The Failure Gauge: The Foundation of Success

Americans generally do not tolerate high school failure. As of recently, most states' education policy now advocates embracing failure, but this may take years to implement.

But let us try to implement this new strategy. Let's learn from the "failures," from difficulty and low performance to plan for the future. To find the student's strengths, we need to look at the student's challenges. Perfect grades are less informative than understanding the struggle to learn something hard or new and the value of mastering tough material through persistence and resilience.

Failing or low performance reveals volumes. (Check all that apply) Make copies, because everyone has more than one subject they are not best at. If they are perfect at everything, as the saying goes, then they are not challenging themselves enough.

Learn from Failures: Reasons for Course Struggles
The teen accepted a hard challenge and learned the material in the end—conventional grades may not fully interpret real growth.
That level course was too difficult for the teen.
The teen loves the subject but would respond to an experiential course, not textbook-based teaching.
The teen's strengths are not in that direction.
The teen really hates the material.
The teen was bored and not mature enough to follow rules.
Your teen is an egotistical know-it-all who thinks he is too good to do the homework so got an F while getting an A on the final—the course may have been too basic.

Love It or Hate It

COURSES YOU LOVE

COURSES YOU HATE

ACTIVITIES YOU LOVE

ACTIVITIES YOU HATE

A parent does not want to find out their kid hates math when the teen arrives at college and immediately changes from the engineering major to theatre because of it. This kind of thing happens all the time. That costs money, time, and trust on both sides.

Learning Styles

How do the above subjects, classes, and activities your teen loves match up with their learning style?

Identifying the student's learning style is important in planning: visual, auditory, and tactile. Neither one is better or worse, smarter or "dumb." But it can seem that way. Our education system has been based on "visual" learning—reading books, interpreting charts, doing math. That is great if you are a visual learner.

Now, high schools and colleges offer different kinds of learning experiences. Experiential learning is usually more suited to the tactile learner, and in some ways, the auditory learner. They will have to make accommodations to thrive in the old-style academic courses.

LEARNING STYLE TEST		
VISUAL	**AUDITORY**	**TACTILE**
Love reading	Love teacher lectures	Love to make and build
Hard to focus on lectures	Love discussions	Fidget and move
Remember faces, not names	Remember names, not faces	Remember actions, dances
Remember visual details	Will remember music, sounds	Love projects
Description Learn from reading and looking at pictures and charts. In a debate, lecture, or discussion, may process information more slowly.	Description Learn & remember by hearing and listening. Great lectures help overcome reading and writing portion of learning.	Description Learn by doing, touching, or hands-on learning. Will learn advanced math, etc., by using it to solve visual problems.

That is the most basic test. There are amazing tests online. EducationPlanner.org has a ten-question test.[64]

It is important to favor the right learning environment or use tools to compensate for any disadvantage. Everyone is a blend, so if the student is having trouble learning, try these suggestions.

Kids are not dumb, but they can seem so. Many learn complex material differently.

LEARNING	STYLE STUDY	TOOLS
VISUAL	AUDITORY	TACTILE
Take notes at lectures	Read back notes aloud	Take hands-on courses
Make flash cards	Read assignments aloud	Take frequent breaks studying
Try to visualize at lectures	Have someone read to you	Learn by typing
Color-code	Computers can "read aloud"	Fidget, which aids learning

Teens' Time for Honesty

Print these questionnaires twice—one so the parent knows the questions and one for the student to rip out and keep confidential. Teens, share as much as you want with your parent. Being honest with them is important. But it is you who has to live your life.

What are you doing when you lose all track of time?
1.
2.
3.

What do you love to do in your spare time?
1.
2.
3.

What websites and Twitter accounts do you follow?
1.
2.
3.

What subjects do you love?
1.
2.
3.

Which subjects do you hate?
1.
2.
3.

What would your life look like if you could do anything?
1.
2.
3.

When you look ahead to being forty, what do you want to be doing?
1.
2.
3.

When you are falling asleep at night, what worries do you have?
1.
2.
3.

When you are falling asleep at night, what do you daydream about doing?
1.
2.
3.

What is something you are proud of?
1.
2.
3.

What are your goals?
1.
2.
3.

What is your vision for your future?
1.
2.
3.
4.
5.

What are your strengths?
1.
2.
3.
4.
5.

What are you naturally good at? Your aptitudes?
1.
2.
3.
4.
5.

What are your interests? Passions?
1.
2.
3.
4.
5.
6.

What are your personality traits?
1.
2.
3.
4.

5.
6.

What are your core values?
1.
2.
3.
4.
5.
6.

What challenges or causes do you want to solve?
1.
2.
3.
4.

What material things would be important to you as an adult?
1.
2.
3.
4.
5.

What activities or places make you feel safe and valued?
1.
2.
3.

4.
5.
What kind of people make you feel comfortable?
1.
2.
3.
4.
5.
What activities do you find hard to stick to?
1.
2.
3.
4.
What do you have coming in your future that you dread?
1.
2.
3.
4.
Where would you want to work?
Inside or outside
In an office or at home
In a lab, factory, museum, studio, gallery, hospital
Working in groups
Noisy or quiet

Public contact or closed office
40-hour work week, 50-hour, 80-hour, 120+ work week
After high school, what do you want to do?
Go to college
Go to work
Go to work and college
Do more professional certification
Take a year off
Whether you are planning on college or career, what do you worry will go wrong?
1.
2.
3.
4.
5.
Do you think your current passions and your strengths match your career/college plans right now?
Where do they match?
1.
2.
3.
Where are they misaligned?
1.
2.
3.

Survival Skills

Critical thinking and problem-solving
Collaboration across networks and leading by influence
Agility and adaptability
Initiative and entrepreneurship
Effective oral and written communication
Accessing and analyzing information
Curiosity and imagination[65]

Being academically smart doesn't automatically mean that a student has mastered the above survival skills. Taking over the group project because the others are "dumb" or "lazy," is not leading. Taking over a group in order "to beat" other smart kids is not collaboration, persuasion, communication.

"I wish they would introduce a 'Charm' course in middle school," said a robotics and coding teacher. She sees smart kids who variously feel superior, have no people skills, or lack self-confidence. No one would hire these kids who have no desire to get along with anyone. Many are not even nice, while others are too nice. People skills need to be developed.

Here are some goals from Edutopia, from the George Lucas Education Foundation, just one example of initiatives across the country.

Comprehensive Assessment[66]

This should measure the full range of student ability—social, emotional, and academic achievement. Through various measures, including portfolios, presentations, and tests, multiple learning styles are supported.

Integrated Studies[67]

To increase engagement and retention, academic subjects are presented in an interdisciplinary fashion that reflects modern knowledge and society. For instance, history, literature, and art can be interwoven and taught through text, images, and sound.

Project-Based Learning[68]

Long-term and student-centered, project-based learning is a rigorous hands-on approach to learning core subject matter and basic skills with meaningful activities that examine complex, real-world issues. Project-based learning helps students develop and retain useful, working knowledge of subjects that are often taught in isolation and abstraction.

Social and Emotional Learning[69]

When students work together on teams, they learn to collaborate, communicate, and resolve conflicts. Cooperative learning and character development support the social and emotional development of students and prepares them for success in the modern workplace.

Technology Integration[70]

Through the intelligent use of technology, combined with new approaches to education, a more personalized style of learning can be realized.

Academic Routes and Professional Routes

Academic routes can lead to great jobs.
Professional routes can lead to great jobs.
Many jobs can be reached by either professional or academic routes.
All jobs need academic and professional expertise.

CareerWise, described as an upcoming major player in reforming US high school education, works with schools and businesses to provide high school apprenticeships starting junior year, where students attend high school and start a career with a part-time salary of $35,000. The third year is spent working for the company, then often the company contributes to funding this top employee's college. The student starts a real career in a growth business or industry in junior year.

A familiar response is, "That's wonderful…for other kids. But my teen isn't aiming for blue-collar. My teen doesn't want to fix cars, or be a plumber. My teen is going to a selective college." But these apprenticeships are in medicine, IT, engineering, even finance at JP Morgan in New York City.[71]

High school experiential courses and career exploration can enhance that college degree.

Lockheed Martin

Lockheed Martin offers coding internships in drone research in the virtual reality department. That is a great job and start of a career at coveted Lockheed Martin. Or a great three years spent before applying to MIT or the Colorado School of Mines.[72]

Aviation

An aviation career can be reached by two paths, academic and professional. A public high school in the Denver area, for example, offers an aviation specialty: aviation maintenance—outside of the plane, aviation maintenance internal, and flight training. These can be attained for free in high school.

The starting salary on external plane maintenance for high school grads is $55,000; the starting salary for internal is $65,000–$85,000; pilot starting salary is $20–$40,000 but dramatically increases to $60,000–$190,000 based on experience and airline. The aspiring pilot could work aviation maintenance, a fifty-hour-a-week job, while building the flight hours.

The University of Georgia boasts the same training plan of the two certifications and pilot training. It is an amazing university with campuses on all continents, including Antarctica. The four-year degree, if done in four years, will cost approximately $100,000 in-state and $190,000 out of state.

If the family has the money and the student the time, college is an amazing, rich experience. But the college grad will be four years "behind" that professionally qualified high school grad. At twenty-three, the college grad pilot could be making $20,000, while the professionally qualified could be up to $120,000 or higher, at age twenty-three, having earned $60,000–$85,000 a year while racking up flight time with no debt.

Maybe one feels more "elite," but that comes with a price—which may or may not be fine. The high school-trained pilot can also travel the world, read Socrates, and listen to jazz (considered the hallmark of the college-educated).

Ditch College Elitism and Stop "Random Acts of College"[73]

Choose the route best for the student.

The traditional college path of self-paying a bachelor's and then a master's leaves a student hoping to get a job is "costly, risky, with few jobs for the inexperienced grad."[74]

College Is Not Proof of Intelligence or Class

The "elitist" ideas of college as bestowing "class" or college as a "degree in intelligence" needs to end.

Is a top career at places like JP Morgan or Lockheed Martin less good if one got there for free via an internship and college paid for by the company, or if one self-paid for college costing $100,000–$350,000 and then applied and got the job?

College has got to stop being a status symbol. Careers have a multitude of pathways requiring intelligence and expertise. Career success at any level should be its own "status" symbol, deserving of respect.

Strong parenting can stop many college financial disasters.

A parent can insist that a college student finish the degree in four years.

Strong parenting can limit the choice of colleges to those that can be afforded.

Strong parenting can stop paying for college for the D and F student who has lost his or her scholarship from partying, etc.

Strong parenting can allow a student to do what they really want to do.

Strong parenting can also allow a student to change their mind for valid reasons and help point them to the better career choice.

A strong parent can accept who their student is, whether he or she is headed to an elite college or straight to a job.

College and Advanced Training for Life

I assure you I am not trying to discourage *anyone* from going to college. College is vital. Lifelong learning is the new lifestyle.

Those who hate studying and books and just want to get out to work will have to do college-level work. Learning is the new way of life for future prosperity. Whether starting with an academic or professional focus, both groups will have to retrain or upskill for new careers not yet imagined.

The University of Florida has a new pathways degree that is academically rigorous but *in an experiential form* targeted at careers in growth industries.

Most of the rest of the world call the professional route "degrees" and treat them as equal to academic degrees. Washington is in the process of doing this.

Getting the Most Out of High School to Set Up Academic and Career Success

Surveys show a group of parents "more" satisfied with the overall high school experience. These are parents of students who have done experiential courses, where students apply what they have "book learned."[75]

Some students may say, "I hate differential equations," but use them daily in experiential mechanical engineering high school courses. Some courses involve onsite work like internships, trying out a real job, making connections with employers that they can use after high school or after college. These teens get the ability to explore careers in high school *while often receiving core, elective, or college credit*. These students participate in a national program available in most states, called CTE (Career and Technical Education).

The average parent still thinks CTE (Career and Technical Education) is vocational training for those on a non-college, working-class, lower-paid, blue-collar track. 86 percent of CTE students go on to college and usually with more dual college credit completed when they arrive at college than the average student, unlike APs where exam results and college policy will determine whether or not the student gets credit.

There is a bias against CTE courses. But with these courses, a pre-med student can work in a hospital ward. The future financier can work in finance or with a top entrepreneur and may get a nationally recognized business certification. The future teacher can get classroom-certified. The future mechanical engineering major can work designing his or her vision of a new airplane, hands-on, or patent a nanotech process. Electrical engineering can be reached without college—but the student must be smart!

These courses should be a no-brainer for all students.

Know Your Options

What if high school could give your student…

- core credit or college credit to explore and start careers

- internships through a CTE course or externships and job shadowing—like internships but a few hours to a few days

- a recognized certificate (in pre-law, teaching, therapy, medicine, engineering, design…in four hundred fields)

- proof of workplace success that will impress employers after college graduation

- hands-on implementation of book learning—to the academic teen to get real-world experience and for the kid who is fed up with books

- high school and apprenticeship program (with a $35,000 a year salary)

- job exposure before college to inspire the student to innovate and direct his or her college study

- networking that could lead to additional financial aid for college

- ongoing part-time work in a career field during college

- a career certification in high school that means an immediate career after high school that can be a near-six-figure starting salary (at age seventeen or eighteen), or a career start until college can be afforded

- verifiable proof of maturity for college admissions

for *free*…during high school.

Those are amazing things that the American high school public school system offers.

Usually, these courses are *electives*. Some are new core courses that may be better for a certain career or taught in an alternative learning style (rather than an academic style) for students who learn differently (but are not "less smart").

But only about 27 percent of parents know about these high school course offerings.[76]

Overcoming Professional-Route Bias

Parents and teens want a dignified path to be proud of. College bestows dignity. "Professional" has the stigma of low-class, vocational, manual work, even though that is far from the truth in the Technology Age.

But we can change our mindset to make these valuable courses "acceptable."

Here is an activity. One: name six careers that can be reached via college but equally reached by a professional route. Two: research advanced manufacturing. Name six subjects studied for advanced manufacturing—it is no longer-labor intensive, it is knowledge-intensive. Just look it up on the internet—changing a life-long mindset takes effort. Or cheat—the answer key is below.

Careers Reached by Both College and Professional Routes (name six)
a.)
b.)
c.)
d.)
e.)
f.)
Advanced Manufacturing Is Knowledge Not Labor Intensive-name six subjects
a.)
b.)
c.)

d.)
e.)
f.)

Answer key:

1. a.) Medicine b.) Finance and banking c.) STEM d.) Aviation e.) Engineering

2. a.) Nanotechnology b.) Advanced materials c.) automation, d.) computer technologies e.) process technologies f.) information technologies

Nearly every high school student should take one or more of these courses to enrich their high school experience.

Here is a to-do list to open eyes to opportunities.

Career and Technology	Exploration
Activity	**Completed**
Watch virtual job shadows online	
Go to a CTE information session at your high school	
Visit CTE classes at high school in the teen's field of interest	
Talk to at least three teachers at a CTE fair	
Tour one of the new high schools with professional education or technical college	
Attend a career fair virtually, or at your high school or community college. Ask three employers there to contrast the college and professional routes	

Academic kids need professional courses and professional kids need academic courses!

Singapore, a small country of 5.6 million, has the goal that everyone earn above a middle-class salary. Their national goal is for everyone to earn an upper-middle-class salary.[77]

Singapore acknowledges the two paths, academic and professional. Professional high schools, like those springing up in America, are established. Getting a professional qualification has the dignity of an academic degree.

For those on the academic track, upskilling and reskilling is now part of what the University of Singapore offers. Attend undergraduate and the student can return to retrain for a new career over the next twenty years.

Both paths are equally promoted.

The Value of Experiential Learning

Experiential courses fulfill many student needs:

- Maturity through real-working-world immersion
- Face-to-face communication (even if through Google chat, Facetime or Zoom)
- Group project-solving
- Learning to use new technologies to solve problems
- Training and certification in a high-earning stable career
- Career "tasters"
- Academically challenging courses taught experientially—so enhancing the impact
- Instills purpose to bachelor's study
- Early networking
- On-the-job training in high school, not grad school

CTE can be trying out careers or it can be actual job training. It is both and more.

Career exploration:

- Recognized as ideal intellectual preparation for four-year college
- Reveals what would be most important to learn in college that would solve problems the student saw when "working" in the field in the experiential course
- Leads to innovations or inventions
- Kickstarts a career or allows for part-time career work if taking the college route

Summer jobs one can get from CTE experience are real career-building, not low-paid fast-food work.

"Child Support"

Thinking about adulthood and careers sounds overwhelming. "It's too soon." Whether that discussion seems too much in eighth grade, in high school or in college, it isn't.

75 percent of parents financially help their grown children. As a parent, is that in your plans?[78]

Kid-centered parents do so much to support their children, but do they really want literally to support their child for life—or the next twenty years after high school?

Twenty years ago, many parents didn't expect a young person to be independent until twenty-five. Today many parents feel their child will not be financially independent until age thirty.

Now, 33 percent of young adults up to twenty-five still live at home. Over 15 percent are still at home at thirty. The reason listed is rarely economic. Parents could be robbing the "child" of a chance at real independence, self-respect, accomplishment. Some parents love having their grown kids live with them. Some love it when their "child," his or her spouse, and the kids move in permanently (and this happens at all economic levels).

Do what works for the family! I love to have my kids around a lot, but I would like them to have pride in their own endeavors.

But what if you don't want your child and their new family to move in upstairs or take over the basement, or you don't have a "west wing" for them to take over for life? Then maybe we should start talking about careers a bit sooner than age twenty-five or thirty. At eighteen, teens are legally adults. Resist the urge to keep them dependent or childlike.

Work can feel like "a life sentence" or it can be something we would do without being paid. So let's help find something amazing for our kids to do, that they want to do.

Help them find a great life they will love.

Contract Work—The New Normal

A national wine label with a wide variety of nationally and internationally well-known wines shows how companies are now structured. They contract to buy the grapes from a vineyard that they do not own. They contract another company to press the grapes. They hire another specialist company to blend the wine. They hire a bottling plant to bottle, a storage company to store. Label designers are independently contracted. A distributor is contracted. A marketing firm is contracted.

The company has two owners. There is no staff, no vineyard. Independent contractors are hired only when needed. This is efficient. No health care, no pension program, no idle employees in off seasons. This is the way for efficiency, innovation, and quick response.

The company hires companies that do the work best on short-term contracts.

Planning Early Years

The more words that a baby hears in the first two years correlates with academic achievement. Instilling a love of learning will drive the child more than punishment or reward, as aspirational goal-setting is for the older child after establishing delayed gratification. Parents showing curiosity about everything they see is a free way to promote an atmosphere of learning. Ask questions and listen to your child's answers.

Reading: Encourage reading. Computer time often drives reading. Watching Japanese anime with subtitles is a gateway to reading. Psychologists attest that listening to audio books, even without following along, helps with reading. Playing some video games can help rewire synapses in the brain using similar methods as some expensive brain therapy treatment for some forms of dyslexia.

Math: But math must be learned. *Not getting As in math means failing math.* Math knowledge builds. A student can't be shaky on fractions, or pre-algebra, or graphs. He or she might be able to skip William Faulkner's *The Sound and the Fury* and not impact his or her ability to create an effective written argument. Missing a foundational piece of math will lead to failure.

Homework

Stop pages of repetitive homework. Repetitive homework, once a concept is learned and understood, leads to lower grades—even in math. Fifteen pages of repetitive homework isn't a productive use of time. A few pages for reinforcement is great, but if the student doesn't know the concept, homework won't help; if they do know, then boredom will set in.[79]

Planning High School and Beyond

High School Graduation Is the First Priority

Chart your graduation requirements and college prerequisites. They can change. Revise each year of high school.

How many credits do you need?	High School Graduation	College 1/ Higher Ed	College 2/ Higher Ed	College 3/ Higher Ed	College 4/ Higher Ed	College 5/ Higher Ed
English						
Math						
Social Studies						
US Government						
Science						
Gym						
Health						
Foreign Language						
Electives						
Math Test						
English Test						

Check with your school for their requirements. Learn what credits they accept. College or other high school summer credits may not go toward graduation but a separate transcript can be sent to college admissions.

Usually high schools require:

> English—four years
> Math—three years
> Social Studies—three years (including one semester US Government)
> Science—three years
> Gym—three semesters
> Health—one semester
> Foreign Language—optional
> Electives—six semesters

For twenty-two credits.

Many school districts require additional competency tests in math and English

High School/College Credit Options

What credits does your high school accept?	Yes /No
Own high school	**yes**
District	
Outside district online school	
Varsity sports for gym credit	
APs (advanced placement)	
Dual enrollment	
Summer school	
College summer school	
College credit	

Starter Career Ideas

Essential Questions
What do you love doing so much that you would do it without being paid?
What do you daydream about doing when you are lying in bed at night? (Teens don't have to tell parents exactly— but it is a great way for them to be honest with themselves.)
Where do you see yourself at age forty?

Budget Your Dream Life

At an "Evening with the Deans" at a high school, deans said that the students entering college were "almost *overprepared* academically," but had a serious lack of life skills, like budgeting, reading a map, advocating for themselves, self-regulation, resilience, etc.[80]

Picturing adult responsibilities can make them manageable and reveal real, favorable paths. That low-paid archeology career earning $28,000 may include travel, living quarters and food at the dig in China six months of the year, and cost of living at the Wyoming lab may be extremely low. The cruise line entertainment manager job or singing cast member, earning seventeen to twenty-five dollars an hour, will include room and board so virtually all the salary can go into savings—$50,000 to $75,000 going into savings for three to ten years is a pretty great nest egg doing what one loves. The finance job earning $200,000 will be eaten up quickly with high-cost city living and high taxes, and twenty years of paying off elite college student loans. A military career can pay for college, guarantee a job usually in a Technology Age growth field—but it means becoming a "soldier," whether a JAG, drone pilot, or mechanical engineer. Plan it out.

What will real life really look like? Can the young adult do with basic cable or slow internet? Daily Starbucks at $6.87 or is a $0.99 Big Gulp acceptable? Expensive hobby, sport? Gym memberships aren't free. Fashionista? Movie buff? Newest computer, latest phone? Car repair, gas? An Uber, bus pass? Look at photos of the cheapest apartment—look at the neighborhood amenities, transportation, crime rate.

Whether for cost of living during higher education, college, or out in the world working, the teen should choose several places to live and research online to fill in the following chart.

Fill out for the first independent living experience and for ten years on. Then plan for ten years on. For ten years in the future, factor in buying a house and a car. Make it location-specific.

Budget Notes

Cost of Living	Example	Example ten Years	Locale 1 Now	Locale 1 Future	Locale 2 Now	Locale 2 Future
Housing	$1,555	$1,000				
Utilities	n/a.	$175				
Electricity	$95	$175				
Heating/Water	$65	$65				
Phone	$20	$0				
Cable	$70	$149				
Internet	$40	$55				
Cell Phone	$95	$97				
Food	$815	$1,300				
Transportation	$160	$375				
Clothes	$150	$150				
Health	$99	$127				
Entertainment	$45	$200				
Personal Care	$35	$35				
Student Loans	$280	$280				
Total Monthly Cost	$3,524	$4,183				
Yearly	$42,288	$50,196				
Savings	$8,077					
Miscellaneous	$3,000	$8,0770				
Taxes	**	**				
Salary Needed	$53, 365	$97,000*				

Example amounts—$250 is based on a $25,000 ten-year loan. $150 is for a week-daily Starbucks.

Savings should be 20 percent of income. Transportation is insurance plus forty dollars for gas. Housing is for a one-bedroom apartment in a medium-sized community. That is living on the edge with no savings. For average savings of 20 percent, the person would need a salary of at least $53,000. Do not rely on the example. In some metropolitan areas, a studio apartment could range from $700 to $4,000.

Miscellaneous	Example	Future 1	Future 2
House down payment	$55,000		
Car down payment	$5,000		
Child one yearly	$13,000		
Medical deductible	$7,000		
iPhone	$770 with trade-in		
Yearly	$80, 770		

Ten years in the future, the $400,000 house down payment is in the region of $55,000. The medical deductible may be $7,000. More insurance may be $500 to $2,000. The car deposit may be $5,000.

So, this student needs to work toward an $80,770 salary by saving substantially from Year One—the recommended median salary to support a $400,000 house with property taxes, income taxes.

Tax rates vary per state and can make a significant difference. No state tax is greater than a 27 percent rate. Property taxes vary, but are usually not a factor when renting. Federal taxes must be included.

Location, Location, Location—State Job Growth Trends

Where you want to live should be a big factor in college and career choice.

"Where" is crucial to future success. Some careers will not be offered in some states. Some locations will favor certain careers.

For some careers, where you live or study doesn't matter. All growth areas will need more medical staff, teachers, utility technicians. Those careers are more "portable." But openings will be few in communities with static growth.

Pick a college where he or she can get internships in their choice career— successful internships can result in job offers. Internship experience and that network of contacts can be portable to other locations, but it is still harder to start a career thousands of miles from the network you have established with college internships.

Mineral engineering in Georgia, probably no, but in Rocky Mountain states, local industry leads to internships and jobs. Submarine design in Georgia, with a thriving, expanding submarine design and manufacturing industry, yes. Don't make attaining "the dream" career harder than it already is.

High-paying growth jobs are not necessarily *where* you would expect. Wind farm development is huge in Iowa. Tech companies are relocating from current famous tech valleys to Oregon or Montana. Many careers will use 100 percent teleworking so the employees with expertise can live anywhere.

If the student is keen on working at a specific company, see what professional schools and colleges they recruit from.

Growth Careers by State

The chart below shows a general snapshot of each state's growth industries. Support industries often accompany the creation of new jobs. If a state is adding 20,000 employees for a new aerospace division, then obviously that area will usually need more teachers, more healthcare services, personal services, construction, and infrastructure but these are not counted as new growth fields.

Chart what interests the student where he or she lives, wants to live, and wants to go college. Or, let the career openings guide college location choice.

State Growth Industries	College Location	Future Location Choice
Alabama		
Construction		
Rocket engines		
Airbus		
Alaska		
Energy		
Construction		
Food services		
Arizona		
Healthcare		
Financial: called the "Fintech Sandbox"		
Allstate, Freedom Financial, etc.		
Construction		
Surface mining		
Arkansas		
Walmart, Coca-Cola expansion		
Leisure and hospitality		

Southland Gaming		
Construction		
California		
Construction		
Hospitality		
Decline in incoming population		
Negatives: Trade war		
High housing prices, high taxes		
Fire risk		
Tech companies relocating		
Colorado		
NEED SKILLED WORKERS		
Increasing wages		
400 Aerospace companies		
Space command		
Construction		
Payroll Processing: Gusto		
Amazon		
Negatives: high house prices		
Connecticut		
Manufacturing:		
Electric boat (submarines)		
High Tech		
Infosys		

Aerospace		
Genomics		
Healthcare		
Construction		
Delaware		
Higher scale job growth		
Finance:		
J.P. Morgan Chase (example)		
Logistics		
Biopharmaceuticals		
Tourism		
Washington DC		
Government		
Business support		
Tourism		
Hospitality		
Florida		
No state income tax		
Highest in-migration— Northeast & International		
Big service industries		
Healthcare		
Construction		
Tourism		

Georgia		
Construction—6 percent jobs increase		
Health care—3 percent jobs increase		
Negative: Trade war slowdown		
Hawaii		
Half of jobs are in hospitality:		
Hotel, food and real estate		
Construction		
Idaho		
Technology:		
Examples: Paylocity		
Clearwater analytics		
Start-up robotics		
Construction		
Low cost of living attracting companies		
Illinois		
Boeing		
Abbott Laboratories		
Caterpillar		
All hiring: Software developers		
Computer engineers		
Data analytics		
Telecommunications experts		
Construction		

Indiana		
Construction		
Healthcare		
Leisure and hospitality		
High tech		
Amazon		
US Steel		
Negative: Weakening manufacturing		
Iowa		
Biotech research		
Wind energy—second-largest industry in US		
Negative: Trade war affecting agriculture		
Kansas		
Aerospace		
Aviation		
Negatives: Trade war (agriculture declining)		
No job diversity		
Kentucky		
Automotive industry		
Russian investment		

Louisiana		
Moderate health services		
Moderate tourism		
Industrial projects:		
Ethane cracker		
Alpha olefins plant		
Maine		
NEED SKILLED WORKERS		
Defense industry		
Manufacturing start-ups		
Low-paying tourism jobs		
Maryland		
SHORTAGE: TECHNOLOGY JOBS		
NURSING JOBS		
Cybersecurity—expanding hub		
Healthcare		
Construction		
Infrastructure projects		
Massachusetts		
High tech		
Financial		
Biotech		
Pharmaceuticals		
Transportation hub		

Companies: Verizon		
Google		
Apple		
Amazon		
Healthcare		
Education		
Accounting		
Fact: Draw from talented New England grads		
Michigan		
Amazon		
Only Midwest state with automotive slowdown		
Minnesota		
Strongest Midwest in-migration		
Housing construction		
Manufacturing—no growth		
Healthcare—no growth		
Has first US city to ban single-home construction		
Multi-family home construction (to lower costs)		
Mississippi		
Global automakers		
Leisure and hospitality		
Shipbuilding/modernizing US Navy projects		

Missouri		
Manufacturing		
Transportation		
Pharmaceuticals		
Animal health		
Montana		
High tech		
Tourism		
Healthcare		
Decline: Oil		
Farming		
Nebraska		
Construction		
Business and professional services		
Warehousing		
Negative: Agriculture impacted by trade war and bad weather		
Nevada		
BOOM ECONOMY		
3 percent payroll increase		
NEED SKILLED WORKERS		
ESPECIALLY CONSTRUCTION WORKERS		

New Hampshire		
Fastest New England growth		
WORKFORCE SHORTAGE:		
Factories and restaurants especially		
Defense production		
Electronic warfare		
High tech start-ups from venture capital funding		
Negative—Tariffs problems for:		
Manufacturing & construction		
New Jersey		
Leisure and hospitality growth		
Pharmaceuticals		
Biotechnology		
New Mexico		
Mineral industry (modest hiring)		
Mining, oil, natural gas		
US airbases		
Leisure and hospitality		
Solar energy growth area		
Film industry: Netflix TV & film production		

New York		
Shrinking population due to high taxes		
Venture capital funding		
Facebook		
Apple		
Google		
Pool of highly educated workers		
North Carolina		
Big banks		
North Dakota		
LABOR SHORTAGE		
Construction up 10 percent		
Healthcare up 4 percent		
Cancer treatment		
Oil pipeline (short-term jobs)		
Ohio		
Automotive industry		
Steel industry		
Negative: Chinese trade conflict		
Oklahoma		
Oil		
Natural gas		
Tech: Google, etc.		

Amazon		
Construction		
Oregon		
Fastest-growing state		
Intel chip factory		
Big construction projects (Portland)		
Construction (commercial, affordable residential)		
Pennsylvania		
Professional services		
Healthcare		
Construction		
Transportation		
Energy		
Gene therapy		
Tech Hub: Software developers like		
Apple and Lucas Systems		
Rhode Island		
Healthcare		
Construction		
High tech/innovative tech		
Recruiting internationally		
Declining manufacturing		

South Carolina		
Export-driven		
BMW, Volvo, Mercedes		
Samsung, Boeing		
New port for big ships		
South Dakota		
Shrimp hatchery		
Cheese processing		
Wind farms		
Tennessee		
No income tax		
Amazon		
Orthodontics		
Volkswagen electric cars		
Texas		
Energy		
High tech		
New Apple campus		
Military contracts		
Energy-related industries		

Utah		
Great economy		
The "Silicon Slopes"		
High tech (one in seven jobs are high tech)		
Cloud computing		
"Bionic Valley" bioengineering		
Life sciences		
Aerospace		
Tourism		
Low-cost housing		
Vermont		
Aviation		
Manufacturing		
Aerospace		
Health services		
Tourism		
Virginia		
Amazon (25,000 well-paying jobs)		
Government jobs		
Washington		
Highly competitive		
High tech		
Amazon		
Microsoft		

Costco		
PACCAR truck building		
Starbucks		
West Virginia		
Toyota		
Intuit		
Gas pipeline		
Negative: 2012–2016—26,000 lost coal jobs		
Wisconsin		
NEED SKILLED WORKERS		
Manufacturing		
Liquid crystal displays		
Construction		
Hospitals		
Amazon		
Wyoming		
Manufacturing		
Retail		
Warehousing		
Negative: Energy down		
2015–2016: 20,000 energy jobs lost		
Shrinking healthcare sector[81]		

Personal Preferences Job Test

What does your perfect workday lifestyle look like? Some offices will only allow one family photo and a company coffee mug. Some allow dogs. What would stop you being happy in a job? Early mornings, teamwork, dress code? Twenty-four hour shifts? Three day shifts? Be honest and be real. Look at "job shadow videos" to reality check your career choices.

Job	Average Hours	Work Place	Casual Strict	Work at Home	Work w Public	Contract Work	Hates

What are the average hours? Lawyers, doctors, financiers, often work over 120 hours a week. Comcast technician managers are salaried, so get no extra pay for overtime. Can you bring your dog to work? Can you occasionally work at home? Everyone works with people, but would the job mean constant work with the general public? What are the less likeable features? You may want to be a game character designer but because the game is top secret, you work in a locked cubicle alone refining hair dynamics for one character's ponytail for two years… job shadow—virtual or real.

Knowing All the Options for a Better High School Schedule: Core Classes

Traditional, Advanced, Honors, AP, IB, CTE, Dual Enrollment

Core classes are the foundation courses for high school: English, math, science, and social studies. Students need core classes, electives courses, in addition to health, fitness, and US government/civics. The reader should have filled out the numbers of each subject your high needs for graduation.

Most high school course catalogues will show "track" progressions per subject. However, sometimes these do not list the wider list of CTE and dual enrollment classes—become aware of those.

Choosing the right level of class is extremely important. For a challenging class, try to select classes that are about one year advanced from where you are!

Planning English Core Classes

Choose four, one per year (or two if one-semester classes)

Ninth Grade
English 1
English 1 Honors
Tenth Grade
English 2
English 2 Honors

Eleventh Grade
English 3
English Honors 3
AP English Language
Twelfth Grade
A variety of regular or CP (college prep) courses like
Science Fiction
Short Story Writing
Shakespeare
Poetry
World Literature
AP Literature
CTE English core credit options (varies per district)
Health and Wellness: Behavioral Health
Business Services
Hospitality and Tourism
Medical Writing
Science/Technical Writing

These CTE courses are not some easy alternative. They meet core requirements. "Content in these courses is designed to provide learners with real-world skills, context, and industry terminology to succeed in today's workplace."[82]

Planning Math Core Classes

Math planning can look different for each student. Many middle schools will offer Algebra 1 or Geometry 1 or even Algebra 2.

Traditionally high schools will offer

Ninth Grade
Algebra 1
Algebra 1 Accelerated
Algebra 1
Tenth Grade
Geometry 1 standard
Geometry 1 Accelerated
Geometry Honors
Eleventh Grade
Algebra 2
Algebra 2 Accelerated
Algebra 2 Honors
Twelfth Grade:
Pre-Calculus
Calculus
Statistics
AP Calculus AB
AP Calculus BC
AP Statistics

CTE Math core options (varies per school district)
Infrastructure Engineering
Advanced Manufacturing
IT & STEAM
Aviation Maintenance

"Students will gain the confidence and necessary procedures to solve industry-related math problems and will eventually become leaders in their field."[83]

Performance-Based Simulations with Assessment

Solving algorithms, equations, and word problems is traditional. Now students are broken into groups and given real-life scenarios to solve. Locate hurricane victims who sent a message from an oil rig off Louisiana. Students work as air traffic controllers, pilots, meteorologists, transport dispatchers, making medical personnel decisions, facing communications challenges, fitting a relief budget, to arrange an island medical evacuation, near the oil rig, in high winds, to facilities they have located. This is math- and physics-intensive, but also gets the teens working real jobs, across fields, where they must communicate and innovate. These projects will serve the student better in the long run than repetitive solving of algorithms and equations.[84]

Planning Science Core Classes

The traditional science plan follows this progression:

Ninth Grade
Earth and Space Science

Tenth Grade
Biology—standard
Biology—honors
Eleventh Grade
Chemistry—standard
Chemistry—honors
Twelfth Grade
Physics
Other options
Environmental Science
AP Biology
AP Chemistry
AP Physics 1
AP Physics 2
AP Physics C1
AP Physics C2
AP Environmental Science
CTE Science Core Options (varies per school district)
Health & Wellness—Intro to Health & Wellness
Health & Wellness—Certified Nurse Aide
Health & Wellness—Pharmacy Technician
Health & Wellness—Intro to Physical Therapy / Occupational Therapy
Automotive Technology—MLR 1
Automotive Technology—MLR 2

| STEAM—Advanced Robotics |
| STEAM—Innovative Design |
| Other |
| Other |

"The scientific approach teaches students how to critically evaluate current research, define measurable outcomes, and work in an industry setting."[85]

Career Exploration Courses

High school career exploration courses don't guarantee the student will patent a new invention in that "application of knowledge" class—though many have. He or she may hate the course and the career—that may be just as valuable. All show accepting a challenge and mature career exploration. That means a lot to colleges and employers in the future.[86]

Dual Enrollment Options: CTE Courses for College Credit (Core or Electives)

Instead of AP options, here are some examples of dual enrollment options that are often offered within the high school or available within the district or local colleges.

These courses earn high school *and* college credit. With AP courses, the student must pass an end-of-year nationally standardized AP test. If the student scores from 3 to 5, the college may give credit. Selective colleges do not give credit but, sometimes, allow the next level class.

Almost all colleges accept the dual enrollment credit. That course may not count toward the college GPA. But it will count toward graduation.

Taking advantage of these courses, the student may be only a couple of credit hours short of an associate degree when graduating from high school. A summer course could complete the two-year degree.

Check courses that might interest you.

Dual Enrollment: Common High School and College Credit Courses
Business and Marketing:
Accounting 2
Business Law
Entrepreneurship
Intro to Business
Marketing Co-op
Principles of Business
Marketing 2
Computer Applications
Commercial Art and Design
Graphic Design 2
Digital Photography 2
Photography/Digital Mixed Media
Applied Technology
Computer Aided Design
Engineering Drawing/Design
Health Sciences
Advanced Health Sciences
Principles of Health Sciences

Computer Science
Programming Game Design
Computer Applications
Intro to Computer Programming
Criminal Justice
Crime Science: Investigation
Intro to Criminal Justice
Engineering Technologies
Engineering Design/Drawing
Computer-Aided Design
Family and Consumer Science
ProStart Hospitality 1
ProStart Culinary Program 2
Visual Arts and Design
4-D Design Film and Animation
Graphic Design 1 and 2
Cosmetology
Cosmetology
Automotive Technology
Each school district has its own program. Check with your school district.

Now find those courses in your own school district catalog for these offerings.

Certifications

Certifications—The Free Job Safety Net

Any student can obtain a certificate(s) that will guarantee entry into a well-paying high-demand career while in high school, without undermining academic excellence.

Obtaining a certificate is attractive to college admissions and future employers as the certificate verifies experience doing the work, which is the top consideration of employers, more than a college degree.

Use that certificate to get a part-time job and kick-start a career. Money, experience, and networking!

Devoting one to four (or more) of the forty-eight total class periods in four years of high school to ensuring a well-paid career launch pad while still in high school is not an overwhelming time commitment. The teen could already walk into a full- or part-time career job with or without college. Even if college is the plan!

Some reasons to choose a certificate course:

- Try out a career. He or she may find that career isn't the right one by working in the field.
- The student will have real practical experience in the career of choice.
- The student will have started networking and accumulating "social capital" for employment after college.
- The employer may fund or part-fund college.
- If the student finds they need extra money, they are not working in the college cafeteria or bookstore but are accumulating real career experience.

Cosmetology counts as a college-level chemistry course (so weighted credit) and could be an amazing background for a dermatologist or plastic surgeon, and be a money earner in college. It's an obvious background for innovating skin treatments and procedures.

A hobby or interest, backed by a certificate, is peace-of-mind insurance that is free, that colleges like, and that employers like, even if a different field is pursued. A certificate in editing, animation, or animation character rigging can lead to part-time, per project, remote work. (My son loved editing and takes on editing jobs in his spare time for spare cash.)

That drone course can lead to that Lockheed Martin paid apprenticeship.

Getting certificates should be a no-brainer. Certifications tell employers that the person has completed special training and is qualified to do specific work or jobs.

Cherry Creek School District, near Denver, Colorado, offers the following certifications for high school students. Below these are certificates offered at Arizona high schools.

Manufacturing Fundamentals
National Institute of Metalworking Skills (NIMS) upon completion of pathway
Computer Numeric Control (CNC) Machining
National Institute of Metalworking Skills (NIMS) upon completion of pathway
Fundamentals of Manufacturing II
National Institute of Metalworking Skills (NIMS)
CNC Machining II
National Institute of Metalworking Skills (NIMS)
Project Management for Entrepreneurs I (PM4EI)
Certified Associate Project Management (CAPM) upon completion of PM4EI and PM4EII (may be earned in grade twelve only)

Project Management for Entrepreneurs II (PM4EII)

Certified Associate Project Management (CAPM) upon completion of PM4EI and PM4EII (may be earned in grade twelve only)

Project Management for Entrepreneurs III (PM4EIII)

Certified Associate Project Management (CAPM) upon completion of PM4EI, PM4EII, & PM4EIII (may be earned in grade twelve only)

CTE Capstone

Certified Associate Project Management (CAPM) upon completion of PM4EI and PM4EII (may be earned in grade twelve only)

HEALTH

Behavioral Health Technician

Behavioral Health Technician Certification

Certified Nurse Aide

Certified Nurse Aide Certification

Introduction to Physical & Occupational Therapy

Certification under development

Pharmacy Technician

Pharmacy Technician

Lodging & Resort Management

GOLD Certified Guest Service Professional, ServSafe Food Handler, Workforce Readiness Certificate and CHTMP (Certified Hospitality & Tourism Management Professional). Includes a hundred-hour internship

ProStart I / ProStart II

ServSafe Food Handler

Workforce Readiness Certificate

Gold Certified Guest Service Professional

ProStart National Certificate of Achievement

ProStart Youth Apprenticeship

ServSafe Manager

Workforce Readiness Certificate

Gold Certified Guest Service Professional

ProStart National Certificate of Achievement

ServSuccess Certified Restaurant Professional

Infrastructure Engineering

Construction I

OSHA-10 Construction

HBI PACT (Pre-Apprenticeship Certificate Training)

NCCER (National Center for Construction Education and Research)

Construction II

National Center for Construction Education and Research (NCCER) Carpentry

Electrical

Plumbing

Home Builders Institute Pre-Apprenticeship Construction Training (PACT) Carpentry

Electrical

Plumbing

Construction III: Future Course

IT STEAM

Cybersecurity I: Computer Systems

CompTIA A+

TestOut PC Pro

Cybersecurity II: Networks & Security

CompTIA Network+

TestOut Network Pro

CompTIA Security+

TestOut (Security Pro)

Cybersecurity III: Ethical Hacking
Computer Aided Design I
SOLIDWORKS Certified Associate—CSWA Mechanical Design
SOLIDWORKS Certified Associate—CSWA-AM Additive Manufacturing
Drone Pilot
FAA Small UAS Rule (Part 107)
Production Design I
Society of Manufacturing Engineers ADDITIVE MANUFACTURING FUNDAMENTALS
SOLIDWORKS Certified Associate—CSWA Mechanical Design
Productions Design II
SOLIDWORKS Certified Associate—CSWA-AM Additive Manufacturing
SOLIDWORKS Certified Expert—CSWE Mechanical
SOLIDWORKS Certified Professional—CSWP Mechanical Design
Advanced Robotics & Automation Systems
Virtual Reality
No certifications yet but possibly coming
Auto Maintenance and Light Repair (MLR) I
Auto Maintenance and Light Repair (MLR) II
Auto Service Technology MLR III High Performance

Auto 1

Snap-on Certifications

    Multimeter

    Torque

    Precision Measurement

    Scanner

    Diagnostics

ASE Student Automobile Certifications

    Brake Systems

    Suspension & Steering Systems

    Electrical/Electronic Systems

    Engine Performance

Auto 2

Certifications:

Snap-on Certifications

Wheel Service & Alignment

Advanced Scanner Diagnostics

Pro-Cut on-car Rotor Machining

Battery Starting and Charging

ASE Student Automobile Certifications

Brake Systems

Suspension & Steering Systems

Electrical/Electronic Systems

Engine performance

Auto 3
Continuation of Snap-on Certifications: Wheel Service & Alignment Advanced Scanner Diagnostics Pro-Cut on-car Rotor Machining, Battery Starting and Charging
ASE Student Automobile Certifications: Brake Systems Suspension & Steering Systems Electrical/Electronic Systems Engine performance
Two-Year Pathway: Accelerated General Aircraft Maintenance I & II
Snap-on Multimeter
Two-Year Pathway: Airframe I (Summer Course)
Snap-on Torque and Snap-on Precision Measurement
Two-Year Pathway: Accelerated Airframe II & III
Three-Year Pathway: General Aircraft Maintenance 1
Snap-on Multimeter
Three-Year Pathway: General Aircraft Maintenance 2
Snap-on Precision Measurement
FAA 750 hours
Three-Year Pathway: Airframe I (Summer Course)
Snap-on Torque and Snap-on Precision Measurement
Three-Year Pathway: Accelerated Airframe II & III
Maintenance and Airframe

The Arizona State Board of Education linked these industry certifications with CTE programs offered in the state.

CTE Program	Accounting
Industry Certification	**Sub-Certifications**
Microsoft Office Specialist (MOS)	MOS Office 365—Word, Excel, PowerPoint MOS Office 2019—Word, Excel, PowerPoint MOS Office 2016—Word, Excel, PowerPoint
NAFTrack Certification	Academy of Finance
QuickBooks Certified User (QBCU)	QBCU Desktop—2019 Pro QBCU Desktop—2017 QBCU Desktop—2016 QBCU Desktop Online—US
A*S*K* (Assessment of Skills and Knowledge for Business) Certification[87]	A*S*K* Fundamental Business Concepts A*S*K* Fundamental Marketing Concepts A*S*K* Concepts of Finance A*S*K* Concepts of Entrepreneurship and Management A*S*K* Fundamentals of Ethics

CTE Program	Animation
Industry Certification	**Sub-Certifications**
Adobe Certified Associate (ACA)	ACA CC—ACA Video Design Specialist
	ACA CC—ACA Visual Design Specialist
	ACA CC—ACA Web Design Specialist
Autodesk Certified User (ACU)	ACU AutoCAD
	ACU Inventor-Imperial
	ACU Inventor-Metric
	ACU Revit Architecture-Imperial
	ACU Revit Architecture-Metric
	ACU 3ds Max
	ACU Maya
	ACU Fusion 360CAD
	ACU Fusion 360CAD/CAM
Certified Expert Technical Artist Rigging and Animation[88]	

CTE Program	Business Management
Industry Certification	**Sub-Certifications**
Microsoft Office Specialist (MOS)	MOS Office 365—Word, Excel, PowerPoint
	MOS Office 2019—Word, Excel, PowerPoint
	MOS Office 2016—Word, Excel, PowerPoint
NAFTrack Certification	Academy of Finance
QuickBooks Certified User (QBCU)	QBCU Desktop—2019 Pro
	QBCU Desktop—2017
	QBCU Desktop—2016
	QBCU Desktop Online—US

A*S*K* (Assessment of Skills and Knowledge for Business) Certification	A*S*K* Fundamental Business Concepts
	A*S*K* Fundamental Marketing Concepts
	A*S*K* Concepts of Finance
	A*S*K* Concepts of Entrepreneurship and Management
	A*S*K* Fundamentals of Ethics
RISE-UP—Retail Industry Fundamentals New 2019	
RISE-UP-The Business of Retail New 2019	
RISE-UP-Customer Service and Sales New 2019[89]	

CTE Program	Business Operations
Industry Certification	**Sub-Certifications**
Microsoft Office Specialist (MOS)	MOS Office 365—Word, Excel, PowerPoint
	MOS Office 2019—Word, Excel, PowerPoint
	MOS Office 2016—Word, Excel, PowerPoint
QuickBooks Certified User (QBCU)	QBCU Desktop Online—US
A*S*K* (Assessment of Skills and Knowledge for Business) Certification[90]	A*S*K* Fundamental Business Concepts
	A*S*K* Fundamental Marketing Concepts
	A*S*K* Concepts of Finance
	A*S*K* Concepts of Entrepreneurship and Management
	A*S*K* Fundamentals of Ethics

CTE Program	Digital Communication
Industry Certification	**Sub-Certifications**
Adobe Certified Associate (ACA)	ACA CC—ACA Video Design Specialist
	ACA CC—ACA Visual Design Specialist
	ACA CC—ACA Web Design Specialist
PrintEdUSA Student Certification[91]	PrintEdUSA Student Certification-Graphic Designer
	PrintEdUSA Student Certification-Introduction to Graphic Communication
	PrintEdUSA Student Certification-Digital File Preparation/Digital File Output
	PrintEdUSA Student Certification-Digital Production Printing
	PrintEdUSA Student Certification-Offset Press Operations/Binding and Finishing
	PrintEdUSA Student Certification-Screen Printing Technology

CTE Program	Digital Photography
Industry Certification	**Sub-Certifications**
Adobe Certified Associate (ACA)[92]	ACA CC—ACA Video Design Specialist
	ACA CC—ACA Visual Design Specialist
	ACA CC—ACA Web Design Specialist

CTE Program	Digital Printing
Industry Certification	**Sub-Certifications**
Adobe Certified Associate (ACA)	ACA CC—ACA Video Design Specialist
	ACA CC—ACA Visual Design Specialist
	ACA CC—ACA Web Design Specialist
PrintEdUSA Student Certification[93]	PrintEdUSA Student Certification-Graphic Designer
	PrintEdUSA Student Certification-Introduction to Graphic Communication
	PrintEdUSA Student Certification-Digital File Preparation/Digital File Output
	PrintEdUSA Student Certification-Digital Production Printing
	PrintEdUSA Student Certification-Offset Press Operations/Binding and Finishing
	PrintEdUSA Student Certification-Screen Printing Technology

CTE Program	Film and TV Production
Industry Certification	**Sub-Certifications**
Adobe Certified Associate (ACA)	ACA CC—ACA Video Design Specialist
	ACA CC—ACA Visual Design Specialist
	ACA CC—ACA Web Design Specialist
Apple Certified Pro (ACP)[94]	Apple Certified Pro (ACP)—Final Cut Pro 8
	Apple Certified Pro (ACP)—Logic Pro 8

CTE Program	Finance
Industry Certification	**Sub-Certifications**
Microsoft Office Specialist (MOS)	MOS Office 365—Word, Excel, PowerPoint
	MOS Office 2019—Word, Excel, PowerPoint
	MOS Office 2016—Word, Excel, PowerPoint
NAFTrack Certification	Academy of Finance
QuickBooks Certified User (QBCU)	QBCU Desktop—2019 Pro
	QBCU Desktop—2017
	QBCU Desktop—2016
	QBCU Desktop Online—US
A*S*K* (Assessment of Skills and Knowledge for Business) Certification[95]	A*S*K* Fundamental Business Concepts
	A*S*K* Fundamental Marketing Concepts
	A*S*K* Concepts of Finance
	A*S*K* Concepts of Entrepreneurship and Management
	A*S*K* Fundamentals of Ethics

CTE Program	Graphic Design
Industry Certification	**Sub-Certifications**
Adobe Certified Associate (ACA)	ACA CC—ACA Video Design Specialist
	ACA CC—ACA Visual Design Specialist
	ACA CC—ACA Web Design Specialist
PrintEdUSA Student Certification[96]	PrintEdUSA Student Certification-Graphic Designer
	PrintEdUSA Student Certification-Introduction to Graphic Communication
	PrintEdUSA Student Certification-Digital File Preparation/Digital File Output
	PrintEdUSA Student Certification-Digital Production Printing
	PrintEdUSA Student Certification-Offset Press Operations/Binding and Finishing
	PrintEdUSA Student Certification-Screen Printing Technology

CTE Program	Business Management
Industry Certification	**Sub-Certifications**
Microsoft Office Specialist (MOS)	MOS Office 365—Word, Excel, PowerPoint
	MOS Office 2019—Word, Excel, PowerPoint
	MOS Office 2016—Word, Excel, PowerPoint
Beginning Jewelry Sales	
RISE-UP—Retail Industry Fundamentals New 2019 RISE-UP-The Business of Retail New 2019 RISE-UP-Customer Service and Sales New 2019[97]	

CTE Program	Music and Audio Production
Industry Certification	**Sub-Certifications**
Certified Radio Operator[98]	

Part Eight

Career Pathways–Careers, Starting Salaries, and Education Requirements

State departments of education with industry and business have come up with pathways to enter growth careers. These align with workforce needs to deliver entry to higher-wage, in-demand careers.

Here is a distillation of pathway information for hundreds of growth careers, with median entry salaries, projected sector growth, and what training is required for the job path you choose.

Figure out the best educational entry point to the dream career and how to advance. If you can't immediately afford four-year college, look at entries to the career.

Pick the entry point that works for you. Careers are specialized. Enter the career early, fine tune ambitions, target further education, and often the employer will subsidize additional education. Choose an early career entry-point for summer or part-time jobs while in a four-year degree to be professionally relevant.

Agriculture, Food, & Natural Resources

Agribusiness Systems

High School	One to Three Years	Bachelor's	Advanced
Dairy Herd Supervisor $58,000	Agricultural Chemical Dealer	Agricultural Commodity Broker (and license) $64,000 4 percent	Agricultural Economist (bachelor's-PhD) $104,000 8 percent
Entrepreneur	Agricultural Products Buyer-Distributor	Agricultural Economist (bachelor's-PhD) $104,000 8 percent	Agricultural Educator—Post-secondary $84,000 4 percent
Farm Manager $58,000	Bank/Loan Office $63,000 11 percent	Agricultural Educator $69,000	
Farmer-Rancher-Feedlot Operator $58,000	Feed-Supply Store Manager	Agricultural Lender $63,000 11 percent	
	Field Representatives for Bank, Insurance Company or Government Program	Banker/Loan Officer $63,000 11 percent	
	Livestock Manager (HS, bachelor's) $67,000	Farm Investment Manager $63,000 11 percent	
	Salesperson $22,000 7 percent	Livestock Manager (HS, bachelor's) $67,000	
		Produce Commission Manager $67,000	
		Sales Manager $67,000	

Animal Systems

High School	One to Three Years	Bachelor's	Advanced Degree
Livestock Management (HS-bachelor's) $67,000	Animal Caretaker-Poultry Manager Certificate needed	Agricultural Educator	Physiologist (bachelor's, MA, PhD depending on employer—from pharmaceuticals to farming) $80,000 8 percent
	Aquaculturalist	Animal Nutritionist	Wildlife Biologist (bachelor's, certification, MA, PhD) $77,000 8 percent
	Artificial Insemination Technician	Livestock Geneticist (BS-PhD) $93,000 11 percent	Livestock Geneticist (BS-PhD) $93,000 11 percent
	Dairy Producer (one to two years exp) $67,000, -1 percent	Meat Science Researcher	
	Equine Manager (associate, BS) $35,000 16 percent	Physiologist (bachelor's, MA, PhD depending on employer—from pharmaceuticals to farming) $80,000 8 percent	
	Feed Sales Representative	Wildlife Biologist (bachelor's, certification, MA, PhD) $77,000 8 percent	
	Livestock Buyer $58,000	USDA Inspector $75,000	
	Livestock Inspector	Veterinarian (BA through PhD)	
	Livestock Producer $58,000		
	Veterinary Assistant (HS or certification)		

	Veterinary Technician (two years post HS)		
	Veterinarian Technologist (four years post HS)		

Environmental Service Systems

One to Three Years
Employee Assistance Plan Manager
Occupational Analyst
Pay Equity Officer
Payroll Professional (APA certification) $40,000 4 percent

Bachelor's
Affirmative Action Coordinator $107,000 8 percent
Compensation and Benefits Manager/Administrator $119,000 5 percent
Conciliator/Mediator/ Arbitrator (bachelor's, Law Degree, MBA, five years' experience) $62,000
Corporate Trainer $60,000 5 percent
Employer Relations Representative $101,000 9 percent
Employment and Placement Manager $101,000
Equal Employment Opportunity Specialist $60,000 15 percent
Human Resources Consultant (bachelor's or master's, plus four to five years' experience) $66,000
Human Resources Coordinator (bachelor's or master's) $66,000
Human Resources Manager $110,000 9 percent
Industrial Relations Director $113,000

International Human Resources Manager $113,000
Labor and Personnel Relations Specialist $60,000 7 percent
Organizational Behaviorist $78,000 (bachelor's, master's, doctorate)
Organizational Development Specialist (bachelor's, master's, doctorate) $78,000
OSHA/ADA Compliance Officer (bachelor's, master's, doctorate) $68,000 6 percent
Personnel Recruiter $60,000 7 percent
Training and Development Manager $108,000 10 percent

Advanced
Conciliator/Mediator/ Arbitrator (bachelor's, Law Degree, MBA, five years' experience) $62,000
Human Resources Consultant (bachelor's or master's, plus four to five years' experience) $66,000
Human Resources Coordinator (bachelor's or master's) $66,000
Organizational Behaviorist $78,000 (bachelor's, master's, doctorate)
Organizational Development Specialist (bachelor's, master's, doctorate) $78,000
OSHA/ADA Compliance Officer (bachelor's, master's, doctorate) $68,000 6 percent

Food Products & Processing Systems

High School
Livestock Management (HS-bachelor's) $67,000

One to Three Years
Animal Caretaker-Poultry Manager Certificate needed
Aquaculturalist
Artificial Insemination Technician
Dairy Producer (one to two years exp) $67,000, -1 percent
Equine Manager (associate, BS) $35,000 16 percent
Feed Sales Representative
Livestock Buyer $58,000
Livestock Inspector
Livestock Producer$58,000
Veterinary Assistant (HS or certification)
Veterinary Technician (two years post HS)
Veterinarian Technologist (four years post HS)

Bachelor's
Agricultural Educator
Animal Nutritionist
Livestock Geneticist (BS-PhD) $93,000 11 percent
Meat Science Researcher
Physiologist (bachelor's, MA, PhD depending on employer—from pharmaceuticals to farming) $80,000 8 percent
Wildlife Biologist (bachelor's, certification, MA, PhD) $77,000 8 percent
USDA Inspector $75,000
Veterinarian (BA through PhD)

Advanced Degree
Physiologist (bachelor's, MA, PhD depending on employer—from pharmaceuticals to farming) $80,000 8 percent
Wildlife Biologist (bachelor's, certification, MA, PhD) $77,000 8 percent
Livestock Geneticist (BS-PhD) $93,000 11 percent

Natural Resources Systems

High School
Commercial Fisherman (Certification, Internship) $29,000
Fisheries Technician (HS to associate) $53,000
Forest Technician (HS to associate to bachelor's) $53,000
Geology Technician (HS to associate) $53,000
Log Grader $40,000 -14 percent
Logger $40,000 -14 percent
Park Manager
Pulp and Paper Manager
Range Technician
Water Monitoring Technician

One to Three Years
Fisheries Technician (HS to associate) $53,000
Forest Technician (HS to Associate to bachelor's) $53,000
Geology Technician (HS to Associate) $53,000

Park Manager
Wildlife Manager (Associate to bachelor's) $64,000 4 percent

Bachelor's
Agricultural Educator
Ecologist (BS master's-PhD) $69,000 11 percent
Fish and Game Officer
Fisheries Technician
Forest Technician $67,000
Geologist
Mining Engineer ($94,000, 8 percent growth)
Wildlife Manager (associate to bachelor's) $64,000 4 percent

Advanced Degree
Ecologist (BS master's PhD) $69,000 11 percent
Hydrologist (MS, PhD) $79,000 10 percent growth over ten years

Plant Systems

High School
Landscaping and Groundskeeping workers
Tree trimmers and pruners $38,000 (HS, associate)

Less than one year

Pesticide handlers, sprayers, applicators $35,000 8 percent

Supervisors of farm workers, fish workers, and forestry workers $31,000

One to Three Years

Agricultural Journalist

Biotechnology Lab Technician

Commodity Marketing Specialist

Custom Hay/Silage Operator

Farmer (through PhD)

Farm workers and laborers

Golf Course Manager

Grain Operation Superintendent

Green House Manager

Precision Agriculture Technicians

Rancher

Tree Surgeon

Bachelor's

Agricultural Educator (bachelor's, master's, PhD)

Bioinformatics Specialist

Botanist

Conservation Specialist

Plant Breeder and Geneticist

| Plant Pathologist |
| Soil and Water Specialist |

Power, Structural, & Technical Systems

High School
Machine Operator $36,000
Machinist $36,000
Recycling Technician $46,000
Welder $41,000

Under one year
Agricultural Equipment Operators (4H certification) $31,000
Communication Technician—certification $50,000, -8 percent

One to Three Years
Database Administrator $90,000 9 percent
Electronic Systems Technician $57,000 -1 percent
Equipment/Parts Manager
Farm equipment mechanic $42,000
GPS Technician $56,000 -8 percent
Heavy Equipment Maintenance Technician $42,000
Information Lab Specialist
Mobile Heavy Equipment Mechanic $42,000

Bachelor's
Agricultural Applications Software Developer/Programmer $81,000 24 percent
Agricultural Educator (bachelor's, master's or PhD) $60,000 2 percent
Agricultural Engineer $79,000
Remote Sensing Specialist $32,000 10 percent
Wastewater Treatment Plant Operator $65 -5 percent

Advanced
Agricultural Educator (master's or PhD) $84,000 4 percent Post-secondary

Architecture & Construction

Construction

High School
Carpenter (Apprenticeship) $43,000 8 percent
Code Official (Experience license) $59,000 10 percent
Concrete Finisher $43,000
Construction Foreman/Manager (Experience or associate) $93,000 10 percent
Construction Inspector (associate) $59,000 10 percent
Contractor (associate or BA) $60,000
Design Builder (apprenticeship or associate) $46,000 8 percent
Drywall Installer (apprenticeship) $46,000 8 percent
Electrician license $53,000 20 percent

Electronic Systems Technician certification one year of training
General Contractor/Builder associate and management exp.$97,000
Heating, Ventilation, Air Conditioning and Refrigeration Mechanic
Mason apprenticeship three to four years (physically demanding) $50–50,000 20 percent
Painter $50,000 7 percent
Paperhanger $38,000 20 percent
Plumber apprenticeship $51,000 16 percent
Project Inspector
Roofer (apprenticeship of three years) $40,000 11 percent
Safety Director
Sheet Metal Worker $47,000
Superintendent (associate or bachelor's, ten years' experience) $85,000
Tile and Marble Setter $38,000

Bachelor's
Construction Engineer $93,000 6 percent
Contractor (associate or BA) $60,000
Equipment and Material Manager
Project Estimator (bachelor's plus certification) $64,000
Project Manager $103,000 11 percent
Specialty Contractor Superintendent (associate or bachelor's, ten years' experience) $85,000

Design/Pre-Construction

High School
Building Code Official (certification) $59,000
Code Official (certification) $59,000
Drafter (associate) $69,000 8 percent
Electrical Engineer (HS plus apprenticeship, certification, years' experience) $94,000, electrician starting median $52,000 9 percent)
Specification Writer
Surveying and Mapping Technician $47,000 5 percent

Bachelor's
Architect (professional, bachelor's through PhD plus internship) $79,000 8 percent growth
Building Designer $79,000 8 percent
Cost Estimator $69,000 8 percent
Environmental Designer (bachelor's through master's) $68,000 4 percent
Civil Engineer $83,000 8 percent growth
Electronic Engineer $102,000 -1 percent (decline)
Environmental Engineer $84,000 12 percent growth
Fire Prevention and Protection Engineer (license) $93,000
Industrial Engineer $84,000 10 percent
Interior Designer (license) $54,000
Landscape Architect $68,000 4 percent
Regional and Urban Planner/Designer $57,000 6 percent

Materials Engineer $93,000 2 percent
Mechanical Engineer $87,000 4 percent
Safety Director (OSHA certification) $50,000 6 percent
Structural Engineer $86,000 6 percent

Advanced
Architect (professional, bachelor's through PhD plus internship) $79,000 8 percent growth
Environmental Designer (bachelor's through master's) $68,000 4 percent
Landscape Architect $68,000 4 percent

Maintenance/Operations

High School
Carpenter $46,000
Code Official (certification) $59,000
Commissioning Agent
Construction Foreman/Manager (with management exp.) $93,000 10 percent
Construction Inspector (certification) $59,000
Demolition Engineer $50,000
Estimator $69,000 9 percent
Hazardous Material Remover $40,000
Manufacturer Representative (HS or bachelor's) $60,000 6 percent
Mason (apprenticeship three to four years) $40,000–$50,000 2–39 percent
Safety Director (associate or bachelor's) $69,000

Security and Fire Alarm System Installer (associate and training) $47,000 11 percent
Service Contractor and Field Supervisor
Subcontractor $35,000 11 percent
System Installer
Wastewater Maintenance Technician (associate & certification) $46,000

Bachelor's
Construction Engineer $93,000 6 percent
Equipment and Materials Manager $108,000
Environmental Engineer $84,000 12 percent
Manufacturer Representative (HS or bachelor's) $60,000 6 percent
Safety Director (associate or bachelor's) $69,000

Arts, A/V Technology & Communications

A/V Technology & Film

High School
Audio Systems Technician (certification CTS, CTS-D, CTS-1) $49,000 10 percent
Audio-Video Designer and Engineer (certification CTS, CTS-D, CTS-1) $49,000 10 percent
Audio-Video System Service Technician (certification CTS, CTS-D, CTS-1) $49,000 10 percent
Technical Computer Support Technician: Film, Video, and DVD
Video Systems Technician (associate or BA) $49,000 10 percent

Bachelor's
Videographer: Special Effects and Animation $78,000
Video Systems Technician (associate or BA) $49,000 10 percent

Journalism & Broadcasting

High School
Audio-Video Operator
Control Room Technician (certification preferred) $53,000
Copymarkers
Radio Operators

One to Three Years
Broadcast Technician
Radio and Television Announcer

Bachelor's
Art Director $92,000 5 percent
Control Room Technician
Design Director $102,000 1 percent
Editor $62,000 14 percent
Journalist (BA preferred, $55,000, -10 percent declining)
Light Director $61,000 5 percent
Producer (BA preferred with extensive experience) $71,000 12 percent

Proofreaders $41,000
Publisher (BA preferred or certification) 69,000 -1 percent
Reporter (usually BA) $41,000 -12 percent declining
Researcher
Station Manager (bachelor's and experience) $123,000 7 percent
Writer $62,000 no growth

Performing Arts

High School
Costume attendants
Actor $17.54 per hour

One to Three Years
Actor $17.54 per hour
Athletes and sports competitors $53,000
Choreographers $22.98 per hour
Costume Designer (associate or bachelor's) $72,000

Bachelor's
Actor $17.54 per hour
Coach (bachelor's or master's) $33,000 11 percent
Composer $49,000
Conductor $$9,000
Costume Designer (associate or bachelor's) $72,000

Dancer $18.17 per hour
Film/Video Editor $62,000 11 percent
Lighting Designer $61,000
Makeup Artist
Music Directors (bachelor's or master's) $50,000 6 percent
Music Instructor $69,000
Musician $28.15 per hour
Performer $18.70 per hour
Performing Arts Educator
Playwright $62,000
Production Manager: Digital, Video and Stage
Scenic Designer (Exhibit designer) $61,000
Scenic Painter min wage
Sound Designer $49,000

Advanced Degree
Agents of artists, performers, and athletes
Music Directors (bachelor's or master's) $50,000 6 percent
Coach (bachelor's or master's) $33,000 11 percent
Composers $49,000
Film/Video Editor $62,000 11 percent
Lighting Designer $61,000
Producer $71,000 12 percent
Director $71,000 12 percent

Printing Technology

High School
Print binding and technology
Computer Typography and Composition Operator (certification) $44,000–$66,000
Graphics Equipment Operator $40,000
Lithographer $36,000

One to Three Years
Desktop Publishing Specialist $37,000
Paper Salesperson $23,000
Plate Maker $40,000
Pre-Production Technician $40,000 -1 percent
Printing Equipment Operator $35,000 -10 percent
Production Coordinator
Production Manager $103,000
Web Page Designer (associate or bachelor's) $69,000 12 percent

Bachelor's
Web Page Designer (associate or bachelor's) $69,000 12 percent

Telecommunications

High School
Customer Service Representative
Network Designer
Sales Representative $24,000
Systems Designer
Telecommunication Computer Programmer and Systems Analyst
Telecommunication Equipment: Cable, Line Repairer and Installer $54,000
Telecommunication Technician $54,000

Visual Arts

High School
Artist $42,000
Commercial Artist $42,000
Commercial Photographer: Digital, Still, Video, Film
Commercial/Residential and Home Furnishing Coordinator
Computer Animator
Curator and Gallery Manager
Fashion Designer
Fashion Illustrator
Graphic Designer (BA preferred) $48,000 4 percent
Illustrator $42,000

Interior Designer $51,000 4 percent
Textile Designer $52,000 1 percent

Bachelor's
Art Director $92,000 5 percent
Graphic Designer (BA preferred)
Interior Designer $51,000 4 percent

Business Management & Administration

Administrative Support

High School
Administrative Assistant $38,000 -7 percent
Communications Equipment Operator
Customer Service Assistant $33,000 -2 percent
Data Entry Specialist $32,000 -21 percent
Desktop Publisher $37,000
Dispatcher (certification) $38,000 -3 percent
Executive Assistant (associate or certification) $59,000 -17 percent
Information Assistant
Legal Secretary $50,000 -21 percent
Library Assistant and Order Processor

Medical Front Office Assistant (certification) $30,000
Receptionist (certification) $29,000 5 percent
Records Processing Assistant
Shipping and Receiving Clerk $33,000
Stenographer (court) $59,000 7 percent
Typist (certification) $39,000
Word Processor $29,000–$36,000 -25 percent

One to Three Years
Computer Operator (associate and one to two years' experience) $45,000
Court Reporter (certification) $49,000
Executive Assistant (associate or certification) $59,000 -17 percent
Medical Transcriptionist (associate or certification) $34,000 -9 percent
Office Manager $55,000 -1 percent
Paralegal (associate) $50,000 12 percent

Business Information Management

Human Resources Management

One to Three Years
Employee Assistance Plan Manager
Occupational Analyst
Pay Equity Officer
Payroll Professional (APA certification) $40,000 4 percent

Bachelor's
Affirmative Action Coordinator $107,000 8 percent
Compensation and Benefits Manager/Administrator $119,000 5 percent
Conciliator/Mediator/ Arbitrator (bachelor's, Law Degree, MBA, five years' experience) $62,000
Corporate Trainer $60,000 5 percent
Employer Relations Representative $101,000 9 percent
Employment and Placement Manager $101,000
Equal Employment Opportunity Specialist $60,000 15 percent
Human Resources Consultant (bachelor's or master's, plus four to five years' experience) $66,000
Human Resources Coordinator (bachelor's or master's) $66,000
Human Resources Manager $110,000 9 percent
Industrial Relations Director $113,000
International Human Resources Manager $113,000
Labor and Personnel Relations Specialist $60,000 7 percent
Organizational Behaviorist $78,000 (bachelor's, master's, Doctorate)

Organizational Development Specialist (bachelor's, master's, Doctorate) $78,000
OSHA/ADA Compliance Officer (bachelor's, master's, Doctorate) $68,000 6 percent
Personnel Recruiter $60,000 7 percent
Training and Development Manager $108,000 10 percent

Advanced
Conciliator/Mediator/ Arbitrator (bachelor's, Law Degree, MBA, five years' experience) $62,000
Human Resources Consultant (bachelor's or master's, plus four to five years' experience) $66,000
Human Resources Coordinator (bachelor's or master's) $66,000
Organizational Behaviorist $78,000 (bachelor's, master's, Doctorate)
Organizational Development Specialist (bachelor's, master's, Doctorate) $78,000
OSHA/ADA Compliance Officer (bachelor's, master's, Doctorate) $68,000 6 percent

Operations Management Education & Training

One to Three Years
Employee Assistance Plan Manager
Occupational Analyst
Pay Equity Officer
Payroll Professional (APA certification) $40,000 4 percent

Bachelor's
Affirmative Action Coordinator $107,000 8 percent
Compensation and Benefits Manager/Administrator $119,000 5 percent
Conciliator/Mediator/ Arbitrator (bachelor's, Law Degree, MBA, five years' experience) $62,000
Corporate Trainer $60,000 5 percent
Employer Relations Representative $101,000 9 percent
Employment and Placement Manager $101,000
Equal Employment Opportunity Specialist $60,000 15 percent
Human Resources Consultant (bachelor's or master's, plus four to five years' experience) $66,000
Human Resources Coordinator (bachelor's or master's) $66,000
Human Resources Manager $110,000 9 percent
Industrial Relations Director $113,000
International Human Resources Manager $113,000
Labor and Personnel Relations Specialist $60,000 7 percent
Organizational Behaviorist $78,000 (bachelor's, master's, Doctorate)
Organizational Development Specialist (bachelor's, master's, Doctorate) $78,000
OSHA/ADA Compliance Officer (bachelor's, master's, Doctorate) $68,000 6 percent
Personnel Recruiter $60,000 7 percent
Training and Development Manager $108,000 10 percent

Advanced
Conciliator/Mediator/ Arbitrator (bachelor's, Law Degree, MBA, five years' experience) $62,000
Human Resources Consultant (bachelor's or master's, plus four to five years' experience) $66,000
Human Resources Coordinator (bachelor's or master's) $66,000
Organizational Behaviorist $78,000 (bachelor's, master's, Doctorate)
Organizational Development Specialist (bachelor's, master's, Doctorate) $78,000
OSHA/ADA Compliance Officer (bachelor's, master's, Doctorate) $68,000 6 percent

Education

Administration and Administrative Support

Bachelor's
Assessment Specialist
CareerTech Administrator
Curriculum Developer $93,000 10 percent
Education Researcher
Instructional Media Designer bachelor's or master's (one to five years' experience. ASTD certification) $64,000
Test and Measurement Specialist

Advanced
Administrator $91,000
College Dean
College President
Instructional Media Designer bachelor's or master's (one to five years' experience. ASTD certification) $64,000
Principal $95,000 4 percent
Superintendent $95,000
Supervisor and Instructional Coordinator $63,000 11 percent

Professional Support Services

Bachelor's
Parent Educator $44,000
Social Worker (bachelor's, master's) Fed: $76,000 State $52,000 Family $48,000
Speech-Language Pathologist (bachelor's, master's) $80,000 27 percent
Testing Specialist

Advanced
Clinical Psychologist $70,000 15 percent
Counselor (master's) $56,000
Developmental Psychologist (doctorate) $100,000
Social Psychologist (master's, Doctorate) $100,000 14 percent
Social Worker (bachelor's, master's) Fed 76,000 State $52,000 Family $48,000
Speech-Language Audiologist (master's, Doctorate) $82,000 16 percent
Speech-Language Pathologist (bachelor's, master's) $80,000 27 percent

Teaching/Training

High School
Physical Trainer $44,000 13 percent

One to Three Years
Child Care Worker entry $23,000
Child Care Director (associate, bachelor's) $47,000
Daycare Teacher (associate) entry $24,000
Early Childhood Aide (associate)
Elementary Aide (associate)
Group Worker and Assistant (associate)
Nanny
Preschool Teacher's Assistant $22,000 entry

Bachelor's
Child Care Director (associate, bachelor's) $47,000
Child Life Specialist $52,000
Coach
Early Childhood Teacher (certification ECE, bachelor's)
Early Intervention Specialist $35,000
Elementary School Teacher $39,000 ($40,000–80,000 range)
High School Teacher
Human Resource Trainer $59,000
Kindergarten Teacher $37,000

Middle School Teacher $52,000
Preschool Director $37,000
Reading Specialist (bachelor's, master's) $42,000
Special Education Teacher $41,000

Advanced
Board Certified Behavior Analyst $55,000
College/University Faculty (master's, PhD) Math $87,000, arts $82,000–103,000

Accounting

Banking Services (Finance)

High School
Abstractor (certification) $49,000
Bill and Account Collector $36,000 -3 percent
Compliance Officer $70,000
Credit Report Provider
Customer Service Representative
Data Processor (certification) $43,000
Debt Counselor (certification)
Financial Manager
Financial Planner $121,000

Loan Processor $40,000 4 percent
Operations Manager
Relationship Manager
Repossession Agent (certification) $33,000
Teller $30,000 -12 percent

One to Three Years

Title Researcher and Examiner $51,000 4 percent

Bachelor's

Accountant (CPA certification)
Acquisitions Specialist $125,000 -6 percent
Branch Manager (bachelor's, CPA, CFS) five or more years' experience $127,000
Credit Analyst $71,000 8 percent
Internal Auditor (certification) $70,000 11 percent
Loan Officer $64,000
Mortgage Broker $61,000 3 percent
Network Services Technician $62,000 6 percent
Trust Officer $68,000

Business Finance

High School
Claims Clerk $49,000
Customer Service Agent $16.23 per hour
Direct Marketing Representative
Examiner $65,000 -4 percent
Insurance Agent (license) $50,000 10 percent
Insurance Appraiser $62,000 4 percent
Insurance Broker (license) $50,000 10 percent
Investigator $65,000 -4 percent
Loss Control Manager (certification) $65,000 ($39,000–$98,000)
Producer
Product Manager
Sales Agent (sometimes college) $50,000 10 percent
Special Investigator $65,000 -4 percent

One to Three Years
Benefits Consultant (state license) $50,000
Claim Adjuster $49,000 -1 percent
Claims Agent $52,000 -1 percent
Processing Clerk (associate) $37,000 11 percent
Sales Agent (sometimes college) $50,000 10 percent

Bachelor's
Actuary (certification) $116,000 20 percent
Branch Manager five years' experience $127,000
Compliance Specialist $68,000 6 percent
Financial Planner (bachelor's, master's) $81,000
Underwriter $56,000 8 percent
Underwriter (Life Insurance) $69,000

Master's
Financial Planner (bachelor's, master's) $81,000

Government & Public Administration

Foreign Service

High School
Administrative Officer
Concierges (certification) $30,000
Criminal Investigators $81,000
Consular Officer
Detectives (HS, bachelor's) $81,000
Development Assistance Officer
Diplomatic Courier

Foreign Service Officer, age twenty to fifty-nine when applying, US citizen (bachelor's, master's) $88,000

Political Officer

Program Officer

Public Affairs Officer

Tour Guides and Escorts $28,000 7 percent

One to Three Years

Criminal Investigators $81,000

Detectives (HS, bachelor's) $81,000

Interpreters $47,000 18 percent

Translators $47,000 18 percent

Bachelor's

Customs Bankers

Detectives (HS, bachelor's) $81,000

Financial Analysts $85,000 6 percent

Foreign Service Officer (age twenty to fifty-nine when applying, US citizen) bachelor's, master's $88,000

Advanced Degree

Ambassador

Economic Officer (master's) $104,000 8 percent

Foreign Service Officer (age twenty to fifty-nine when applying, US citizen) bachelor's, master's $88,000

Intelligence Officer (bachelor's, master's) $68,000

Political Scientist (master's) $117,000 3 percent

Governance

High School
Assistant, Deputy, or Chief of Staff
Cabinet Level Secretary
Commissioner (County, Parish, City)
Commissioner (State Agency)
Congressional Aide
Governor
Legislative Aide
Legislative Assistant
Lieutenant Governor
Mayor
Representative (Fed/State) $174,000 (Fed)
Senator (Fed/State) $174,000 (Fed)
Specialist

Bachelor's
Lobbyist (certification) $68,000–$72,000 6 percent
Policy Advisor $117,000 5 percent
President
Vice President

National Security

High School

Agent/Specialist (HS to PhD)
 	
    FBI bachelor's plus three or more years, or bachelor's and a master's plus two years' experience. $64,000 age twenty-three to thirty-seven
 	
    Drug Enforcement Admin $66,000 age twenty-one to thirty-six
 	
    Border Patrol $54,000 under forty

Air Force careers in demand
 	
    Aircraft Mechanic $56,000
 	
    Combat Aircraft Crew
 	
    Explosive Ordnance Disposal Specialist $52,000
 	
    Infantry

Law Enforcement Specialist $50,000
 	
    Missile Security Specialist $46,000
 	
    Radio Operators
 	
    Special Forces $50,000
 	
    SERE (tactical training specialists) $74,000

Rank E-1, making just over $20,000 per year, while a recent college graduate will start at an E-3 rank making almost $24,000. Keep in mind the military also pays toward housing, insurance, and other items for those who are serving.
Military jobs in demand
Infantry $44,000
Musician $68,000
Artillery or Missile Crew Member $54,000
Communications Equipment Repairer $66,000
Electrical Instrument or Equipment Repairer $55,000
Survival Equipment Specialist $49,000
Special Forces $49,000

US Navy and US Army jobs in high demand
Human Intelligence Officer $59,000
Signals Intelligence Specialist $60,000
Network and Database Administrator $54,000
Geospatial Imaging Specialist $55,000

Under One year
Artillery
Missile Crew
Radar and Sonar Technicians

One to Three Years
Air Crew Supervisor $103,000
Detective and Criminal Investigators $81,000
Special Forces $50,000
Airborne Warning/Control Specialist
Combat Aircraft Pilot/Crew
Combat Control Officer
Combat Engineer
Cryptographer
Emergency Management Directors
Intelligence Analyst
Intelligence/Counterintelligence
National Security Advisor (HS to PhD)

Officer/Specialist:
•   Combat Operations
•   Electronic Warfare Operations
•   Military Intelligence
•   Missile and Space Systems
•   Munitions
•   Nuclear Weapons
•   Signals Intelligence
•   Special Forces
Staff or Field Officer
Submarine Officer
Surface Ship Warfare Officer

Bachelor's
Air Crew Officer
Infantry Officer
System Software Developer
Cryptographer (bachelor's to master's) $101,000 26 percent

Advanced Degree
Signals Intelligence Officer $109,000
Agent/Specialist (HS to PhD) $59,000

Planning

High School
Business/Enterprise Official
Census Clerk
Census Enumerator
Chief of Vital Statistics
Commissioner
County Director
Director (Various Agencies)
Economic Development Coordinator
Federal Aid Coordinator
Planner $70,000
Program Associate

Public Management & Administration

High School
City Council Member
City Manager
City or County Clerk
County Administrator or Clerk
Executive Director $78,000 6 percent

Officer/Associate: $58,000 5 percent
•   Association
•   Chamber of Commerce
•   Charitable Organization
•   Foundation
•   Industrial Foundation
General Service Officer
Management Analysis Officer
Program Administration Officer

Regulation

High School
Code Inspector/Officer experience $59,000 10 percent

One to Three Years
Bank Examiner $80,000 10 percent
Cargo Inspector (associate or bachelor's) two to four years' experience $70,000
Chief Bank Examiner (associate or bachelor's) two to four years' experience $80,000

Bachelor's
Aviation Safety Officer (FAA certification) $62,000 3 percent
Bank Examiner $80,000 10 percent
Border Inspector $59,000
Business Regulation Investigator $60,000 8 percent
Cargo Inspector (associate or bachelor's) two to four years' experience $70,000
Chief Bank Examiner (associate or bachelor's) two to four years' experience $80,000
Chief of Field Operations
Director
Election Supervisor
Enforcement Specialist $64,000 8 percent
Equal Opportunity Officer
Immigration Officer
Inspector Investigator/Examiner (High school or above) $65,000 -4 percent declining

Revenue & Taxation

High School
Assessor High school, or above with experience $55,000 14 percent

Bachelor's
Assessor HS or above with experience $55,000 4 percent
CPA (bachelor's) $68,000 11 percent
Internal Revenue Investigator (High school or above) $65,000 -4 percent declining

Revenue Agent/Officer $54,000
Tax Auditor bachelor's with CPA certificate preferred $70,000 6 percent
Tax Examiner/Assistant/Clerk $54,000 -1 percent declining
Tax Policy Analyst $58,000

Advanced degree
Tax Attorney PhD Law degree $118,000 6 percent
Inspector General

Health Sciences

Biotechnology Research & Development

High School
Animal Services Technician $34,000 19 percent
Data Entry Clerk $30,000 -21 percent
Lab Assistant-Genetics (certification or more) $52,000 11 percent
Medical Lab Assistant (certification or more) $52,000

One to Three Years
Clinical Trials Research Associate (certification through bachelor's) $49,000 7 percent
Lab Technician (associate) $53,000
Maintenance and Instrument Technician (associate) two to five years' experience $62,000

Process Technician $50,000 1 percent
Quality-Control Technician (associate) $55,000 1 percent

Bachelor's
Animal Services Technologist $34,000 19 percent
Bioinformatics Associate
Biomedical Chemist $95,000 14 percent
Biostatistician (bachelor's through PhD) $75,000 31 percent
Clinical Trials Research Associate (cert through bachelor's) $49,000 7 percent
Clinical Trials Research Coordinator $118,000 10 percent
Geneticist $93,000 11 percent
Microbiologist $71,000 5 percent
Molecular Biologist (bachelor's through PhD) entry $48,000 to $114,000 median
Pharmaceutical Scientist $84,000 8 percent
Quality Assurance Technician $63,000
Regulatory Affairs Specialist $64,000 8 percent
Research Assistant $38,000
Research Associate $59,000 13 percent
Toxicologist (bachelor's through PhD) $83,000 8 percent

Advanced Degree
Biochemist (Doctorate) $59,000 8 percent
Biochemist (PhD) $83,000
Bioinformatics Scientist adv degree, plus three to five years' experience $79,000
Bioinformatics Specialist $83,000

Biostatistician (bachelor's through PhD) $75,000 31 percent
Cell Biologist (PhD) $67,000 Molecular Biologist (bachelor's through PhD) entry $48,000 to $114,000 median
Research Scientist (master's to PhD) $82,000 13 percent

Diagnostic Services

One to Three Years
Cardiovascular Technologist (associate) $56,000 7 percent
Central Supply Technician (one year) $36,000 4 percent
Computer Tomography (CT) Technologist $52,000 11 percent
Diagnostic Medical Sonographer (associate) $72,000 19 percent
Electrocardiographic (ECG) Technician (certification, associate) $31,000 7 percent
Histotechnician (associate) $54,000
Magnetic Resonance (MR) Technologist (associate) $72,000 11 percent
Mammographer (associate, bachelor's) $58,000 12 percent
Nuclear Medicine Technologist (associate, bachelor's) $73,000 2 percent
Phlebotomist (certification) $34,000
Radiologic Technologist/ Radiographer (associate) $59,000 9 percent

Bachelor's
Clinical Lab Technician $52,000 11 percent
Cytogenetic Technologist $51,000 13 percent
Cytotechnologist (ASCP) $47,000–$79,000

Exercise Physiologist $49,000
Geneticist $93,000 11 percent
Histotechnologist $54,000
Medical Technologist/Clinical Laboratory Scientist $52,000 11 percent
Nutritionist $84,000 14 percent
Pathology Assistant $81,000 14 percent
Positron Emission Tomography (PET) Technologist $59,000

Advanced
Pathologist (medical degree) $199,000 15 percent
Radiologist (medical degree, three to seven years' residency) $295,000 13 percent

Health Informatics

High School or GED
Medical Biller $33,000 11 percent

One to Three Years
Community Services Specialist
Data Analyst (associate) $40,000 11 percent
Data Information Manager (certification to PhD) $84,000 39 percent
Health Information Coder (certification) $37,000 15 percent
Medical Assistant (certification) $29,000
Medical Information Technologist

Patient Financial Services Representative (certification) $36,000 10 percent
Pharmacy Services Associate/Tech (certification) $23,000
Reimbursement Specialist (certification in medical coding) $47,000
Transcriptionist (certification, associate) $35,000 -3 percent
Unit Coordinator (certification, associate) $35,000

Bachelor's
Admitting Clerk $33,000 3 percent
Applied Researcher
Epidemiologist $69,000 5 percent
Ethicist $99,000 18 percent
Health Care Administrator
Health Educator $54,000 10 percent
Medical Librarian/Cybrarian (master's) $59,000 6 percent
Public Health Educator $44,000–$53,000
Risk Manager (bachelor's, master's) and five years' business experience $127,000
Utilization Manager $72,000 18 percent

Advanced
Data Information Manager (certification to PhD) $84,000 39 percent
Health Informatics (PhD) $99,000 18 percent
Medical Ethics Professor $144,000 23 percent
Medical Ethics Lawyer (law degree) $120,000 6 percent
Medical Librarian/Cybrarian (master's) $59,000 6 percent
Risk Manager (bachelor's, master's) and five years' business experience $127,000

Support Services

One to Three Years
Biomedical/Clinical Technician (associate) $49,000
Dietary Aide (certification) $27,000
Hospital Maintenance Engineer (certification, associate) $38,000 6 percent
Material Agent
Transport Technician/Coordinator (associate) $94,000 6 percent

Bachelor's
Biomedical/Clinical Engineer $88,000 4 percent
Central Services Manager $99,000 18 percent
Environmental Health and Safety Technician (one to three years' experience) $73,000
Facilities Manager (bachelor's, master's) $61,000 7 percent
Food Service Administrator
Industrial Hygienist
Materials Manager

Advanced
Central Services Manager (bachelor's, Master) $99,000 18 percent
Environmental Services Manager (master's, PhD) $107,000 7 percent
Epidemiologist (master's, PhD) $76,000 9 percent
Facilities Manager (bachelor's, master's) $61,000 7 percent

Therapeutic Services

High School
Data Entry Coordinator $30,000 -21 percent
Pharmacy Technician (HS, associate) $32,000

One to Three Years
Anesthesiologist Assistant (bachelor's, master's) $167,000 17 percent
Certified Nursing Assistant (CNA certification) $28,000 9 percent
Clinical Medical Assistant (on job training, certification) $33,000 23 percent
Dental Assistant/Hygienist $33 an hour, 20 percent
Dental Lab Technician (certification) $40,000 11 percent
EMT/Paramedic (license, certification, associate) $34,000 7 percent
Home Health Aide (opt certification) $24,000 37 percent
Licensed Practical Nurse (license, eleven to twelve months) $46,000 11 percent
Massage Therapist $41,000 22 percent
Pharmacy Technician (HS, associate) $32,000
Radiologic Technician $61,000 13 percent
Registered Nurse (certification, associate, bachelor's) $71,000 15 percent
Respiratory Therapist (two-year certification) $60,000 23 percent
Surgical Technician (Diploma, certification, associate) $47,000 9 percent

Bachelor's
Anesthesiologist Assistant (bachelor's, master's) $167,000 17 percent
Athletic Trainer
Dietician
Exercise Physiologist
Occupational Therapist
Physician's Assistant
Recreation Therapist
Registered Nurse (certification, associate, bachelor's) $71,000 15 percent
Social Worker $77,000 Fed, $52,000 State, $48,000 family/school

Advanced Degree
Anesthesiologist Assistant (bachelor's, master's) $167,000 17 percent
Audiologist (Doctor in Audiology) $75,000 21 percent
Chiropractor (BA plus four-year chiropractic degree, state certification) $66,000
Dentist (BA plus professional or doctoral degree & residency for specialties, license) $158,000
Nurse Practitioner (master's) $92,000
Optometrist (bachelor's and four-year optometry degree) $110,000 18 percent
Pharmacist (bachelor's and PharmD) $124,000 6 percent
Physical Therapist (PhD) $88,000 34 percent
Physician (MD/DO) $208,000
Psychiatrist $203,000 16 percent
Psychologist $79,000 ($100,000)
Registered Nurse (certification, associate, bachelor's) $71,000 15 percent

Speech-Language Pathologist (master's) $80,000 27 percent
Veterinarian (Doctor of Veterinary Medicine, and recertification) $90,000 19 percent

Hospitality & Tourism

Lodging

High School
Front Desk Employee $10 an hour 7 percent
Front Desk Supervisor (HS or bachelor's) $62,000 1 percent
Laundry Attendant $10 an hour 7 percent
PBX Operator $10 an hour 7 percent
Valet Attendant $10 an hour 7 percent

One to Three Years
Bell Captain
Catering Manager $48,000 11 percent
Concierge $30,000
Front Desk Supervisor (HS or bachelor's) $62,000 1 percent Front Office Manager (HS, associate) experience or more $106,000 7 percent
Laundry Supervisor
Maintenance Worker

Bachelor's
Chief Engineer $62,000
Director of Human Resources $85,000 6 percent
Director of Operations $87,000 -1 percent
Director of Sales and Marketing (bachelor's, master's) plus exp. $53,000 1 percent
Executive Housekeeper
Food and Beverage Director $45,000 11 percent
Food and Beverage Manager $54,000 11 percent
Front Office Manager (HS, associate) experience or more $106,000 7 percent
General Manager $60,000 7 percent
Lodging Manager $53,000 7 percent
Owner
Reservations Manager
Revenue Manager $39,000
Rooms Executive $39,000 7 percent
Services Manager $39,000

Recreation, Amusements & Attractions

High School
Bartender (less than high school) $23,000 8 percent
Club Personnel
Family Centers
• Manager
• Equipment Operator
• Maintenance Personnel
Facilities Manager
Fairs/Festivals
• Event Planner
• Supervisor
• Manager
• Promotional Developer
Gaming and Casino
• Manager (bachelor's) $74,000 7 percent
• Supervisor $49,000 10 percent
• Dealer $20,000 4 percent
• Maintenance Personnel
• Security and Safety Personnel $33,000 4 percent
Historical/Cultural/ Architectural/ Ecological
• Guide $29,000
• Ranger $40,000 3 percent

Museums/Zoos/ Aquariums Personnel
Resort Trainer and Instructor (bachelor's) $46,000
Theme Parks/Amusement Parks Personnel
Ticket Vendor

Bachelor's
Gaming and Casino
•   Manager (bachelor's) $74,000 7 percent
Resort Trainer and Instructor (bachelor's) $46,000
Sports Promoter $132,000 8 percent

Advanced
Parks and Gardens Ranger (master's) $40,000 3 percent

Restaurants & Food/Beverage Services

High School
Banquet Server $20,000
Banquet Set-Up Employee $20,000
Bus Person
Cocktail Server $20,000
Counter Server $20,000
Host $22,000 11 percent
Kitchen Steward

| Line Cook (certification) $22,000 |
| Restaurant Server $21,000 |
| Room Service Attendant $21,000 |

| **One to Three Years** |
| Baker $23,000 |
| Brewer |
| Pastry and Specialty Chefs (certification) $48,000 |
| Restaurant Server $25,000–$45,000 |
| Wine Steward $49,000 |

| **Bachelor's** |
| Caterer $37,000 6 percent |
| Catering and Banquets Manager |
| Executive Chef, seven to eight years' experience $48,000 11 percent |
| Food and Beverage Manager $65,000 |
| General Manager $65,000 9 percent |
| Kitchen Manager (any education) $54,000 9 percent |
| Maître d' $44,000 |
| Restaurant Owner |
| Services Manager $53,000 |

Travel & Tourism

High School
Motor Coach Operator $33,000
Tour and Travel Coordinator/Guide $42,000–$59,000

One to Three Years (most travel jobs at this level in $40,000–$62,000 range)
Convention Services Manager $49,000 7 percent
Destination Manager $48,000
Director of Communication (associate, bachelor's)
Director of Convention and Visitors Bureau (associate, bachelor's)
Director of Meetings (associate, bachelor's)
Director of Membership Development (associate, bachelor's)
Director of Tourism Development (associate, bachelor's)
Director of Visitor Services (associate, bachelor's)
Director of Volunteer Services (associate, bachelor's)
Eco-System Tourism Coordinator (associate, bachelor's)
Interpreter (associate or Fluency) $47,000 18 percent
Meeting Planner/Director $49,000 11 percent
Tour and Travel Consolidator
Travel Agent $42,000–$59,000

Bachelor's
Director of Marketing and Advertising (bachelor's, master's) $134,000
Director of Communication (associate, bachelor's)
Director of Convention and Visitors Bureau (associate, bachelor's)
Director of Marketing and Advertising (bachelor's, master's) $134,000
Director of Meetings (associate, bachelor's)
Director of Membership Development (associate, bachelor's)
Director of Tourism Development (associate, bachelor's)
Director of Visitor Services (associate, bachelor's)
Director of Volunteer Services (associate, bachelor's)
Eco-System Tourism Coordinator (associate, bachelor's)
Events Manager/Planner (bachelor's) $49,000
Tourism Marketing Specialist $134,000 8 percent
Transportation Specialist $55,000

Advanced
Director of Marketing and Advertising (bachelor's, master's) $134,000

Human Services

Consumer Services

High School
Banker $38,000
Consumer Goods or Services Retail Representative $24,000
Consumer Research Department Representative
Customer Service Representative $33,000 -2 percent
Employee Benefits Representative
Event Specialist
Field Merchandising Representative
Hospital Patient Account Representative (certification) $36,000 16 percent
Inside Sales Representative $58,000
Insurance Representative
Investment Broker (HS-bachelor's) $50,000 10 percent
Real Estate Service Representative (HS, bachelor's) $48,000
Sales Consultant $24,000
Small Business Owner

Bachelor
Account Executive (Advanced) $127,000 9 percent
Banker (commercial) $93,000
Banker (investment) $98,000
Buyer $54,000 -9 percent
Certified Financial Planner five to nine years, $71,000
Consumer Advocate $42,000
Consumer Affairs Officer experience $49,000 9 percent
Consumer Credit Counselor experience $49,000
Financial Advisor $90,000 14 percent
Investment Broker (HS-bachelor's) $50,000 10 percent
Market Researcher (bachelor's, master's) $63,000 23 percent
Real Estate Service Representative (HS, bachelor's) $48,000

Advanced
Market Researcher (bachelor's, master's) $63,000 23 percent

Counseling & Mental Health Services

High School
Substance Abuse and Behavioral Disorder Counselor (HS-master's) $49,000 22 percent

Bachelor
Substance Abuse and Behavioral Disorder Counselor (HS-master's) $49,000 22 percent
Residential Advisor (college student) $27,000 12 percent

Advanced Degree
Career Counselor $60,000 8 percent
Clinical and Counseling Psychologist (MD) $74,000 20 percent
Employment Counselor (master's) $56,000 8 percent
Industrial-Organizational Psychologist (master's, PhD) $97,000 13 percent
Marriage, Child and Family Counselor $54,000 2 percent
Mental Health Counselor $44,000 22 percent
School Counselor/Psychologist $60,000 8 percent
Sociologist (master's) $73,000
Substance Abuse and Behavioral Disorder Counselor (HS-master's) $49,000 22 percent
Vocational Rehabilitation Counselor (MA plus two years licensing or four thousand hours experience, for example) $39,000

Early Childhood Development & Services

High School
Nanny (HS, associate) $33,000
Teacher Assistant (certification) $26,000

One to Three Years
Childcare Assistant/Worker (certification, license) $24,000
Nanny (HS, associate) $33,000
Teacher Assistant (certification) $26,000

Bachelor's
Assistant Director, Childcare Facilities
Director, Childcare Facilities (CDA credential) $47,000
Educator for Parents $44,000
Elementary School Teacher $58,000 3 percent
Preschool Teacher $29,000 7 percent

Advanced Degree
Elementary school counselor $56,000 8 percent

Family & Community Services

High School One to Three Years
Adult Day Care Coordinator
Adult Day Care Worker
Community Housing Service Worker
Coordinator of Volunteers $38,000 5 percent
Emergency and Relief Worker (certification, associate, bachelor's) $33,000 15 percent
Geriatric Services Worker (certification, bachelor's, master's)
Human Services Worker

| Leisure Activities Coordinator |
| Religious Leader |
| Residential Advisor |
| Social and Human Services Assistant |
| Social Services Worker |

Bachelor's

| Career Counselor $60,000 8 percent |
| Child Life Educator $52,000 |
| Child Life Specialist (certification) $52,000 |
| Community Service Director (bachelor's, master's) $64,000 18 percent |
| Dietician $57,000 |
| Director, Religious Activities/ Education Programs (bachelor's, master's) five years' experience $40,000 |
| Geriatric Services Worker (certification, bachelor's, master's) |
| Social Worker $77,000 Fed, $52,000 State, $48,000 family/school |
| Vocational Rehabilitation Counselor $37,000 20 percent |

Advanced Degree

| Community Service Director (bachelor's, master's) $64,000 18 percent |
| Director, Religious Activities/Education Programs (bachelor's, master's) five years' experience $40,000 |
| Employment Counselor $56,000 8 percent |
| Geriatric Services Worker (certification, bachelor's, master's) |
| Licensed Professional Counselor $44,000 22 percent |
| Marriage and Family Counselor, two years' experience $48,000 |
| Vocational Rehabilitation Counselor $37,000 20 percent |

Personal Care Services

High School
Barber $31,000
Companion (associate, bachelor's) $30,000
Cosmetologist, Hairdresser and Hairstylist $24,000–$34,000
Electrologist $31,000
Electrolysis Technician
Embalmer (associate) $45,000
Esthetician (certification, associate, diploma) $33,000
Funeral Attendant (HS, associate) $23,000
Funeral Director (associate) $52,000 4 percent
Home Care Aide $24,000 36 percent
Massage Therapist (five hundred hours training, certification) $41,000
Nail Technician, Manicurist and Pedicurist $20,000
Personal Aide $24,000 36 percent
Shampooer
Spa Attendant

One to Three Years
Companion (associate, bachelor's) $30,000
Embalmer (associate) $45,000
Esthetician (certification, associate, diploma) $33,000
Funeral Director (associate) $52,000 4 percent

Mortician (associate, bachelor's) $52,000 4 percent
Skin Care Specialist (certification, associate) $31,000

Bachelor
Companion (associate, bachelor's) $30,000
Exercise Physiologist $49,000
Mortician (associate, bachelor's) $52,000 4 percent
Personal Fitness Trainer $39,000 14 percent

Information Technology

Information Support & Services

High School
Barber $31,000
Companion (associate, bachelor's) $30,000
Cosmetologist, Hairdresser and Hairstylist $24,000–$34,000
Electrologist $31,000
Electrolysis Technician
Embalmer (associate) $45,000
Esthetician (certification, associate, diploma) $33,000
Funeral Attendant (HS, associate) $23,000
Funeral Director (associate) $52,000 4 percent

Home Care Aide $24,000 36 percent

Massage Therapist (500 hours training, certification) $41,000

Nail Technician, Manicurist and Pedicurist $20,000

Personal Aide $24,000 36 percent

Shampooer

Spa Attendant

One to Three Years

Companion (associate, bachelor's) $30,000

Embalmer (associate) $45,000

Esthetician (certification, associate, diploma) $33,000

Funeral Director (associate) $52,000 4 percent

Mortician (associate, bachelor's) $52,000 4 percent

Skin Care Specialist (certification, associate) $31,000

Bachelor's

Companion (associate, bachelor's) $30,000

Exercise Physiologist $49,000

Mortician (associate, bachelor's) $52,000 4 percent

Personal Fitness Trainer $39,000 14 percent

Network Systems

High School
Barber $31,000
Companion (associate, bachelor's) $30,000
Cosmetologist, Hairdresser and Hairstylist $24,000–$34,000
Electrologist $31,000
Electrolysis Technician
Embalmer (associate) $45,000
Esthetician (certification, associate, diploma) $33,000
Funeral Attendant (HS, associate) $23,000
Funeral Director (associate) $52,000 4 percent
Home Care Aide $24,000 36 percent
Massage Therapist (five hundred hours training, certification) $41,000
Nail Technician, Manicurist and Pedicurist $20,000
Personal Aide $24,000 36 percent
Shampooer
Spa Attendant

One to Three Years
Companion (associate, bachelor's) $30,000
Embalmer (associate) $45,000
Esthetician (certification, associate, diploma) $33,000
Funeral Director (associate) $52,000 4 percent

Mortician (associate, bachelor's) $52,000 4 percent
Skin Care Specialist (certification, associate) $31,000

Bachelor
Companion (associate, bachelor's) $30,000
Exercise Physiologist $49,000
Mortician (associate, bachelor's) $52,000 4 percent
Personal Fitness Trainer $39,000 14 percent

Programming & Software Development

One to Three Years
Software Applications Tester (certification) $55,000
Tester (certification) $55,000

Bachelor's
Applications Analyst $64,000
Applications Engineer $103,000
Business Analyst $81,000 14 percent
Computer Engineer $102,000 24 percent
Data Modeler $88,000 9 percent
Game Developer (associate, bachelor's) $65,000
Operating System Designer/Engineer $110,000
Program Manager $111,000

| Programmer $68,000 |
| Programmer Analyst $68,000 |
| Project Lead |
| Software Design Engineer $110,000 |
| Systems Administrator $142,000 |
| Systems Analyst $63,000–$93,000 |
| Test Engineer (bachelor's, master's) $72,000 |

| **Advanced** |
| Software Applications Specialist/Scientist $123,000 |

Law, Public Safety, Corrections & Security

Emergency & Fire Management Services

| **High School** |
| Dispatcher $39,000 8 percent |

| **Under One to Three Years** |
| Emergency Management and Response Coordinator (EMT certification) years' experience $74,000 5 percent |
| EMT (EMT Certification, associate) $34,000 7 percent |
| Fire Fighter $49,000 |
| Forest Fire Fighter $49,000 7 percent |

Forest Fire Inspector and Investigator (Natl Fire Academy) $62,000 6 percent
Hazardous Materials Responder (Firefighter II certification) $49,000
Manager/Supervisor of Fire Fighters or Forest Fire Fighters (associate, bachelor's) $76,000 5 percent
Rescue Worker

Bachelor's
Emergency Planning Manager $64,000
Manager/Supervisor of Fire Fighters or Forest Fire Fighters (associate, bachelor's) $76,000 5 percent
Training Officer

Law Enforcement Services

High School & Under One to Three Years
Animal Control Officer $38,000 6 percent
Bailiff (HS, associate) $45,000 -1 percent
Bomb Technician (law enforcement training, associate, bachelor's) $61,000 7 percent
Criminal Investigator and Special Agent
Evidence Technician (associate, bachelor's) $57,000 17 percent
Game Enforcement Officer (HS-bachelor's) $57,000 2 percent
Gaming Investigator (certification) $36,000 4 percent
Gaming surveillance $36,000
Highway Patrol Officer (one to two years' college, training) $72,000 5 percent
Park Ranger $40,000
Police and Patrol Officer (HS, twelve to fourteen weeks at Police Academy) $61,000 7 percent

Police Detective and Criminal Investigator (experience, training) $81,000
Police, Fire and Ambulance Dispatcher $40,000 6 percent
Private Detective and Investigator (associate) $50,000
Sheriff (associate, certification, one to five years' experience) $62,000 7 percent
Training Officer $70,000
Transit and Railroad Police
Unemployment Fraud Investigator (associate, bachelor's) $65,000 -4 percent

Bachelor's
Evidence Technician (associate, bachelor's) $57,000 17 percent
Federal Marshal (bachelor's, grad, one to three years' experience) $36,000–$41,000 entry
Game Enforcement Officer (HS-bachelor's) $57,000 2 percent
Immigration and Customs Inspector (Professional training) $53,000
Park Ranger $40,000
Unemployment Fraud Investigator (associate, bachelor's) $65,000 -4 percent

Legal Services

High School through One to Three Years
Case Management Specialist $38,000
Court Reporter (associate) $49,000
File and Document Manager $38,000 6 percent
Information Officer $38,000 6 percent
Investigator (certification) $56,000 8 percent

Legal Assistant (certification) $54,000 12 percent

Legal Secretary (associate, bachelor's) $50,000 -21 percent

Negotiator (police academy) $62,000

Paralegal (certification, associate) $50,000 12 percent

Bachelor's

Law Clerk (bachelor's, JD) $53,000 3 percent

Legal Secretary (associate, bachelor's) $50,000 -21 percent

Mediator/Arbitrator (bachelor's, master's, Law degree, five to ten years' experience) $62,000

Advanced

Administrative Lawyer (law degree, pass bar exam) $115,000 6 percent

Attorney $120,000 6 percent

Criminal Lawyer (law degree, pass bar exam) $115,000 6 percent

Judge (JD and experience) $133,000

Law Clerk (bachelor's, JD) $53,000 3 percent

Magistrate (JD and experience) $54,000 12 percent

Mediator/Arbitrator (bachelor's, master's, Law degree, five to ten years' experience) $62,000

Security & Protective Services

High School through One to Three Years
Armored Car Guard $40,000 4 percent
Computer Forensics Examiner (two to three years' experience) $72,000
Executive Protection Officer/Specialist $56,000
Gaming Surveillance Specialist $36,000 4 percent
Industrial Espionage Security Officer/Specialist
Lifeguard $22,000
Private Investigator $50,000
Security Officer (on-job training) $24,000
Transportation Security Officer/Specialist (opt one year experience) $41,000
Uniformed Security Officer $26,000

Bachelor's
Computer Security Specialist $102,000 32 percent
Corporate/Agency Security Director $65,000 7 percent
Information Security Assistant $90,000–$102,000 32 percent
Information System and Security Specialist $102,000 32 percent
Loss Prevention Specialist $69,000 9 percent
Physical Security Specialist/Consultant (with training) $60,000 (retail $30,000)
Security Director (bachelor's, master's) $175,000 11 percent

Manufacturing

Health, Safety & Environmental Assurance

One to Three Years
Safety Coordinator (associate, bachelor's, five years' experience) $48,000
Safety Technician (associate, bachelor's) $49,000

Bachelor's
Environmental Engineer $87,000
Environmental Specialist (bachelor's, master's) $66,000
Health and Safety Representative (one to three years' experience) $73,000
Safety Coordinator (associate, bachelor's, five years' experience) $48,000
Safety Engineer (two to five years' experience) $89,000
Safety Technician (associate, bachelor's) $49,000

Advanced
Environmental Specialist (bachelor's, master's) $66,000

Logistics & Inventory Control

High School
Dispatcher $39,000 8 percent
Freight, Stock, and Material Mover $27,000 8 percent
Materials Handler $28,000
Materials Mover $27,000 8 percent

Under One to Three Years
Industrial Truck and Tractor Operator (certification, associate, Apprenticeship) $36,000
Process Improvement Technician (associate) $50,000
Quality-Control Technician (associate) $55,000
Traffic Manager
Traffic, Shipping, and Receiving Clerk $27,000 5 percent

Bachelor
Communications, Transportation and Utilities Manager $94,000 6 percent
Logistical Engineer (bachelor's, master's) $74,000
Logistician (bachelor's, master's) $74,000
Materials Associate $77,000 2 percent
Process Improvement Engineer $71,000

Advanced
Logistical Engineer (bachelor's, master's) $74,000
Logistician (bachelor's, master's) $74,000

Maintenance, Installation & Repair

High School through One to Three Years
Most of these jobs require some advanced study or training
Biomedical Equipment Technician (associate) $99,000 4 percent
Boilermaker (Apprenticeship) $62,000 9 percent
Communication System Installer/Repairer (associate, bachelor's) $53,000 -8 percent
Computer Installer/Repairer (certification, associate) $38,000
Computer Maintenance Technician
Computer Systems Installer (certification, associate) $82,000
Electrical Equipment Installer/Repairer $58,000
Facility Electrician $59,000
Industrial Electronic Installer/Repairer/Manager $58,000
Industrial Machinery Mechanic (HS, associate, on job) $52,000 5 percent
Industrial Maintenance Electrician (HS, associate) $55,000
Industrial Maintenance Technician/Mechanic (HS, associate) $62,000
Instrument Calibration and Repairer (associate, two to five years' experience) $62,000
Instrument Control Technician (two to five years' experience) $62,000
Maintenance Repairer $38,000
Major Appliance Repairer $39,000
Meter Installer/Repairer $39,000–$58,000
Plumber, Pipe Fitter and Steam Fitter $53,000 16 percent
Security System Installer (associate) $47,000 11 percent

Bachelor's
Job/Fixture Designer $71,000
Laser Systems Technician $63,000

Manufacturing Production Process Development

High School
Manufacturing Technician (HS, associate) $52,000 5 percent
Power Generating and Reactor Plant Operator (HS, associate) $52,000 5 percent
Precision Inspector, Tester and Grader $31,000
Process Improvement Technician
Purchasing Agent (HS, bachelor's, master's) $62,000

Under One to Three Years
Electrical and Electronic Technician and Technologist (associate) $64,000
Engineering and Related Technician and Technologist (associate) $64,000
Manufacturing Technician (HS, associate) $52,000 5 percent
Power Generating and Reactor Plant Operator (HS, associate) $52,000 5 percent

Bachelor's
Design Engineer (bachelor's entry level) $87,000
Electronics Engineer $77,000
Industrial Engineer $84,000 10 percent
Labor Relations Manager (bachelor's, master's) $91,000 7 percent

Manufacturing Engineer $47,000
Production Manager $46,000
Purchasing Agent (HS, bachelor's, master's) $62,000
Supervisor $90,000

Advanced Degree
Labor Relations Manager (bachelor's, master's) $91,000 7 percent
Purchasing Agent (HS, bachelor's, master's) $62,000

Production

High School through Three Years
Most of these jobs require some training or certification
Assembler (certification) $61,000 -1 percent
Automated Manufacturing Technician (certification, associate) $57,000 1 percent
Calibration Technician (certification, associate) $61 -1 percent
Electrical Installer and Repairer (associate)
Electromechanical Equipment Assembler (certification) $57,000 1 percent
Extruding and Drawing Machine Setter/Set-Up Operator $33,000
Foundry Worker (associate)
Grinding, Lapping, and Buffing Machine Operator $35,000 -7 percent
Hand Packer and Packager
Hoist and Winch Operator (apprenticeship) $43,000 -1 percent
Instrument Maker (associate, two to five years' experience) $62,000

Large Printing Press Machine Setter and Set-Up Operator (on job) $36,000 -12 percent
Machine Operator (on job) $31,000 -21 percent
Medical Appliance Maker (certification, associate) $40,000 13 percent
Micro and Nano Fabrication Technicians
Milling Machine Setter and Set-Up Operator (tech certification) $43,000 -21 percent
Millwright (apprenticeship) $52,000 10 percent
Pattern and Model Maker $44,000 9 percent
Precision Layout Worker $47,000 9 percent
Sheet Metal Worker $47,000 9 percent
Solderer and Brazier (associate) $38,000–$44,000 3 percent
Tool and Die Maker (apprenticeship) $52,000 3 percent
Welder (certification American Welding Society) $44,000 3 percent

Quality Assurance

High School
Calibration Technician (CCT certification) $61,000 -1 percent
Inspector $52,000 18 percent
Lab Technician (HS, certification, associate) $52,000 11 percent
Process Control Technician (certification, associate) $58,000 11 percent
Quality-Control Technician $38,000, -18 percent
Quality Engineer $68,000

Bachelor's
SPC Coordinator $93,000

Marketing

Marketing Communications

High School
Administrative Support Representative $35,000–$90,000
Customer Service Representative $33,000 -2 percent
Receiving Clerk $33,000
Sales Associate $28,000 -2 percent
Stock Clerk (on job) $24,000 5 percent
Visual Merchandise Manager (on job) $28,000 2 percent

Bachelor's
Department Manager $110,000
Merchandise Buyer $67,000
Merchandising Manager $118,000
Operations Manager $99,000 8 percent
Retail Marketing Coordinator $118,000 5 percent
Sales Manager $117,000 5 percent
Store Manager $46,000 5 percent

Marketing Information

Management and Research

High School
Account Executive $59,000 -3 percent declining
Administrative Support Representative (HS, certification) $38,000 7 percent
Circulation Manager
Co-op Manager
Creative Director $86,000
Customer Service Representative $33,000 -2 percent
Interactive Media Specialist (associate) $43,000 27 percent
Research Specialist (master's) $117,000 5 percent
Sales Representative $41,000 6 percent

Bachelor's
Account Manager $53,000–131,000 9 percent
Account Supervisor $72,000 6 percent
Advertising Manager $110,000 5 percent
Analyst (digital) $51,000 23 percent
Art Director $89,000 2 percent
Contract Administrator (bachelor's, master's) $81,000 10 percent
Copywriter $61,000 2 percent
Creative Director $86,000

Graphics Director $47,000 1 percent
Marketing Associate $97,000
Media Buyer/Planner $60,000
Promotions Manager (bachelor's, master's) $117,000 5 percent
Public Information Director (years' experience) $86,000
Public Relations Manager (several years PR) $114,000
Research Assistant $46,000
Sales Promotion Manager (bachelor's)
Trade Show Manager $53,000 7 percent

Advanced
Sales Representative (bachelor's, master's) $117,000 5 percent
Sales Promotion Manager (bachelor's, master's) $117,000 5 percent
Contract Administrator (bachelor's, master's) $81,000 10 percent
Promotions Manager (bachelor's, master's) $117,000 5 percent

Marketing Research

One to Three Years
Administrative Support Representative $38,000 7 percent
Customer Service Representative $33,000 -2 percent
Frequency Marketing Specialist (HS, bachelor's) $37,000 23 percent
Research Project Manager (associate, bachelor's, master's) $49,000

Bachelor's
Agile Project Manager $91,000 12 percent
Analyst $56,000 23 percent
Brand Manager $51,000 23 percent
CRM (Customer Relations Mgr.) $105,000
Customer Satisfaction Manager $64,000 8 percent
Database Analyst (bachelor's plus two years' experience) $90,000
Database Manager (one to five years' experience) $90,000
Forecasting Manager $91,000 12 percent
Frequency Marketing Specialist (HS, bachelor's) $37,000 23 percent
Interviewer
Knowledge Management Specialist $142,000 11 percent
Marketing Services Manager $107,000 9 percent
Planning Analyst (bachelor's, master's) $85,000
Product Planner
Research Associate
Research Project Manager (associate, bachelor's, master's) $49,000
Research Specialist/Manager (bachelor's, master's) $93,000
Strategic Planner $71,000 9 percent

Advanced
Director of Market Development (master's) $104,000 7 percent
Planning Analyst (bachelor's, master's) $85,000
Research Project Manager (associate, bachelor's, master's) $49,000
Research Specialist/Manager (bachelor's, master's) $93,000

Buying and Merchandising

High School through Three Years
Agent $34,000
Customer Service Representative $32,000 -2 percent
Field Marketing Representative (HS, bachelor's) $49,000
Inbound Call Manager (certification)
National Account Manager (HS, bachelor's) $42,000 11 percent
Outside Sales Representative $41,000 6 percent
Regional Sales Manager $41,000 6 percent
Retail Sales Specialist $24,000
Salesperson $24,000
Sales/Marketing Associate (associate) $64,000
Telemarketer $25,000

Bachelor's
Account Executive $59,000 -3 percent
Administrative Support Representative $38,000 -7 percent
Agent $34,000
Broker (one to three years' experience) $65,000 7 percent
Business Development Manager $71,000
Channel Sales Manager $117,000
Client Relationship Manager (two to five years' experience) $114,000
Field Marketing Representative (HS, bachelor's) $49,000
Field Representative $49,000
Industrial Sales Representative $61,000 2 percent
Key Account Manager $72,000
Manufacturer's Representative $60,000 6 percent
National Account Manager (HS, bachelor's) $42,000 11 percent
Pharmaceutical Sales $80,000
Sales Engineer $58,000–$165,000 median $101,000
Sales Executive (two years' experience) $110,000
Solutions Advisor
Technical Sales Specialist $89,000
Territory Representative/ Manager (experience) $49,000

Professional Sales

Bachelor's
Account Executive $59,000 -3 percent
Administrative Support Representative $38,000 -7 percent
Agent $34,000
Broker (one to three years' experience) $65,000 7 percent
Business Development Manager $71,000
Channel Sales Manager $117,000
Client Relationship Manager (two to five years' experience) $114,000
Field Marketing Representative (HS, bachelor's) $49,000
Field Representative $49,000
Industrial Sales Representative $61,000 2 percent
Key Account Manager $72,000
Manufacturer's Representative $60,000 6 percent
National Account Manager (HS, bachelor's) $42,000 11 percent
Pharmaceutical Sales $80,000
Sales Engineer $58,000–$165,000 median $101,000
Sales Executive (two years' experience) $110,000
Solutions Advisor
Technical Sales Specialist $89,000
Territory Representative/Manager (experience) $49,000

Science, Technology, Engineering & Mathematics

Engineering & Technology

One to Three Years
CAD Technician
Electrical Engineer $96,000 2 percent
Electronics Technician (associate) $57,000 1 percent
Manufacturing Technician $38,000
Survey Technician (HS, associate) $44,000 11 percent

Bachelor's
Aeronautical Engineer (bachelor's, master's) $113,000 6 percent
Aerospace Engineer (bachelor's, master's) $117,000 2 percent
Agricultural Technician $41,000
Application Engineer (one to two years' experience) $103,000
Architectural Engineer $84,000 11 percent
Agricultural Engineer $77,000 5 percent
Automotive Engineer $87,000
Biotechnology Engineer (bachelor's through PhD) $88,000 4 percent
Biotechnology Engineer (bachelor's through PhD) $88,000 4 percent
Chemical Engineer $98,000 8 percent
Civil Engineer $86,000 6 percent

Communications Engineer (bachelor's, master's) $72,000 4 percent
Computer Engineer $114,000 6 percent
Computer Programmer $82,000–$132,000
Construction Engineer $93,000 6 percent
Electrical Engineer $96,000 2 percent
Geothermal Engineer $78,000 4 percent
Industrial Engineer $87,000 8 percent
Manufacturing Engineer $97,000 8 percent
Marine Engineer $92,000 9 percent
Mechanical Engineer $87,000 4 percent
Metallurgist $71,000 2 percent
Mining Engineer $94,000 8 percent
Nuclear Engineer (bachelor's through PhD) $101,000 -1 percent
Petroleum Engineer $137,000 3 percent
Product/Process Engineer $71,000 8 percent
Systems Engineer $110,000 21 percent
Transportation Engineer $66,000 67 percent

Advanced Degree
Aeronautical Engineer (bachelor's, master's) $113,000 6 percent
Aerospace Engineer (bachelor's, master's) $117,000 2 percent
Biotechnology Engineer (bachelor's through PhD) $88,000 4 percent
Communications Engineer (bachelor's, master's) $72,000 4 percent
Nuclear Engineer (bachelor's through PhD) $101,000 -1 percent

Science & Mathematics

Bachelor's
Analytical Chemist (bachelor's through PhD) $78,000 4 percent
Atmospheric Scientist (bachelor's through PhD) $89,000 9 percent
Biologist $77,000
Botanist $49,000 4 percent
Chemist $73,000 3 percent
Ecologist $71,000 8 percent
Economist $71,000 8 percent
Environmental Scientist $71,000 8 percent
Geneticist $93,000 11 percent
Geologist $58,000 10 percent
Geophysicist $88,000
Marine Scientist $91,000 6 percent
Math Teacher $50,000
Meteorologist $52,000 21 percent
Nanobiologist (bachelor's, master's) $60,000
Nuclear Chemist/Technician $73,000
Programmer $88,000 9 percent
Quality-Control Scientist
Research Technician $44,000 7 percent
Science Teacher $50,000
Scientist $70,000

Statistician (master's) $80,000 34 percent
Zoologist $60,000 11 percent

Advanced
Analytical Chemist (bachelor's through PhD) $78,000 4 percent
Anthropologist (master's) $48,000 4 percent
Applied Mathematician (master's) $105,000 21 percent
Archeologist (master's) $47,000 4 percent
Astronomer (PhD) $97,000 5 percent
Astrophysicist (PhD) $81,000 8 percent
Atmospheric Scientist (bachelor's through PhD) $89,000 9 percent
Mathematician (master's) $105,000 21 percent
Nanobiologist (bachelor's, master's) $60,000
Physicist (PhD) $115,000 8 percent
Statistician (master's) $80,000 34 percent

Transportation, Distribution & Logistics

Health, Safety & Environmental Management

High School through Three Years
Department of Transportation (DOT) Inspector (one year security experience) $41,000
First Responder (certification in NREMT, CPR) $34,000
Hazardous Materials Manager (associate) $42,000–$58,000
Health and Safety Manager (one to three years' experience) $73,000

Bachelor's
Environmental Compliance Inspector $54,000
Environmental Compliance Specialist $73,000
Environmental Engineer $87,000 5 percent
Environmental Manager $107,000 7 percent
Environmental Protection Specialist $61,000
Environmental Scientist (bachelor's, master's) $66,000
Industrial Health and Safety Engineer $86,000 6 percent
Industrial Hygienist $71,000 8 percent
Risk Manager (five years' experience) $127,000
Safety Analyst (bachelor's, master's) $73,000

Advanced
Environmental Scientist (bachelor's, master's) $66,000
Safety Analyst (bachelor's, master's) $73,000

Logistics Planning & Management Services

One to Three Years
Logistician (associate, bachelor's) $74,000 7 percent

Bachelor's
International Logistics Specialist $74,000 7 percent
Logistician (associate, bachelor's) $74,000 7 percent
Logistics Analyst (bachelor's, master's) $56,000 26 percent
Logistics Consultant (bachelor's, master's) $56,000 5 percent
Logistics Engineer (bachelor's, master's, five years' experience) $74,000 5 percent
Logistics Manager (HS, bachelor's, private five to fifteen years' experience; military one to two years' experience) $66,000

Advanced
Logistics Analyst (bachelor's, master's) $56,000 26 percent
Logistics Consultant (bachelor's, master's) $56,000 5 percent
Logistics Engineer (bachelor's, master's, five years' experience) $74,000 5 percent

Course Preview: What Courses You Will Need to Take for Your Career

Some careers interest you. It would be smart to check out what courses you will be taking to get there. Don't aim for a medical administration job that requires three accounting courses if you absolutely wouldn't want to do those courses. If you want to be a beautician, chemistry courses are required to excel in the profession. There are artists who refuse to use Adobe Photoshop and artists who refuse to use anything but Adobe Photoshop. If you are useless at computer design, you might want to take an additional course or make sure you have some exposure in high school.

Those "I refuse to take…" teen complaints we parents hear are not trivial if disliked courses could derail a major. Know what you are going to have to study. You may find that, if you complete some courses in high school or in the first year or two of college, you could get an entry job in your career, for part-time work during college. That company can help guide your course choice and may even subsidize it. Or the company may not. But that experience will help you focus your career ambitions.

High School

High school is free. Try out courses to make sure that this is a possible career area for you. Find out you really, really hate the career in high school and not in your second or third year of college, when you might have to add a year for the change of major.

On the curriculums online, no, your high school is probably not going to have a course called "Principles of Governance & Public Administration" for preparation for a government job or national security career. Nor will your high school have Health Science IV: Introduction to Biotechnology Research and Development for a biotech career, but something similar will be offered at a high school in the school district—just under the name your school district applies to it. Or your local community college may offer that content. Most high schools must allow you to take that community college course if it is not offered in your high school.

Project Management for Entrepreneurs is a course being offered in many school districts. Completing those courses in high school leads to a Certified Associate Project Management (CAPM) certificate. That means that, upon high school graduation, you can apply for careers as a Business Analyst, Relational Administrator, Operational Support Associate, a job in a government project management office, Senior Project Manager in IT, or Marketing Coordinator for Communications. This certificate impresses colleges and doing contract work in the summers off college is better than working fast-food jobs.

A traditional education is solid. But there are courses that can be equally valuable and more relevant to the student's interest and to what is useful for a job. The science research writing course may be a better tool than English 12. Cosmetology is a dual-credit chemistry course. An insurance regulations high school or dual-credit course may put that finance career into perspective. Again, I know parents often recoil at the thought of their baby trying out careers, but allow them to try—it can make them a standout for college admissions.

Getting a head start on a career, with in-depth knowledge, experience, or just for career exploration, will impress colleges and set you ahead in real career learning. A mature approach to a career, beyond "I wanted to be a vet since I was four," is appreciated by college admissions—*even* if you change your mind later.

Reading these, the student may feel rather daunted. "I am going to have to learn all that?!?" That is why the student needs to choose a career they are interested in. College should be for a purpose beyond maturing. If the student really isn't ready for serious learning, they should take a gap year. But again, add the student's passions to the career to keep enthusiasm fueling success. Business administration can sound dry, but not if the student combines it with an interest in sports for team manager, sports agent, recreational manager. Art curator in a museum takes a PhD, but the bachelor's level translates into art buyer for a hotel chain, wedding event planner, advertising executive, fashion runway manager. But you need to take all the courses as a foundation.

Go to www.collegeneedtoknow.com and create your account for access to curriculums, high school to graduate school, and for information on over a thousand jobs.

Career exploration or career certification courses in high school signal maturity to college admissions officers.

No, students probably won't really know what they really want to do until they are twenty-six, but unless parents will support them into their thirties, choose a "starter career" they are passionate about.

Don't spend all the education budget on the four-year degree.

The "starter career" needs academic and practical courses—whatever it is. So, go to the website, and look at what courses are required and which ones the student can do in high school.

Check the courses needed, high school, college, and beyond for the choice careers to make sure the student really wants to take all those courses.

Part Nine

Action Plan

Let's turn all that self-discovery into an action plan.

Action planning requires honesty. It means facing realities. But when the student completes the action plan, facing realities honestly, the student can look at the best career entry paths to reach a life they would find acceptable or even love.

These are the final steps:

1. What do I want?

2. What are my assets?

3. Map my networking connections.

4. Be honest about the pros and cons for six careers.

5. Choose the primary career focus.

6. Lay out the next steps.

Let's First Look at Some Sample Students to See How This Works

Here are examples of real students being real with themselves. Following the examples, the parent and student get a real picture of real students and the dilemmas and opportunities they face. Using the charts simplifies a world of worry to show what are good feasible goals.

After the examples are the chart templates for the student. Most school districts in the US have something like this being rolled out. Most states are working on training people to work with parents and students to use this tool. But this tool is in your hands now. It will only work if you are honest, realistic, and not worrying about what others think.

Examples

Read down the Student One column and then down the Student Two column, or compare as you go. Both are real students.

The Student One information comes from the Colorado Career Conversation Training from the Colorado Education Leadership Council. Student Two is a student interviewed for the purposes of this book.

What Do I Want?

Student One	Student Two
What are my dreams for the future?	
Want to be financially independent and able to help support my family	Travel
Want to make a difference in my community	Love art and fashion

What are my goals? Core values	
Social justice, dignity, respect	Importance of art in how I see things
Work with a team of committed people	Love helping people with art
Want to work to mean something	

What are my needs? What are my realities?	
Must have job on graduation	Want to be good enough to get a job
Want to live at home first, then move out	Want to live in NYC or London
Could do part-time school or training	Could work part-time

What Are My Assets?

What are my strengths?	
Hard worker	Editor of art/writing magazine
Empathetic	Leader (state academic pageant winner)
Detail-oriented, neat, organized	State debate qualifier
Like to solve problems in a team	I work hard following my passions

What are my interests? Hobbies?	
Hip hop dance	New York Fashion week model 2019
Cultural experiences	Design my own clothes
Travel	Have my own charity
	Worked in Vietnam hospital

What are my personality traits?	
Gold-blue dominant	Leader
Introspective	Love public speaking
Coordinator	Not a great team player
Education/ Social/ Logistics	Can "read" people and help them

Mapping My Networking Connections

Student One Network Map

Social	Educational	Professional	Personal	Recreational
UMA Church Youth Group	Ms. Martinez Counselor	Smith Family Babysitting	Ms. Holmes CEO neighbor	Dance Cra-z Team
	Mr. Knox Math & Business	Ms. Olivas Volunteer Super	Amy & Adam Spicer mentors	
	Ms. Olsen Model UN	Mr. Beck, Mgr. @ McDonald's	Eric Hughes lawyer/godparent	

Student Two Network Map

Social	Educational	Professional	Personal	Recreational
Girls Care service work	Ms. Deck AP Research	Dr Smiths, Dir. Health Charity	Dick Oster NYC famous artist	US Miss Director J Watt
Art Print Magazine	Dr Ngo, Ortho Surgeon Hue Hospital	Dave Waters, Art Gallery Director	Mel Scanton UK art writer/ Family friend	Ms. Stream Debate team
Existentialist Club	Ms. Carls Debate Teacher	Ms. Jules, Mgr. Fashion Place	Jen Shield UK artist agent	All-Family own charity

Choosing Six Possible Careers and the Pros and Cons from My Unique Point of View

Student One: Social Justice Lawyer	Student Two: Museum Curator
Pros	**Pros**
Solve real problems	Love the field
Cons	**Cons**
Four years plus law school	Would require at least a high-level master's
May need to work part-time	Highly competitive field for a big city museum position

Student One: Project Manager at Social Justice-focused Nonprofit	Student Two: Psychologist
Pros	**Pros**
Entry level with growth	Love the field and good at it
Could start part-time	Could get high school training and experience
Really aligned with core values and needs	For part-time work
Cons	**Cons**
Won't pay much at first	Years of education and certification
	I'd probably give up and become a therapist

Student One: Project Manager for Business/Industry or Consultant	Student Two: Art Crime Forensics
Pros	**Pros**
Good money	Love forensics, crime, and art
Uses my strengths	Jobs in military and private sector
Cons	**Cons**
Doesn't align with core values Won't make a difference	BA plus training
Feel like I "sold out"	Or available straight from investigation training but might not be assigned to art crime

Student One: Dance Teacher	Student Two: Fashion Marketing
Pros	**Pros**
Align with my passion	Would love this
Cons	**Cons**
Enough pay? Reliable?	Few jobs
No real growth opportunity	Low pay (though possibility of high pay in sales marketing)

Student One: Day Care Worker	Student Two: Tattoo Artist
Pros	**Pros**
Love kids?	Love drawing and doing face-painting and fake tattoos
Could get work right away	Easy certification at reasonable cost, low supply costs
	Growing demand and high part-time pay
Cons	**Cons**
Really low pay	Wouldn't want to do as career but great part-time

Student One: School Counselor or Social Worker	Student Two: Doctor (Orthopedic)
Pros	**Pros**
Could make a difference every day	Have experience in orthopedic rotations in Vietnam hospital and liked it
Good job security	High-paying
Cons	**Cons**
Need four-year degree	Years of schooling
Not exciting to me	Long hours (over a hundred a week)
	Right now, I don't think I could finish that many years

Chosen Career Focus Conclusions

Student One: Project Manager at Social Justice-Focused Nonprofit
Obtain two-year business entrepreneurship certification and progress to a business management bachelor's degree

Student Two: Event Organizer (at a fashion house or advertising company)
BA in Art: History and Communications would allow to branch into art-related careers

Next Steps to Take

Student One

Continue volunteer work at nonprofits
Concurrent enrollment

Student Two

Work/volunteer in parent's friend's art gallery
Continue as editor of art magazine
Get certified as tattoo artist for spare cash
Will keep doing biology/anatomy/behavioral therapy courses in high school
as back-up

Career Courses

Student One: High School Elective/ Career-Related Courses

For high school planning, need to refine nonprofit field (environmental, social
work, etc.) as that can determine high school options

Options might include:

- Microsoft Office certification for any business field
- Information Technology course

- Health Wellness: Behavioral Health (Senior Year English Core, dual enrollment)
- Health Wellness: Intro to Physical Therapy (Science core)

Student Two: High School Elective/ Career-Related Courses

Goal: Shows depth in art journalism but keeps open other key interests

Adobe Certified Associate certificate courses
Graphic Design 2
AP Art History
AP Art
Publication Journalism
Introduction to Arts, Audio/Video Technology and Communications
Anatomy and Biology 2
Intro to Criminal Investigation

Action Planning: Now It Is Your Turn

Simply summarize your goals and assets from forms you have already completed.

1. What are my assets?
2. Mapping my networking connections
3. Choosing six careers that interest me and the pros and cons from my point of view
4. Chosen career focus
5. Next steps to take
6. Career courses

What Do I Want?

What are my dreams for the future?

What are my goals?

What are my needs? What are my realities?

What Are My Assets?

What are my strengths?

What are my personality traits?

Mapping My Networking Connections

80 percent of jobs are not advertised. Networking is the method to find jobs out there.

Teens have networks. Fill out the names and relationships of the student's network. Think about people the student and the family may know related to career interests and passions. The student may already have a gold mine of connections that were never considered important.

Keep in touch with your network. Call or email your network for advice and contacts. If you don't know anyone in the field, email them for advice, set up a mentorship. They will love being the expert/mentor to help a young person. (It is flattering being asked for advice.) Don't be shy.

Social	Educational	Professional	Personal	Recreational

Choosing Six Careers That Interest Me and the Pros and Cons from My Point of View

Having looked at career pathways, name six jobs that stood out or jobs you know you are passionate about. Include one job you could do with only high school or high school and some college-level training related to career interests and passions.

List the pros and cons for each job from your own point of view. You are the one who must do the work. What do you like about each career, and what would you really hate about doing that job every day?

Career 1:

Pros

Cons

Career 2:

Pros

Cons

Career 3:

Pros

Cons

Career 4:

Pros

Cons

Career 5:

Pros

Cons

Advanced Exercise: Maximizing Outcomes by Finding Transferable Skills

In all of the careers that interest the student, let's look what they have in common to identify transferable skills. What skills or certificates is the student interested in that would be the foundation for several careers? For example, information technology certificates prepare a student for jobs in health care, government, law enforcement.

GIS (geographic information system) certificates, associate degrees, BS degrees, master's, through to GIS PhDs are pathways to an amazing range of careers: tracking the spread of epidemics, finding ancient Peruvian archeological discoveries, understanding historic battlefields, for mining, weather, government intelligence, astronomy, districting, planning highways, civic planning and building projects. It is knowledge and skill that is transferable to many fields and up-scalable.

On the website www.collegeneedtoknow.com, there are course lists where one can compare courses that will work for two or more careers.

Medical technical writing works for medical administration or many medical practitioner careers from entry to physician. Legal ethics courses are a qualification for entering many careers.

Recognizing transferable skills is invaluable to set yourself up for the future. Recognizing the transferable skills you have can allow for a career shift. Look at the certification lists and see what is shared.

See what careers are more closely linked than one imagines.

The student should come away saying, "If I study this, then I can get a job right away if I want in this (internship experience, part-time job or full-time), or with a little/a lot more training, I can do this, but it also prepares me for this…" Or "If I study this, I could do all these jobs in all these different fields." If the student hates one career, or wants to move, or discovers new opportunities, being able to transition has been built in.

Finding Ways into an Industry That Seems Unreachable

Certain career fields may seem out of reach, requiring years of education. But don't ignore jobs in the industry that can lead to advancement within a company.

Curator jobs at the Smithsonian Museum in Washington require a PhD, but there are category creation and data jobs that can get you into the Smithsonian. Once in house, one will have priority access to in-house advertised careers as one adds skills and education.

Disney has a tradition of promoting from within. Lifeguards advance to become the head of cruise line customer relations. Janitors can advance to managing a Disney World park. A jungle cruise operator can become head of a film division. Disney promotes good people from within. It also often pays for graduate degrees.

Companies often retrain contract workers. If the contract worker is excellent, the company would rather keep the worker and retrain them for the next project challenge than go with an unknown.

Two pathways exist to becoming a cosmetic surgeon. If the student doesn't have the money, nor want the debt, and doesn't want to spend eight or more years training, the student could get a dental degree, then take a few MMSD courses and become a cosmetic surgeon. They would not have as wide a training or be able to do the wide range of work that a plastic surgeon can do, but if the specialty was cosmetic surgery anyway, the student will have the credentials for a fraction of the cost and train faster but achieve the same salary as a plastic surgeon doing cosmetic surgery.

Next Steps to Take

For each career choice, look at certifications that the student can get to prove ability, where to get that certification (like in high school as part of the curriculum, community college, from an association), and how long it will take for certification (it could be a few days or a few months).

One may want to get a certification in a field different than the career choice as a way to get a higher-paying job while studying.

Career Idea	Certification Where to get/Duration	Certification Where to get/Duration	Certification Where to get/Duration

Chosen Career Focus

What have you decided is your career choice?
Decision:

Your New Schedule

Let's put it all together in a new schedule.

High School Elective/Career-Related Courses

Now, let's put together your Technology Age high school schedule.

1. Check everything against your own high school graduation requirements list that you filled out earlier.

2. Check everything against your college admissions requirements list.

3. Check everything against your pathways' electives list. You may use one or more pathways.

4. Using your high school handbook, look for courses in each area, English, math, science, social studies, and electives (usually listed by discipline):

Your choices in each area can include:
High school level (often called College Prep courses)
Honors
APs
CTE
Dual enrollment
Dual credit CTE
Certificate courses (job-readiness proof)
Apprenticeships
Internships
Career exploration

Now, in each area, the student can customize the schedule to include his or her interests and careers to explore or advance in.

	English
Ninth Grade	
Tenth Grade	
Eleventh Grade	
Twelfth Grade	

	Math
Ninth Grade	
Tenth Grade	
Eleventh Grade	
Twelfth Grade	

	Science
Ninth Grade	
Tenth Grade	Chemistry—
Eleventh Grade	Biology—
Twelfth Grade	

	Social Studies (must include US Government)
Ninth Grade	
Tenth Grade	
Eleventh Grade	
Twelfth Grade	

	Electives (gym 1½, Health ½)
Ninth Grade	
Tenth Grade	
Eleventh Grade	
Twelfth Grade	

	Electives
Ninth Grade	
Tenth Grade	
Eleventh Grade	
Twelfth Grade	

	Optional extra period or Study Hall
Ninth Grade	
Tenth Grade	
Eleventh Grade	
Twelfth Grade	

Now copy over course codes to the schedule.

	English	Math	Science	Social Studies	Electives	Electives	Elective or Off	Lunch
Ninth Grade								
Tenth Grade								
Eleventh Grade								
Twelfth Grade								

The Best College

So, hopefully, the student has a clearer idea what is important to them and what they are passionately interested in—for now, it can change. Hopefully, parents understand their students even more and recognize what can drive their teen to success through their enthusiasm. Hopefully, both see there are pathways to a great career for any budget, for any learning type. Here are some things to keep in mind.

Location. Choose a location where the student wants to study *and* start a career—*both*.

Cost. Is it affordable? That does not mean affordable with a huge loan, selling the family home, or using the retirement fund.

Scholarships. What scholarships have been offered, already accepted or that the student would qualify for?

Loans. Federally subsidized loans could be used if the student is aware those will have to be repaid starting six months after graduation. Paying back $18,000 is very different than paying back $180,000 simply for a bachelor's degree.

Teaching Style. What is the teaching style of the school? Lectures with breakout seminars with grad students or small professor-led classes; or individual tutorials, etc.

Learning style. Is the student hands-on, so professional courses with applied learning would get better results? (University of Florida has a complete Advanced CTE degree program.) Or are more traditional, reading-led courses better (although application must be available)?

Program. Find a school that has strong departments for your top three career choices so, if you change your mind, you will have strong alternative pathways.

Business, internship relationships

Certifications. Some colleges offer many, some offer none.

Career Services. Is there a good career services office? Job fairs? Internships upon graduation?

Here is an example submitted by a student. Here are the notes on a UK university, New Mexico Tech—a top state university with a fantastic international reputation but less known in the US and an exclusive top liberal arts college with a unique program (it has a 47 percent acceptance rate because its program is so challenging; only those who want extreme rigor will actually apply to the college).

College/University	University of Edinburgh	New Mexico Institute of Mining and Technology	St John's College
Location	Edinburgh, Scotland	Socorro, New Mexico	Santa Fe, New Mexico
Qualifications	Met basic qualifications (awaiting answer) Application submitted early	Met qualifications	Accepted very early through rolling admissions (application open Jan 1 junior year); granted two scholarships
Cost	Four-year BA/ master's combined $65,000 total tuition, room and board for 4 years	Four-year Bachelor of Science $16,000 in-state, $32,000 out-of-state	Tuition $35,000, room & board $16,000 per year, $51,000 per year, $204,000 total
Loan amount	$6,000 per year, $24,000 total	$6,000 per year, $24,000 total	$6,000 per year, $24,000 total
Scholarship offered	None	Scholarships offered $4,000 per year, in-state award	Scholarship $25,000 per year
Immediate out-of-pocket	$10,250 per year; $41,000 4-year total	$12,000 per year, $48,000 total or $12,000 4 year total with work/study	$26,000 per year $104,000 4 year total
Program 1	History—general	Physics	Exceptional, unique Liberal Arts

Program 2	History of Science	Astrophysics	
Program 3	History—Financial Fraud	Above with History (of Science) minor	
Internships	UK corporate financial ethics divisions UK internships in patent pre-law	Astrophysics internships Government science policy internships	Different approach
Certifications	Master's; no professional certifications	Possible engineering certifications	Not generally offered
Teaching method	Lecture, small groups, one-on-one with professor	Lecture, small group, research opportunities	Small group discussion of great books, papers
Career services	Good career advisory services		Career advisory
Job potential	Good corporate connections from internships Would need certificate for teaching if return to US Likely to get PhD program ("free" with teaching assistantship)	Many job opportunities, in physics, astrophysics, or science policy or for law school entry (patent law, etc.) Top degree appealing to grad schools Easily quantifiable credentials	Most graduates go on to grad school—but highly esteemed degree for entry to top grad school, law school, or med school

These are all reasonably affordable "gems." The Scotist Master's degree in four years, a degree in one of the best physics programs in the US that could be virtually free with research work and internships available, or a highly prestigious exceptional liberal arts program that isn't $100,000 a year but as highly recognized.

Even for US students, foreign universities offer top degrees. In the UK, degrees take three years for a bachelor's with overseas tuition ranging from $20,000 to $38,000, room and board ranging from $7,000 for the year (nineteen meals a week, wine parties, etc.) to $25,000 for luxury London studio apartments. But $27,000 for the equivalent of an Ivy degree is amazing. Contrast $81,000 total for three years with $81,000 per year for an Ivy ($324,000 total).

Usually, grades and the GPA are not part of the requirements. Basic requirements can range from five APs with fives (or SAT subject tests of 700) plus 1470 on SAT on down. Others will take several APs with fours or SAT subject tests of 600, and 1250 SAT to be considered, and even less. Those are the minimum requirements and most students exceed the basics. The student will receive a conditional offer before they have taken all their college tests if the college is interested in them, but the student doesn't have to submit all scores until July before college starts in September.

Foreign colleges, in Europe, Asia, and around the world, often have degrees taught entirely in English and tuition costs can be as low as $3,000 per year. The student is responsible for accommodation and food. These are world-class degrees. Students will have to get student visas to study in the country. They may not be allowed to work in the country during college. Some countries allow students to work in the country after graduation; some will allow work for only a few years; others will not allow a work visa unless the company secures it for the graduate.

Your College Shortlists

Whether the plan is for some higher education, a two-year associate degree, a four-year degree, or a four- or five-year BA/MA, chart the student's shortlist of higher education institutions.

Students need to think in terms of Match, Safe, and Stretch colleges or institutions. "Match" is the school where the student meets the requirements and loves what is offered at the school. The "Safe" school is the one where the student exceeds and is virtually certain of being admitted. The "Stretch" school is also known as the dream school. This will usually be the highly selective college where the student may have the qualifications but there are lottery odds for admission, or the student does not quite have perfect qualifications but may have other attributes that could lead to admission.

We know one student who applied to 117 colleges and got into five. I suggest perhaps apply to three in each category. I suggest the student apply early action or early rolling admission to see where he or she gets accepted and what the financial package will be. If the student doesn't get accepted or wants to try for other schools, the student still has regular decision deadlines to add a couple more applications.

Match College Charts

College/University			
Location			
Qualifications			
Cost			
Loan amount			
Scholarship offered			
Immediate out-of-pocket			
Program 1			
Program 2			
Program 3			
Internships			
Certifications			
Teaching method			

Career services			
Job potential			

Safe School Chart

College/University			
Location			
Qualifications			
Cost			
Loan amount			
Scholarship offered			
Immediate out-of-pocket			
Program 1			
Program 2			
Program 3			

Internships			
Certifications			
Teaching method			
Career services			
Job potential			

Stretch School Chart

College/University			
Location			
Qualifications			
Cost			
Loan amount			
Scholarship offered			

Immediate out-of-pocket			
Program 1			
Program 2			
Program 3			
Internships			
Certifications			
Teaching method			
Career services			
Job potential			

Part Ten

Stop Failures Before They Happen

Don't you feel elated that you worked everything out? Yay. Well done. Hurrah. You should be so happy. Perfect college, studying something you are passionate about, little or no debt. On track to graduate in four years and be employable, working somewhere you would love…

The excitement will not last long.

1. Once the student completes all these forms and charts, and selects career paths, high school courses, a college, and making real decisions, *the immediate reaction is to withdraw*. Growing up is frightening, so there can be real "head in the sand" moments, even when the student loves everything about the decision. Teens may withdraw to bed, retreat to video games, and run away from adulthood any way they can.

2. Another response to proclaiming a decision to the world is that the mind processes that as accomplishment—the mind feels that the plan has been completed by sharing and discussing it. The tendency is to never complete the plan because the mind has imagined it and feels the work is done. For example, most are more successful with a New Year's resolution they keep to themselves—a promise to the self of going to the gym every day tends

to be more successful than boasting to everyone you know that your New Year's resolution is to go to the gym every day. The mind processes the announced plan as completion. So, the tendency is not to follow through on decisions.

But there are techniques that can get one over the hurdle of having to actually accomplish what one has planned. These techniques allow the student to troubleshoot what obstacles could come up on the "pathway" and have solutions thought out to help through the tough times ahead.

Pre-Mortem Problems

"Pre-mortem" is a simple technique created by Harvard Business School to save any project from failure. Don't wait to post-mortem what went wrong. Think what can go wrong and devise strategies and remedies so the problems never arise.

Name what could go wrong, name the monster, then you can preload solutions.

So, pre-mortems can really help the student keep on track and act.

The student should write down the "big" decision and then come up with five (or more) things he or she is worried about. Then discuss how to avoid those worries.

For example, when the college is chosen, ask the student what worries him or her. "I don't know if I will make friends." So, come up with strategies like joining a club or making contact with roommates before arriving. "Those are hard courses, I might fail." So, look at campus help options, library resources, professor help hours, etc.

List five worries and three solutions each:

Worry One
Worry Two:
Worry Three:
Worry Four:
Worry Five:

Conclusion

We are now in the Technology Age. That means exponentially accelerating technological change will impact almost every career. It doesn't mean that studying STEM will make a student's future golden. It means that every worker will have to continually retrain as jobs transform and new ones are created.

What was true in the past is often not true today. Coping with change, however needed, is tough. Worse, the coronavirus disruptions have left so many unknowns. Let's recap.

- High test scores are no longer a predictor of college and career success.

- College no longer guarantees career success.

- The prestigious college is not a one-size fits all "best college." It can be the right school for some individuals, but it is no longer the Platinum Ticket bestowing success on anyone who graduates.

- Most colleges offer great educations at the bachelor's level.

- The amazing student will end up with the same earning level whether he or she attends the elite school or goes through the community college and university systems, i.e. engineers will earn similarly, finance managers will earn similarly, at the bachelor's level.

- High rankings are important for graduate school in the specific master's or PhD program but are largely irrelevant when evaluating undergraduate advantage.

- The right-fit college is more important than the prestige school to boost college and career outcomes.

- Great, high-paying, interesting careers can be entered from any education level.

- "Some" college can lead to better career entry than four-year college.

- Those entering the job market will have seven to eleven totally different careers in a lifetime. One job for life is no longer the plan.

- Education doesn't end with the four-year degree.

- All high-paying careers will require some college and continuing higher education.

- Planning and career exploration in high school:

    - Diminishes high school anxiety

    - Increases graduation chances

    - Improves high school and college graduation rates

    - Reduces teen pregnancy

    - Decreases student debt

    - Leads to better career outcomes

- College needs to fit the student, not the student be made to fit the college.

It is a cliché but "Love what you do, and you'll never work a day in your life." But statistics show that loving one's work is the way to higher expertise and innovation. These lead to career advancement, job security, and the highest salaries—on top of happiness and fulfillment.

Developing the child's natural abilities and passions is shown to produce better outcomes than trying to turn them into someone they are not. If you were grooming your child to be a top athlete, a short stocky teen is more likely to become a great wrestler or golfer than a natural basketball player. Work with nature, not against it. Technique is vital, but start with natural ability.

I hope that the student can see himself or herself as the hero of his or her own life, starting a journey he or she has some control over. Success isn't about luck; it isn't that any selective school will be the guaranteed winning ticket. Take control and plan your best routes to success.

Acknowledgements

This book is based on research and statistics vital to making our "best" decisions. It wasn't a foregone conclusion that there would be good solutions to the poor college outcomes, to illegal and unethical competition, to the Depression Olympics created by competition and perceived (not real) failures, to lifelong debt, to career disappointments. I was lucky to discover a world of solutions from schools all the way to Washington, DC, where these challenges are being tackled in a rare bipartisan effort.

So, sincere thanks to the departments of education, local, state, and national, the teachers, the counselors, the principals, the superintendents analyzing, creating, and literally teaching the future in a race against accelerating change.

Colorado Education Initiative (CEI) is responsible for developing and facilitating wider training throughout the state on behalf of the Colorado Department of Education (CDE) and in partnership with additional state agencies and partners, training career "conversationalists" to our kids, and anyone entering the workplace into high-paying careers in growth fields. The Colorado School Counselor's Association introduced me to the "real world" of bad outcomes and amazing outcomes. They put me through "CTE Specialist endorsed school counselor" training hours.

I have met visionaries at every turn—their excitement and commitment were inspiring. Lauren Jones, whose titles and responsibilities are CTE Program Director for Special Populations, Counseling & Equity Middle School CTE Program Coordinator, Career & Technical Education (CTE) in Colorado, Colorado Community College System, sold me on the importance of ICAP (Individual Career and Academic Planning) for students rich and poor. She had a list of "you have to talk to" world-changing educators. Noel Ginsberg, founder of CareerWiseColorado, showed me the world's approach to a fast track to an upper-middle-class career directly or to enhance the university education path through apprenticeships. Dave Fulton, also of CareerWiseColorado, harked back to his days as an assistant principal overjoyed at reaching the targets of enrolling every senior in college but being moved to remedy the problem when he tracked that many did not finish.

That led me to the Innovation Campus of the Cherry Creek School District and thanks to Laura Miller, Counseling Coordinator, Cherry Creek Innovation Campus, a standalone college and career preparedness facility for high school students. Washington bipartisan funding is going to these educational offerings.

I credit those at ACTE, the Association for Career and Technical Education, for training and materials. They made it possible for me to attend the National Policy Symposium, normally in Washington, DC (virtual in 2021), to meet personally with the offices of senators and congressmen including John Hickenlooper, Michael Bennet, and Jason Crow. These are leaders promoting education and workforce development. Bipartisan bills concentrate on funding to CTE pathways, community colleges, apprenticeships, Pell grant money to short-term education, ICAP, PWR—they are committed to pathways to high-paying careers in growth fields.

Thank you to CTE (careertech.org/CTE) and ACTE, the Association for Career and Technical Education (www.acteonline.org) for training me, for their creation of the tools, courses, and information. I thank them for allowing me to use those tools they trained me to use for this book. I thank them for allowing me to share their vision and plans for the future of work and for developing pathways to successful outcomes available to all wanting a great career in growth fields through education offered in public and private schools, community colleges, technical schools, and colleges and universities in every state.

I have met with educational consultants and spent days at therapeutic boarding schools for "troubled teens" and youth psychiatric hospitals.

At my teens' high school, Principal Ryan Silva, named Colorado's high school principal of the year in 2021, is a wise leader driving excellence but committed to balance. Craig Whitgrove, head of Post Grad, is a national expert who has an answer to every college question and the most comprehensive college and career program I have seen in a high school. Lisa Wiese has been the most detail-driven, patient counselor to my triplets, handling the impossibly overwhelming array of responsibilities in every counselor's remit.

Thanks to all high school, college, and career HR professionals, business owners, and Washington DC experts who allowed me into meetings and webinar meetings.

Thank you to my brother Dr. Scott Horn, GIS PhD, for hours of discussion ranging from his university lecturer experience and work with the City of Dallas. Thanks to his daughters, Dr. Megan Horn Orzalli, undergrad at the University of Washington, Harvard medical PhD and post-PhD, now with her own lab at the University of Massachusetts, and Dr. Dara Horn, emergency room doctor in Seattle, for being examples to my kids. Thanks to my wise cousins Kathy Capek and Susan Calonge for listening to my findings with supreme patience and reality-checking me.

Thanks to the inventor of the "video off" feature of Zoom so I could ride my stationary bike during a year and a half of full-day webinars for two years.

And I thank my kids. Thanks to my daughter Leela, determined to make every endeavor a success. Graduating high school with many APs and starting college at fifteen was a mixed blessing. She chose to live her own adventure novel, becoming a television writer, landing a top entertainment agent, returning to college, and supporting herself—at twenty. Thanks to my triplets, Abby, Nathan, and Zach. Originally, I had taught them to strive for a highly selective college but then, starting their high school sophomore year, I found the less-than-hopeful outcome data. We had to wrestle with our beliefs and biases. It has been agonizing to let go of "old truths" that are no longer relevant—but we had to change if we wanted to prepare for better futures. I changed from wanting my children to meet a general ideal for a "top" college and a top job, to wanting them to be their best self for what they wanted to do.

They chose AP classes because they loved the subjects and especially those particular teachers—not because they thought they should do APs. But they deeply regret not doing some CTE and dual enrollment courses! One is planning a gap year; deferring University College London in history. One chose

astrophysics at a top program at a public university in the US. The other decided
to not do the strictly academic art history program, opting for a Criticism,
Curatorship and Communication degree for museum curatorship to event
organizing—practical plus academic—with required internships at museums
and fashion houses, experience organizing street festivals, and learning writing
arts criticism. So, the complete range: one highly academic (but taking a gap
year), one STEM with internships ranging from NASA to government science
policy writing, and one blend of the academic and highly practical. But the best
part of our new approach is to follow your heart—which makes high school and
the whole process an exciting one. In your career lifetime, you will probably be
able to do many careers, or something not yet imagined, if you plan wisely. Do
what you choose with commitment, and have resources to reskill if you need to.
It isn't a race you must win at any cost, it's an engaging journey that, because you
devised it, will be worth your time and energy.

I want to thank every community college, college, institution of higher education,
and university in the US. I would be proud to have my children go to any of them,
if the programs they offer matched that specific child. Every college in America
provides amazing opportunities. Let's try something: hide the name of the college.
Do the unique opportunities at that college fit your individual student? There
isn't a one-size-fits-all magic college that will bestow the perfect future on anyone
who enters but every college can be magical for the right young wizard.

About the Author

Parenting expert Christie Barnes is best known for her acclaimed Paranoid Parents Guides, countering what parents perceive as worries and dangers with facts and statistics to focus their parenting efforts. Appearing in the *New York Times*, on ABC, and across the nation, and even crashing the NPR website, she was honored to help worried parents.

Researching her new book, *What Every Parent Needs to Know about College Admissions*, she was shocked to find that stellar students were not getting even adequate college and career outcomes. She felt more than writing about the problem was needed, so she sought professional qualifications in college and career counseling. Adding to her BA from Mount Holyoke College, graduate study at Oxford, and an MA Hons City University of London, she became a certified High School and College Career "conversationalist," and pursued post-master's education in academic and career planning.

This expertise took her to Washington, DC, for the National Policy Symposium, where she testified and advocated to senators and members of Congress about Career and Technical Education. She has recently appeared in *Forbes* as an expert on college and the future of work and *Reader's Digest* on COVID-19 disruption of college, with Dr. Anthony Fauci.

Barnes had an earlier life in film and television, apprentice directing at the Royal Shakespeare Company, translating plays for the BBC, assistant directing award-winning TV for Channel Four. She married Oscar-nominated, Olivier-award-winning playwright Peter Barnes. His sudden death when their triplets were one and daughter four, left Christie a single mother determined to be the best parent she could be—which led to her career as a respected and well-known parenting expert.

Endnotes

1 The Chronicle for Higher Education, Advanced CTE, Challenge Success and other college think tank and college professional information sessions run from the beginning of March 2020.

2 www.stradaeeducation.org/wp-content/uploads/2020/04/Public-Viewpoint-Report-Week 6.pdf, from Postsecondary CTE Economic Recovery July 2020 pdf Advanced CTE: State Leaders Connecting Learning to Work, 8/20/2020.

3 Michael J. Sorrell, president-Paul Quinn College, 09/09/2020, www.insidehighered.com/news/2020/09/09/what-college-presidents-say-about-leading-covid-19-ra?dnuarrowclick=yes&utm_source=Inside+Higher+Ed&utm_campaign=88ef879cf3-DNU_2020_COPY_02&utm_medium=email&utm_term=0_1fcbc04421-88ef879cf3-236417510&mc_cid=88ef879cf3&mc_eid=d35fa068cc.

4 The impact of legacy status on undergraduate admissions at elite colleges and universities; by Michael Hurwitz The Harvard Graduate School of Education.

5 p. 6, College Admissions during COVID, by Robert Franek, The Princeton Review, Random House, 2020.

6 B. Benson, Cognitive Bias Codex, 2016, https://busterbenson.com/piles/cognitive-biases/.

7 White Paper, 2018, Challenge Success, Stamford University.

8 UC Boulder representative, Highly Selective College Night, October 10, 2019, Cherry Creek High School, Greenwood Village, CO 80111.

9 Zach Friedman, Forbes.com, Student-loan debt statistics, June 13, 2018. www.forbes.com/sites/zackfriedman/2018/06/13 student-loan-debt-statistics-2018.

10 Tony Carnevale, a research Professor and Director of the Georgetown University Center on Education and the Workforce Georgetown Public Policy Institute CEW, Recovery: Job Growth and Education Requirements Through 2020, 2013.

11 Laura Miller, counselor, Innovation Campus, Centennial, CO.

12 CTE future plan, 2019.

13 Dr. Paul Bobrowski, Dean of the Monfort School of Business, University of Northern Colorado, Creek to College, Cherry Creek High School, Jan 7 2019, interview.

14 Principal Ryan Silva, Cherry Creek High School, Greenwood Village CO, interview, Nov 6, 2019.

15 Neil Ginsberg, founder of CareerWise, Interview Denver Colorado, Jan 29th, 2020 speaking of his extensive work with Switzerland and Singapore.

16 US Census Bureau, 2017.

17 Data from: PayScale, www.usnews.com/education/best-colleges/slideshows/10-college-majors-with-the-highest-starting-salaries?onepage.

18 Center on Education and the Workforce (CEW) at Georgetown University.

19 https://money.usnews.com/careers/best-jobs/anesthesiologist/salary.

20 www.glassdoor.com/Salaries/anesthesiologist-salary-SRCH_KO0,16.htm.

21 Talent Pipeline Report, 2015, p. 25.

22 CSCA CTE Specialist endorsed School Counselors training session chaired by Tracey Sanchez, October 11, 2019.

23 The Role of Higher Education in Career Development: Employer Perceptions and American Public Media's Marketplace survey.

24 Careerwise.

25 Career Readiness for All, Spring 2019, Coalition for Career Development, p. 6.

26 Success in the New Economy, Eric Fleming, Video November 12, 2018, YouTube.

27 Source: Georgetown University Center on Education and the Workforce analysis of the US Bureau of Labor Statistics Employment Situation Summary 2020. Note: Columns may not add up to 100 percent due to rounding.

28 The Law of Accelerating Returns: Essays, March 7, 2001 Ray Kurzwell.

29 Tony Carnevale, a research Professor and Director of the Georgetown University Center on Education and the Workforce Georgetown Public Policy Institute CEW, Recovery: Job Growth and Education Requirements Through 2020, 2013.

30 Dr Reyes Gonzolez, President of St Augustine College, *Financial Planning During and Beyond COVID*, The Chronical of Higher Education, seminar, August 12, 2020.

31 Let's Measure What No One Teaches: PISA, NCLB, and the Shrinking Aims of Education David F. Labaree Graduate School of Education Stanford University Stanford, CA 94305-3096 E-mail: dlabaree@stanford.edu Web: http://www.stanford.edu/~dlabaree/ May 15, 2013.

32 Paul Friga,of University of North Carolina at Chapel Hill Kenan-Flagler Business School at an industry appraisal of the impact of COVID-19 on colleges and universities. Chronicle for Higher Education webinar, March 2020.

33 Merriam-Webster Dictionary.

34 Admissions Unplugged, Cherry Creek High School, Dec 9,2019, lecturer University of Colorado, Boulder.

35 www.insider.com/chicago-parents-gave-up-custody-of-kids-college-financial-aid-2019-7.

36 CBS News.

37 calmatters.org/education/higher-education/2019/08/college-scandal-admission-exception-uc-california-side-door-sports-money-diversity-secrecy/

38 www.insidehighered.com/admissions/article/2019/09/05/southern-california-admissions-were-determined-donations-parent.

39 Craig Whitgren, post grad counselor, Cherry Creek High School, Highly Selective Students Night, lecture, Oct. 2019.

40 Let's Measure What No One Teaches: PISA, NCLB, and the Shrinking Aims of Education David F. Labaree Graduate School of Education Stanford University Stanford, CA 94305-3096 E-mail: dlabaree@stanford.edu Web: www.stanford.edu/~dlabaree/ May 15, 2013.

41 www.psychologytoday.com/us/blog/the-science-behind-behavior/201807/why-do-people-brag-social-media.

42 Merriam-Webster Dictionary.

43 www.huffpost.com/entry/tulane-us-news-ranking_n_2395723.

44 Creek to College, Dec 7, 2019, Greenwood Village, CO, Dec 2019.

45 Dr. Paul Bobrowski, Dean of the Monfort School of Business, University of Northern California; lecuture Business School—Understanding the Options of Today, Creek to College, Dec 7, 2019.

46 Christopher Ingraham, Sept. 14, 2015.

47 Markeisha Miner, Dean of Career Studies, Cornell University Law School, MH Alums in Law—The Law School Experience, webinar, 6/23/2020.

48 Markeisha Miner, Dean of Career Studies, Cornell University School of Law; Ellen Cosgrove, vice dean for Academic Administration and the Julio Sosa, MD, Chair of the Department of Medical Education, Albany Medical College, Danetta Bradshaw, MH Alums in Law—The Law School Experience, webinar 6/23/2020.

49 Student Debt and the Class of 2017, 13th Annual report, The Institute for College Access & Success (TICAS) 2017.

50 www.forbes.com/sites/zackfriedman/2018/06/13/student-loan-debt-statistics-2018/#7273edc67310.

51 Dale, Stacy Berg and Alan B. Krueger. 2002. "Estimating the Payoff to Attending a More Selective College: An Application of Selection on Observables and Unobservables." Quarterly Journal of Economics 117(4).

52 Helping or Hovering? The Effects of Helicopter Parenting on College Students' Well-Being Article in Journal of Child and Family Studies 23(3) April 2014 based on 2012 study at Macquarie University in Sydney, Australia.

53 College Admission Cracked. p. 77, p 31.

54 Information workshop—April 2019, Baylor University and University of Iowa, Dean's Night at Creek, Feb 2018.

55 Lauren Jones, Program Director for Special Populations, Counseling & Equity, Middle School CTE Program Coordinator, Career & Technical Education (CTE), Colorado Community College System (CCCS), interview, January 16th, 2020.

56 Mount Holyoke College, webinar, Law School June 2020.

57 Principal Dr Ryan Silva, Principal's Brown Bag lecture, Sept 2019.

58 Will Schiffelbein, Associate Director, Colorado College, Creek to College, Cherry Creek High School, Greenwood Village, December 7, 2019.

59 Will Shifflebein, Associate Director, Colorado College, Creek to College event, Dec 9, 2019.

60 Noel Ginsberg, founder CareerWise, Interview Feb 2020.

61 Graduation Requirements for Students in Missouri Public Schools, Missouri Department of Elementary and Secondary Education, September 2019, p. 4.

62 Gallup State of the American Workplace Report, 2017 www.inc.com/jessica-stillman/how-to-choose-career-business-idea-richard-branson.html.

63 www.wizardingworld.com/news/discover-your-hogwarts-house-on-pottermore.

64 www.educationplanner.org/students/self-assessments/learning-styles.shtml.

65 Harvard's Tony Wagner Getting Real about Career Readiness: A Focus on Cross-sector competencies America Achieves Educator Networks May 2018.

66 www.edutopia.org/assessment.

67 www.edutopia.org/integrated-studies.

68 www.edutopia.org/project-based-learning.

69 www.edutopia.org/social-emotional-learning.

70 www.edutopia.org/technology-integration.

71 Noel Ginsberg, CareerWise interview, Feb 3, 2020.

72 Noel Ginsberg, CareerWise.

73 Laura Miller, Counselor, interview Jan 28, 2020. Innovation Campus, Centennial CO.

74 Noel Ginsberg, CareerWise interview, Feb 3, 2020.

75 The Value and Promise of Career and Technical Education: Results from a National Survey of Parents and Students. Advanced CTE, 2019.

76 CTE report.

77 Noel Ginsberg, Founder CareerWise, interview, Feb 3, 2020.

78 USA Today, www.usatoday.com/story/money/personalfinance/budget-and-spending/2017/12/11/nearly-75-of-parents-help-their-adult-children-financially/108507432/

79 Stanford University, Challenge Success.

80 Evening with the Deans, Cherry Creek High School, Greenwood Village CO, Jan 2019.

81 www.kiplinger.com/slideshow/business/T019-S010-kiplinger-economic-outlook-for-all-50-states-2020/index.html.

82 www.cherrycreekschools.org/site/Default.aspx?PageID=5659.

83 www.cherrycreekschools.org/Page/5660.

84 Inspired by Hampton High School, Allison Park, PA, June 23, 2015, www.youtube.com/watch?v=KZomm-1BbYQ Disaster Mission Relief, math students role-play in a performance-based simulation.

85 www.cherrycreekschools.org/Page/11143.

86 Laura Miller..., Cherry Creek Innovation Campus, Centennial, CO, Interview Jan 28, 2020.

87 Arizona State Board of Education.

88 Arizona State Board of Education.

89 Arizona State Board of Education.

90 Arizona State Board of Education.

91 Arizona State Board of Education.

92 Arizona State Board of Education.

93 Arizona State Board of Education.

94 Arizona State Board of Education.

95 Arizona State Board of Education.

96 Arizona State Board of Education.

97 Arizona State Board of Education.

98 Arizona State Board of Education.

Mango Publishing, established in 2014, publishes an eclectic list of books by diverse authors—both new and established voices—on topics ranging from business, personal growth, women's empowerment, LGBTQ studies, health, and spirituality to history, popular culture, time management, decluttering, lifestyle, mental wellness, aging, and sustainable living. We were recently named 2019 *and* 2020's #1 fastest growing independent publisher by *Publishers Weekly*. Our success is driven by our main goal, which is to publish high quality books that will entertain readers as well as make a positive difference in their lives.

Our readers are our most important resource; we value your input, suggestions, and ideas. We'd love to hear from you—after all, we are publishing books for you!

Please stay in touch with us and follow us at:

Facebook: Mango Publishing
Twitter: @MangoPublishing
Instagram: @MangoPublishing
LinkedIn: Mango Publishing
Pinterest: Mango Publishing
Newsletter: mangopublishinggroup.com/newsletter

Join us on Mango's journey to reinvent publishing, one book at a time.

CPSIA information can be obtained
at www.ICGtesting.com
Printed in the USA
JSHW051931150621
15600JS00002B/2